THE UNITY  OF

WORDSWORTH'S POETRY

Poems
A History of English Literature
A Short History of English Words
The Diction of Poetry from Spenser to Bridges

THE
UNITY OF
WORDSWORTH'S
POETRY

BERNARD GROOM

FORMERLY PROFESSOR OF ENGLISH
MCMASTER UNIVERSITY

MACMILLAN
LONDON · MELBOURNE · TORONTO

ST MARTIN'S PRESS
NEW YORK
1 9 6 6

MACMILLAN AND COMPANY LIMITED
Little Essex Street London WC2
also Bombay Calcutta Madras Melbourne

THE MACMILLAN COMPANY OF CANADA LIMITED
70 Bond Street Toronto 2

ST MARTIN'S PRESS INC
175 Fifth Avenue New York NY 10010

Library of Congress catalog card no. 66–18271

PRINTED IN GREAT BRITAIN

TO MY
FORMER COLLEAGUES
AND STUDENTS OF
McMASTER
UNIVERSITY

Contents

Contents

Preface

THE neglect of Wordsworth's later poetry has been tolerated too long. That changes took place in his work about 1814 cannot be denied, but they were not of a kind to justify the conspiracy of silence in which most critics have joined. Wordsworth's subsequent poetry should at least be candidly and impartially examined. The two main causes which led to its neglect are easily defined. One was a general belief that the production of a 'romantic' poet inevitably deteriorates when he has reached the limits which separate youth from middle age. The other was the myth of the 'Lost Leader', according to which the later Wordsworth was a dull conservative and renegade. Thus there was ready and willing acceptance for Arnold's dictum of 1879: 'Within one single decade, between 1798 and 1808, almost all his really first-rate work was produced.' The pronouncement had consequences probably beyond its author's intention, and it contracted the influence of his own selection,[1] which includes a number of poems suffering from the supposed stigma of having been written after 1808, and now less known than they deserve to be.

Of the various critics who have combated the popular prejudice two are outstanding in their independence of judgement, clearness of vision, and knowledge of Wordsworth's poetry. The first was W. Hale White ('Mark Rutherford'), who in 1898 published *An Examination of the Charge of Apostasy against Wordsworth*. The times were hardly ripe for this work, and Hale White's literary style is somewhat laconic. Wordsworth, he remarks dryly, 'is a man of such mark that all cultivated men and women feel that they must have something to say about him, so they take up "Lucy Gray" and "1815" and pass on, summing him up in a phrase, "inspired poet, dullest of renegades". The antithesis does not exist, and could not have existed; but it saves them much

---

[1] *Poems of Wordsworth.*

trouble, not only in criticism and conversation, but in their own thinking.' The tone is not conciliatory, but the book assuredly attains its limited object: 'My sole aim is to show that he is no apostate, and that to the last he was *himself*.' Some thirty years after, Dr. Edith C. Batho published *The Later Wordsworth* (Cambridge, 1933), a convincing demonstration of the poet's mental activity between 1814 and 1850. This book has made its impact on students of Wordsworth the man, but it does not attempt to reassess his later poetry. It has appeared to me that further progress is possible and desirable in the way opened by these two excellent writers, and in that belief I have written the present book.

In common with other writers on Wordsworth I must acknowledge my debt to the great body of the poet's best critics, from the days of Coleridge, Hazlitt, and De Quincey to the present time. The number of references in the footnotes will indicate my special indebtedness to the five volumes of Wordsworth's *Poetical Works*, edited by E. de Selincourt and Helen Darbishire (Oxford, 1940–9). My chief authority for events in the first half of the poet's life has been Mary Moorman's *William Wordsworth: Early Years 1770–1803*,[1] and I must regret that the second volume of this invaluable work, though announced for publication, was not available for my use. How well Wordsworth's earlier poetry was understood and praised by critics of the nineteenth century and after — Arnold, Lowell, Raleigh, Bradley, Legouis — and by their successors, such as H. W. Garrod and Arthur Beatty, is testified by their enduring influence. To them, as well as to a still later generation of critics and scholars, my indebtedness is gratefully acknowledged.

A more personal expression of gratitude is due to the authorities of McMaster University, Hamilton, Ontario, whose generous grants enabled me to continue my studies of Wordsworth in the United Kingdom during two summer vacations: nor can I fail to associate the book with the hospitality of two of my oldest and dearest friends, who have welcomed me again and again to their home in the heart of Wordsworth's country, where every prospect recalls some memory of the Wanderer, the Solitary, or the Poet.

[1] Hereafter referred to as *Wordsworth: Early Years*.

Introduction

WORDSWORTH's poetry is a unity, but it is seldom so regarded today. To most readers it is known through one of the many anthologies which are the lineal descendants of the selection made by Matthew Arnold in 1879, which has itself been frequently reprinted. At a period when the literary standards of the earlier half-century were being called in question, Arnold's work performed an invaluable service to Wordsworth's reputation. His defence of the poet was based upon a drastic distinction between his earlier and later work, and dates were fixed for marking the divisions. 'Between 1798 and 1808', we are told, 'almost all his really first-rate work was produced.' This sweeping statement, still widely accepted, has led to much misunderstanding. The reputation of some poems is still affected by their date of publication, and this may be seriously misleading. One of the principal poems to suffer in this way is *The Excursion*, which was not published until 1814, though much of the first four books was written by 1806 and a number of earlier passages — some of great beauty — appear in the remainder of the poem. Arnold's selection was indeed a volume of considerable size: 'what strikes me with admiration', he writes, 'is the great and ample body of powerful work which remains to him, even after all his inferior work has been cleared away.' But if Wordsworth's poetry is really of such merit, are his readers to consent, for all time, to the dismissal of the greater part of what he wrote during more than half his life? The tendency to isolate a limited number of poems from the rest shows few signs of weakening, yet it is certain that a strong element of consistency runs through the poet's work from first to last. It deserves, indeed, to be viewed as a whole.

In recent years there has been some protest from critics of Wordsworth against 'the anthology habit'. This means, in effect, discrimination against both the longer poems and the later poems, as such. There was no catastrophic decline in Wordsworth's powers in 1808, and much of what he wrote after that date was, at the lowest, a development of his earlier work or a valuable commentary upon it. For instance, in the final arrangement of his poems, Wordsworth places *Artegal and Elidure* immediately after *The Brothers*, thus inviting a comparison between his treatment of brotherly affection in 1800 with his treatment of the same theme in 1815: it is a juxtaposition from which both poems gain. *The White Doe of Rylstone* fully deserved the admirable editing of Miss A. P. Comparetti in 1940, but it is still little read, having been excluded by Arnold — on account of its length, presumably, for it was finished in 1808, though not published until 1815. *The Waggoner*, written in 1805, and published in 1819, has suffered from a similar neglect. Dr. E. C. Batho's book *The Later Wordsworth* dispelled many prejudices against the character and mind of the poet from about 1815, but hardly did as much justice to his poetry, though she would extend his 'great period' to 1815 at least.[1] Professor F. M. Todd takes a bolder line in *Politics and the Poet*[2] and assures us that Wordsworth's Continental tour of 1837 'prompted a series of poetic compositions often worthy to stand beside the sonnets of 1802'. We must also welcome certain larger anthologies like that of Professor W. M. Merchant, yet on the whole the narrow view of Wordsworth still prevails. One of the most candid witnesses against it is Arnold himself, who in the character of an uninhibited reader admits that he can find 'pleasure and edification' in everything of Wordsworth — with the exception of one poem from which, perhaps, he was deterred only by the title.

The course of Wordsworth studies during the last thirty years might well stimulate us to examine and perhaps to revise our attitude to his poetry. Some admirable editions of separate poems have appeared on both sides of the Atlantic, and the results of large scale scholarship are most impressive. The Letters of William and Dorothy Wordsworth in early, middle, and later life have been collected in six volumes; the entire Poetical Works have been edited with meticulous care and great insight by E. de Selincourt and Helen Darbishire; and an exhaustive biography

[1] p. 314. [2] p. 212 (Methuen, 1957).

has recently been completed by Mrs. Moorman.[1] The time therefore seems ripe for criticism to exert itself in the same way, and by making the whole of Wordsworth's poetic work better known, to bring into view the mutual relations of its various parts. To separate the later work from the earlier is an injury to both. The general course of Wordsworth's poetry, though it includes periods of decline, is one of continuity, development, and revival. Much of the present study consists of a critical description of poems and parts of poems generally omitted from anthologies, and it is hoped that its effect will be to induce some of its readers to explore the neglected work for themselves.

[1] Mary Moorman, *William Wordsworth: A Biography*: vol. i, *The Early Years 1770–1803*; vol. ii, *The Later Years 1803–1850* (Oxford, Clarendon Press, 1957; 1965).

CHAPTER I

The Essential Wordsworth

WORDSWORTH himself believed in the fundamental unity of his poetry. For him the inspiration of his past work survived the changing forms of his philosophy. In his last decade he republished the early poems which had appeared nearly fifty years before, including with them *Guilt and Sorrow* and *The Borderers*, then printed for the first time. All these works were altered so as to conform more closely with his changed views, but their essential character remained. The key to this consistency lies in an unchanged attitude of soul which Ruskin calls 'reverence'. But the form and conscious object of this reverence were modified with the passage of time. It extended from nature to man, and from man to historical Christianity. Hale White, after admitting his superficial inconsistency 'in religious matters', ends with a basic truth: 'Wordsworth worshipped the true God alone, from the days of the *Lyrical Ballads* to his death, and set up no shrine to Baal.'[1]

'I wish to be considered as a teacher or as nothing.' Here is another clue to Wordsworth's unity. The statement was made in 1808 when he was at the height of his imaginative power, and it is to the effect of his imagination that he is referring. He is a teacher, though not a preacher, by inward necessity. From the time of *Tintern Abbey*, when he first came into the full possession of his poetic power, to the end of his life, there is an ethical element in his work, implied or explicit. His most spontaneous outburst of joy has some relation to those moral questions which he once yielded up in despair. Nor is he less natural in the ethics of the *Ode to Duty*, for he could express abstract thought with passion and imagination. Through time and bereavement, and the long

[1] W. Hale White, *An Examination of the Charge of Apostasy against Wordsworth*, p. 61 (Longmans, 1898). Hereafter referred to as *An Examination*.

stress of political anxieties, his teaching kept its main course: he strove to appeal to feelings which were 'sane, pure, and permanent'.

The comparative simplicity of Wordsworth's poetry from 1798 onwards emerges out of an intellectual complexity which remains as the permanent background of his work. These mental and moral origins are in part the subject of *The Prelude* which, besides being a narrative of varied personal and historical interest, is a representative study of a poet's development from boyhood. At times Wordsworth may cast a certain sophistication over his experiences as a child; but his genius lies in his immediate contact with the past. At the age of thirty-four, when he resumed continuous work on *The Prelude* after some five years, he could still feel that for him 'Life's morning radiance hath not left the hills, Her dew is on the flowers'. Indeed, the influences surviving from the past were as much powers as memories: they were 'felt in the blood, and felt along the heart', and they are the source of the poem's greatness. But to appreciate *The Prelude* as a work of art is not the same as using it to discover the essential elements of Wordsworth's poetic character. These are to be found chiefly in the first five books of the poem, and to examine them as an introduction to the study of his poetry as a whole is the task of the present chapter.

Books I and II of *The Prelude* are often considered together: they are continuous and lead to a climax. But the distinction between them must also be emphasized. The psychological difference between the child of Book I and the adolescent of Book II is reflected in the nature of the experiences described. 'Beauty' and 'fear', which Wordsworth names as the fostering powers of his soul, did not come in that order: 'fear' preceded 'beauty' and formed the deepest stratum of his poetic mind. 'Fear' and wonder occupy lines 301–478 of Book I, and when 'beauty' is introduced at line 479, the boy being ten years old, it is a beauty 'old as creation' and his intercourse is 'unconscious', 'a pure organic pleasure'. His earliest distinct memories are of more primitive emotions. There was the feeling of 'strangeness' in the utterance of the loud dry wind as he hung dangerously on the ridge above a raven's nest. There were also the two occasions when a troubled conscience took the form of spectral presences in the solitude of Nature. The long passage describing the adventure in the stolen boat on Ullswater is deservedly famous and has become a *locus classicus* with theologians. 'In this experience', says Dr. C. H. Dodd,[1] 'we can trace most of the various features which Otto records as marks of the "numinous". There is the sense of mystery — "a dim and undetermined sense of unknown modes of being". There is the feeling of the power or energy of the unknown object, and of its "complete otherness". There is the haunting terror, with its universal symbols of darkness and solitude. There is the fascination that keeps the boy looking at the black peak and afterwards keeps him thinking about it to the exclusion of all else.' 'Reverence' is too weak a term for this absorption in an awe-inspiring presence. The boy's experience was an early manifestation of Imagination, in its 'strength of usurpation'[2] — the power 'constructive of *reality*'.[3] Though not alluded to again it is akin to some of the greatest moments of his life. It is the beginning of that power of divination which has made some observers liken him to one of the ancient prophets. It inclines us to rank him in some degree with men greater than himself, and outside the range of his contemporaries. From early childhood Wordsworth was destined to become a man of 'enthusiastic and meditative Imagination'.

In Book II the young boy gives place to the youth or adolescent who now enters upon the conscious quest of natural beauty. No scheme of holiday delight or boyish sport was complete unless it included the sight of some 'winning forms of Nature'. If the day began with the physical enjoyment of the 'galloping steed', followed by the pleasure of strawberries and cream at a smart lakeside inn, such delights yielded to the potent spells of Nature — the 'still spirit shed from evening air', or the calm of the 'shadowy lake', and the 'dead still water' at the approach of night. The beauty of sunset and moonlight and specially the 'holy calm of earliest dawn' — all grew in power with the enlargement of his sympathies. The self-portrait would be incomplete without the

[1] *The Authority of the Bible* (Nisbett, 1928; revised 1938), ch. ii.
[2] *The Prelude*, vi. 599–600.
[3] W. Hale White, *An Examination*, p. 34.

hint of the 'coarser pleasures' which accompanied the growth of aesthetic sensibility.

The adolescent Wordsworth was also entering into the spirit of his age. Love of the picturesque was in the air and 'Nature' was the inspiration of the newer poetry. Wordsworth, however, had a capacity for passion which was denied to the early connoisseurs of landscape beauty, and by the date of his birth he belonged to the generation which learnt the revolutionary force in 'Nature'. It was discovered in other arts by Beethoven and Turner. There was one man of the previous generation in whom 'Nature' worked with comparable force — Rousseau. The parallel between him and Wordsworth brings into view certain aspects of the emotional and aesthetic spirit of the eighteenth century highly characteristic of romanticism. The romantic element in Wordsworth's poetic character was secondary to his 'numinous' inspiration, but it was an 'essential' and was in the main self-developed. He was not a man to derive his feelings from Rousseau or from anyone else.[1]

Rousseau and Wordsworth were both explicit in tracing the stages of their devotion to Nature. Rousseau has been compared with Cowper and with Byron: but both of these were well-to-do men and neither knew what it was to revel in Nature, like Rousseau, with empty pockets, and neither came so near to Nature as Wordsworth, in his indefatigable walking-tours or in the early austerities of Dove Cottage. Both Rousseau and Wordsworth feel an intense emotion for the 'common sights' of nature: Rousseau's rapture on seeing periwinkle-flowers for the first time after thirty years ('Je pousse un cri de joie: Ah! voilà de la pervenche!'[2]) is paralleled by Wordsworth's profound 'thoughts' at the sight of the meanest flower. Rousseau celebrated, as a discovery, what was later called 'Wanderlust' — the sheer joy of 'going forward without knowing whither', purchased by all the discomforts of vagrancy. The same note is struck by Wordsworth:

> who would stop or fear to advance,
> Though home or shelter he had none,
> With such a sky to lead him on?

[1] See Herbert Read, *Wordsworth*, appendix (Faber & Faber, 1965).
[2] *Les Confessions* (1781), Partie I, Livre vi.

Both disliked the manual toil of writing, and the saying that Wordsworth's study was the fields has its parallel in Rousseau: 'c'est à la promenade, au milieu des rochers et des bois ... que j'écris dans mon cerveau.'[1] There is a counterpart to Wordsworth's view that poetry takes its origin from emotion recollected in tranquillity in Rousseau's remark: 'En général les objets font moins d'impression sur moi que leurs souvenirs.'[2] Both writers were unwilling to expose cherished fancies to the cold light of truth. After seeing Mont Blanc, Wordsworth regretted that he had exchanged 'a living thought' for 'a soulless image', and Rousseau felt a like disappointment on first beholding the sea. And, he added, 'la même chose m'arrivera toujours en voyant des spectacles qu'on m'aura trop annoncés: car il est impossible aux hommes et difficile à la nature elle-même de passer en richesse mon imagination.'[3] Finally, Rousseau 'cherished that conception of the true unity of a man's life, which places it in a closely-linked chain of active memories', and Wordsworth, too, wished that his days should be 'Bound each to each in natural piety'. Some of the contrasts between the two writers are striking also, but these need not detain us provided we notice that Rousseau resembles Wordsworth in imaginative sensibility, not in mystical vision.

It was in his adolescent years that Wordsworth became aware of his creative poetic capacity. He regards man himself as in some respects a poetical animal. To babyhood he traces 'the first Poetic spirit of our human life', for the baby, instinctively adopting its mother's feelings, applies them to surrounding objects. If he notices a flower,

> already love
> Drawn from love's purest earthly fount for him
> Hath beautified that flower;[4]

and thus the baby is already both the receiver and the creator of pleasurable perception. Whatever the psychological value of this observation it developed for both Coleridge and Wordsworth into a cardinal truth of general aesthetics: 'We receive but what we give, And in our life alone does Nature live.' What distinguishes

---

[1] Ibid. iii.   [2] Ibid. iv.
[3] Ibid.   [4] *The Prelude*, ii. 246–8.

the active poet from other men, however, is a certain vital
independence of 'the regular action of the world'. Wordsworth
was conscious of possessing this capacity before he could show
any composition to prove it:

> A plastic power
> Abode with me; a forming hand, at times
> Rebellious, acting in a devious mood;
> A local spirit of his own, at war
> With general tendency . . .[1]

Book II concludes with one of Wordsworth's supremely great
passages on his communion with Nature. It is a hymn on his sense
of rapt participation in the creative energy of the natural order —
the feeling 'that God in Nature is one with God in the soul'.[2] In
his revision of *The Prelude*, he distinguished more clearly between
God and the Creation, adding two lines on the gaze of 'every form
of creature'

> Towards the Uncreated with a countenance
> Of adoration, with an eye of love.[3]

No doubt the original form of the passage was truer to the actual
feelings ('those fleeting moods of shadowy exultation') and understanding of adolescence, but by interpreting his early experience
in the light of his later Theism, Wordsworth has given the passage
a greater concreteness, at the same time making it more consistent
with the 'numinous' experience of Book I.

The main essentials of Wordsworth's poetic character were
determined before he left the North of England for Cambridge,
and much of the three following years was spent in an environment
hostile to his enthusiastic nature. Books III–V of *The Prelude* bear
many signs of conscious literary art and are concerned largely
with matters alien to his inner life. At Cambridge he felt the
power of the 'world' to 'lay waste' his powers, and his allegiance
was not undivided. The development of his strictly poetic
character is confined to a few pregnant passages in Book III.

The removal from a landscape so rich in stimulus to sense and

[1] Ibid. 362–6: 'his own' was 'its own' in 1805.
[2] Ibid. 434–5, E. de Selincourt's *Notes*, p. 513.
[3] *The Prelude*, II. 413–4.

imagination as the Lake Country to one of the flattest areas in England, though disappointing, had also its bracing effect. Wordsworth was not born to depend on outward magnificence. It was good for the education of his senses, in relation to his 'moral being', that they should be restricted for a time to the meagre diet of the Cambridge 'flats'. He realized that he had been 'a spoiled child' bred up 'mid Nature's luxuries', and he reacted healthily to the new discipline. His imagination was enlarged and invigorated:

> I looked for universal things; perused
> The common countenance of earth and sky:[1]

and again:

> To every natural form, rock, fruit or flower,
> Even the loose stones that cover the high-way
> I gave a moral life: I saw them feel,
> Or linked them to some feeling.[2]

This new development marks an essential and permanent element in his poetry. It is also the guarantee of its wide appeal. The common sights of nature are those most indispensable to the poet and, in the long run, the most precious to all men.

During Wordsworth's first year at the university, the links with his past remained unbroken, though partly overlaid. On his return to Hawkshead for the summer vacation (Book IV) his feelings were drawn in opposite directions. He was overjoyed to renew old friendships but had become critical and a little superior. Temptations to worldliness, harmless enough at Cambridge, were now more insidious. Nothing could be more natural than the enjoyment of a night spent in 'dancing, gaiety, and mirth', but could he give himself up unreservedly to the social instincts of adolescence? Had his relations with Nature been purely sensuous, little would have been at stake; but his early associations with the stars and fells had been of a sterner kind:

> strong,
> Deep, gloomy were they, and severe; the scatterings
> Of awe or tremulous dread.[3]

There was a danger that such admonitions might be dissipated in a youth so impetuous as Wordsworth. But he was not to be a poet

[1] Ibid. III. 109–10.   [2] Ibid. 130–3.   [3] Ibid. IV. 251–3.

merely by self-election. As he returned from a dance in the early morning and saw in the union of sky and mountain the great yet 'common' drama of dawn in its dazzling splendour, the decision was made, and he describes it to Coleridge in words befitting a supreme moment:

> Ah! need I say, dear Friend! that to the brim
> My heart was full; I made no vows, but vows
> Were then made for me; bond unknown to me
> Was given, that I should be, else sinning greatly,
> A dedicated Spirit.[1]

Following this record and deepening its impression is the incident of the poet's meeting with the Discharged Soldier, on a lonely road by moonlight. It makes one of Wordsworth's most powerful passages — the picture of the tall starving man, his stark human 'simplicity' in strange contrast to the 'trappings of a gaudy world', still visible on his faded uniform. The men who chiefly captured the poet's imagination at this time were the local shepherds, and there was something portentous in this ghastly figure from the wars. Wordsworth's mind was again invaded from without, as it had been in the boat on Ullswater, and again with intimations of mystery. After a moment's weakness he responded with mental alertness and the practical care of a good Samaritan. The test had not been beyond his strength. Full comprehension and interpretation lay in the future, but his instinctive reactions were wholly in accordance with his essential character.

Book v opens with the poet's philosophical dream of an Arab riding in the desert and clasping a shell representing Poetry, and with it a stone, representing 'Euclid's Elements'. The dream adds little to the known essentials of Wordsworth's poetic mind beyond the intimation that he felt strongly the intellectual spell of mathematics. This is not surprising: it appealed to the part of his mind which delighted in abstract reasoning, and no doubt, like the youthful Wanderer, he discerned its relation to astronomy:

> While yet he lingered in the rudiments
> Of science, and among her simplest laws,
> His triangles — they were the stars of heaven, . . .[2]

---

[1] Ibid. 333–7.   [2] *Excursion*, I. 270–2.

The main object of the Book is to represent literature as a vital force — almost as powerful in its influence on the mind and, in the long run, as beneficial as Nature itself. Only the greatest authors are mentioned — Homer, Shakespeare, Milton, and Cervantes — the other references being to anonymous folk-lore and popular ballads. The child absorbed in the stories of Jack the Giant-Killer or Robin Hood is transported to another world and reaps at least 'one precious gain, that he forgets himself'. Imagination may also be a protection against the horrors of the real world.

Some authors have been haunted for life by ghastly memories from childhood: Wordsworth makes a different report. He tells how he once chanced to see the body of a drowned man brought up from a lake, 'a spectre sight of terror', yet

> no soul-debasing fear,
> Young as I was, a child not nine years old,
> Possessed me, for my inner eye had seen
> Such sights before, among the shining streams
> Of faëry land, the forest of romance.[1]

Enthusiasm was the saving power. The very real children of his boyhood, happy as the happiest, were yet 'fierce, moody, patient, venturous, modest, shy'; not over-nourished in arts and letters, but

> Mad at their sports like withered leaves in winds.[2]

And when he returned home from school for the holidays and could read what books he liked, he gave himself up with the same abandonment, forgetful of his fishing-rod, and lying in the glare of the sun on the hot stones of the Derwent,

> Defrauding the day's glory, desperate![3]

From the reading of his childhood is shaped the dream of the Arab who is reverenced for his Quixote-like zeal:

> In the blind and awful lair
> Of such a madness, reason did lie couched.[4]

---

[1] *The Prelude*, v. 451–5.   [2] Ibid. 415–16.
[3] Ibid. 487.   [4] Ibid. 151–2.

One remembers the impression which Wordsworth made at Alfoxden on Hazlitt who thought the poet himself Quixote-like and his manner of reading his own poetry a proof that he was 'either mad or inspired'.

Critics have dwelt much on the immaturity of his early poem, *An Evening Walk*. Émile Legouis tracked down many of its phrases to English and French descriptive poets: others have pointed out its debts to guide-books of the Lake District. The language of the poem, however, is not without signs of effective originality, and Wordsworth himself considered that it contained 'many new images and vigorous lines'. Moreover this early piece is prophetic of much of his later work. In 1815, the poet republished, with two shorter extracts, the long passage beginning:

> Now with religious awe the farewell light
> Blends with the solemn colouring of night;[1]

an unmistakable though distant anticipation of the *Evening Voluntaries* published in the volume *Yarrow Revisited*, in 1835. The early experimenter is linked closely with the mature poet.

[1] *An Evening Walk*, ll. 287–8.

CHAPTER II

Politics and the Early Poems, 1790-7

THE next seven or eight years of Wordsworth's life and the poems composed within that period form a background to the study of his enduring work. It is possible to appreciate some of his greatest qualities without regard to what *The Prelude* tells us of his life between 1790 and 1797. But the relations of his mind to our common humanity would then be less apparent. The best parts of *The Prelude* are woven like a fine tissue into the total fabric of his work. Moreover, the poems of those years, especially *The Borderers*, though of far less intrinsic value than their successors, fill up gaps in his poetic history, and by their very shortcomings illustrate what is characteristic in his mature writing. To any serious study of his poetry as a whole, this background is essential.

It was partly by political thought, at times of an agonizing intensity, that Wordsworth attained that comprehensive view of human nature essential to the writing of great poetry. Some of his beliefs were soon discarded, but they left their effect on his mind, and politics, domestic and foreign, continued to absorb much of his intellectual energy. The young Wordsworth, whose meeting with the Discharged Soldier marked an epoch in his life, knew that his ultimate goal must be one of 'sound humanity;[1] but he could not hasten his progress or foresee its stages. Even when he tried to describe them in retrospect he met 'broken windings' in the way, needing 'the chamois' sinews, and the eagle's wing'. The working of genius cannot be fully explained, though it may be illumined by its own insight. We can at least see that political enthusiasm played a great part in making Wordsworth the poet he became, as did also devoted friendship and passionate love.

[1] *The Prelude*, VIII. 452.

Our present business is with the impact of these forces on his imagination and his poetic response to them, before he discovered the clear road to his characteristic work.

I

We have, as the first stage of this enquiry, to consider that period of Wordsworth's life which includes his tour through France and Switzerland to Italy, his subsequent stay in London, and his residence in France up to the time when he returned to Paris from the Loire in the autumn of 1792. These years are covered by Books vi–ix of *The Prelude*. In setting out on his walking-tour of 1790, with Robert Jones, Wordsworth was obeying an impulse to expend physical energy and to obtain new and striking impressions. Prudence and 'worldly interest' were against the expedition, he says,

> But Nature then was sovereign in my mind,
> And mighty forms, seizing a youthful fancy,
> Had given a charter to irregular hopes.[1]

It has been contended that 'Nature' in these lines is connected with 'natural society' rather than 'the scenery of the Alps'.[2] But surely the obvious meaning is the true one. 'Mighty forms' is the phrase used of the visionary mountains that haunted the poet in childhood,[3] and he tells us elsewhere that for two years more Nature continued to hold a higher place than Man in his 'affections and regards'.[4] He had known beforehand that 'Europe was thrilled with joy', but it was the first physical contact with the new age that changed the course of his life. The arrival at Calais amid the celebrations of the Festival of the Federation he never forgot:

> The senselessness of joy was then sublime!

No doubt there were politics under this ebullition, but it was the ebullition that thrilled the poet. It continued to do so as the friends strode southwards. There was the same 'unruliness of joy' in the 'dances of Liberty', in which the travellers joined:

---

[1] Ibid. vi. 333–5.   [2] F. M. Todd, *Politics and the Poet*, p. 32.
[3] *The Prelude*, i. 398.   [4] Ibid. viii. 346–51.

> All hearts were open, every tongue was loud
> With amity and glee.[1]

Later, these impressions were succeeded by others. When Wordsworth saw the Convent of the Grande Chartreuse — insecure under the new régime — he deeply felt the spell of a dedicated life withdrawn from the world for the sake of 'meditative reason'. The impression was powerfully renewed at intervals in his later life. Crossing the Alps, he gathered memories of rocks, sky, forests, and torrents, to be fused together later, in one of his grandest passages. Switzerland, in its Protestant cantons, showed something of the same republican simplicity he already knew in the Lakeland dales, and he there read 'lessons of genuine brotherhood' more plainly expressed than in the fervours of the Revolution. Another aspect of humanity met his eyes in the gracious life round the Italian lakes:

> ye have left
> Your beauty with me, a serene accord
> Of forms and colours, . . .[2]

The memories of this tour as recorded in *Descriptive Sketches* are darkened by the stern revolutionary creed and the personal depression of two years later. Book VI of *The Prelude* recaptures more faithfully the feelings of the time. Wordsworth rejoiced in the palpable spirit of hope abroad in France but was as yet 'scarcely of the household of social life'. The final impression was left by Nature: 'the ever living universe . . . was opening out its glories'.[3]

II

Book VII, 'Residence in London', does not record much progress in Wordsworth's poetic development. It is a brilliant and largely an objective description of those aspects of the city which pleased his insatiable appetite for sight seeing. At first he was in the mood of the Solitary — without his bitterness — in the New World: content 'to observe and not to feel'. Later, the superficially cosmopolitan aspect of London amused the eye — but how

---

[1] Ibid. VI. 401–2.   [2] Ibid. 677–9.   [3] Ibid. 774–5.

different had been his first impressions of France, where he had
seen

> In a mean city, and among a few,
> How bright a face is worn when joy of one
> Is joy for tens of millions.[1]

Even the normal instincts of human groups — neighbourliness,
for instance — were lost in the vast anonymity of London. 'The
face of every one That passes by me is a mystery!'[2] And his
memory hoarded up a little group of faces, intelligibly meaningful
in an alien setting: the face of a beautiful cottage-child, among
sordid men and women; the looks of 'One Man' bent anxiously
on a sickly child and heedless of the passers-by; the 'upright face'
of a blind beggar sitting motionless against a wall, amid a moving
crowd. Yet his imagination was not utterly overwhelmed by the
'blank confusion' of this Bartholomew Fair. The saving simplicity
of his early life had given him a critical if not a creative detach-
ment. And later, his London memories formed the background
to a group of delightful poems on men and women, aliens in the
metropolis.

In the following four months, which Wordsworth spent at the
Welsh home of his friend Robert Jones, before his second visit to
France, he was able to see more deeply into his London memories.
Some sense of the forces underlying the modern city of commerce
and pleasure came to the surface. He had, on his first approach
to London as a youth of twenty, felt 'the weight of ages' descend
upon him, and his later residence strengthened the impression of
the metropolis as a world-centre. Contemporary man, even in
cities, has his roots and dependencies in remote places and distant
times, and this perception was to grow into the strong sense of
history which marks his later work. The beginnings of this insight
are recognized in *The Prelude* of 1805:

> The Human nature unto which I felt
> That I belong'd, and which I lov'd and reverenc'd,
> Was not a punctual Presence, but a Spirit
> Living in time and place, and far diffus'd.[3]

So too, in this larger view, London appeared a scene of mixed

---

[1] Ibid. 347–9.   [2] Ibid. vii. 628–9.   [3] Ibid. viii. 761–4 (1805).

passions forming a solemn harmony like that of the 'wilds' of his childhood, where his imagination could find a congenial element. The 'great city' was destined to remain as the background of his thought, but it could never become the central 'point of vision' for his interpretation of life.

III

Whatever may have been Wordsworth's practical motives for returning to France in 1791, the intellectual attraction is abundantly clear: 'France lured me forth'. Few could foresee the political crisis which would arise before another year was out, and to the poet France was still the centre of the world's hopes. Though it was inevitable that he should ultimately become a partisan of the people, he had not done so when he crossed the Channel for the second time. He had 'skimmed the master-pamphlets of the day', he says, and sometimes read them with care, but he lived at first in polished circles in Orleans where politics were avoided. For the present he was engrossed in learning the language and ways of a strange people. It might even be supposed, in these surroundings, that revolutionary violence was at an end. When, after a time, he changed his associates and entered 'a noisier world', where army officers debated the news of the day, he realized what passionate divisions lay beneath the surface of society. He again took a decisive turning in the course of his life: he became a 'patriot' and gave his heart to the people.

Wordsworth's tutor in revolutionary politics was Michel Beaupuy, later a General in the Army of the Republic, the poet's senior by some thirteen years. He stood alone among the Royalist officers quartered at Orleans — hated by them 'with an oriental loathing'. But the poet soon found in him the qualities of heart and mind that he loved the most, and seldom does he write of any man with such warmth of affection. Soldier and poet had the same belief in man's 'noble nature', and Wordsworth now began to extend this faith to 'the people':

> Elate we looked
> Upon their virtues; saw, in rudest men,

> Self-sacrifice the firmest; generous love,
> And continence of mind, and sense of right.[1]

He was the more able to feel this enthusiasm since he had seen 'the bravest youth of France' marching to the war on the frontier. In retrospect, Beaupuy seemed the ideal soldier-philosopher, like one of Plato's disciples in active life. It was his mixture of innate gentleness with a capacity for righteous wrath that won the poet's heart. No one can forget the incident of his outburst when they saw the hunger-bitten girl, disconsolately knitting as she led a heifer, picking its food from the lane: ''Tis against *that* That we are fighting'.[2] Yet the poet was only twenty-two: he could not concentrate his thoughts wholly on the stern facts of life, and as the friends walked through the forest glades near the banks of the Loire, his fancy was sometimes tempted by the sound of horse-hooves to stray to one of Tasso's mounted heroines. Thus for a time,

> The meagre, stale, forbidding ways
> Of custom, law and statute

still wore

> The attraction of a country in romance.[3]

But this phase of his imaginative history was nearing its end.

IV

Towards the end of Book ix the direct record of Wordsworth's poetic development is interrupted, and the narrative abruptly takes another course. The book closes with the tragic story of *Vaudracour and Julia,* related fully in the 1805 version of *The Prelude,* but reduced to a mere fragment in 1850. Coleridge, to whom *The Prelude* was addressed, would read the story of Vaudracour as the partial revelation of an event in Wordsworth's life of which the full facts were known only to his closest relatives. Ostensibly the story is introduced by Beaupuy as an illustration of the parental tyranny possible under the *ancien régime.* Vaudracour, a 'high-born youth', falls passionately in love with the daughter of a neighbouring bourgeois family. Their marriage

---

[1] Ibid. ix. 385–8.   [2] Ibid. 517–18.   [3] Ibid. xi. 110–12.

is opposed by his father, and the 'fervent Youth' sees so many obstacles 'to honourable wedlock with his love' that he turns aside 'from law and custom' and entrusts his cause

> To Nature for a happy end of all; . . .[1]

The father, still determined to prevent the marriage, sends armed men to arrest his son under a *lettre de cachet*. Vaudracour kills one of these emissaries, but it is the further severity of both families that brings the story to its end. Finally the lover falls into incurable insanity after the confinement of Julia in a Convent and the subsequent death of their child. The real point of the story in *The Prelude* lies in its partial parallel with the relations of Wordsworth with Annette Vallon, daughter of a surgeon at Blois, where Wordsworth resided after leaving Orleans. A child was born to them at the end of 1792. The situation of Julia has one main resemblance with Annette's, for she also

> without the name of Wife
> Carried about her for a secret grief
> The promise of a Mother.[2]

In 1820 Wordsworth published *Vaudracour and Julia* as a separate poem, and one might have expected that all traces of it would then disappear from *The Prelude*. The change would have caused no difficulty, for Book ix could have been effectively ended just before the beginning of the story. But instead, Wordsworth informs us that the story is irrelevant and then proceeds to give an unsatisfactory synopsis of it in twenty-eight lines. The passage quoted above about Julia is omitted, and instead some new lines are inserted, stronger than anything in the original version, about the mental suffering of Vaudracour —

> supine,
> Save when the stings of viperous remorse,
> Trying their strength, enforced him to start up,
> Aghast and prayerless.[3]

The passage leaps from its context. It is inconceivable that these lines should have been added to strengthen the description of

---

[1] See Moorman, *Wordsworth: Early Years*, p. 185.
[2] *The Prelude*, ix. 609–11 (1805).   [3] Ibid. 575–8.

Vaudracour — who has now hardly any place in *The Prelude* — and they can only be an indirect reference to Wordsworth's own moral history. He was not at liberty to tell the full story of his relations with Annette, nor could he suppress all allusion, however cryptic, to his own state of mind in this vital stage of his life. The depth of his mental despair as described in Book x becomes more real in the light of this passage. Moreover, it emphasizes the importance of remorse as a main theme in *The Borderers*. 'When the winds of war blew them apart, his love for Annette failed to survive enforced absence.'[1] To this accurate summary of the sad story by Mrs. Moorman, little need be added here. Wordsworth's efforts — especially up to the marriage of his daughter Caroline in 1816 — to make reparation for a wrong which could not be undone must be studied in his biography. As a further comment on the relation of this love story to his poetic development, these sentences from Mrs. Moorman's *Life* are invaluable: 'The other people — men and women — to whom he gave his love, were all of them in different ways beings from whom he drew inspiration in the great business of his life, which was to be a poet. He must soon have realized that Annette could not do this — indeed, that she had no conception that such a world even existed as that in which he lived and thought. This, and not merely absence, or difference of nationality or religious upbringing, must have been the real cause of their estrangement.'[2]

The fate of Annette, reflected in various poems of women forsaken by lovers or deprived of protectors, remained as a burden on Wordsworth's mind for the rest of his life. It was, however, not the only cause of his profound disturbance at this time. The prospects of man, which he identified with the more moderate politics of the republican party called the Girondins, seemed to be placed in sudden and terrible peril by events in Paris. He returned to the capital in October to find the Convention in power, after the September massacres, and resolved to inaugurate a new era on its own system. This was the beginning of a fresh challenge which compelled him to plunge deeper and deeper into the recesses of his own mind in quest of basic political principles. Events were moving with extreme rapidity. The

[1] Moorman, *Wordsworth: Early Years*, p. 181.   [2] Ibid., p. 182.

execution of Louis XVI early in 1793 raised an outcry among the governing classes in Great Britain, whose feelings were expressed in Bishop Watson's *Strictures on the French Revolution and the British Constitution*. Wordsworth, who had returned to England, answered this work by writing, though not publishing, his *Letter to the Bishop of Llandaff* 'by a Republican', dwelling on the dangers of indulging the instinct for compassion when vast issues were at stake. 'In a revolutionary age,' he wrote, 'there is a necessary suspension of the mild and social virtues.' 'Political virtues are developed at the expense of moral ones.' The tone of the *Letter* is one of sincere but narrow partisanship, bordering on fanaticism.

The outbreak of war in 1793 greatly intensified the gloom. It was not merely that the poet's own country was in conflict with France, though this is the aspect emphasized later in *The Prelude*. In 1793–4 the evil, for the poet, was war itself. 'The struggle which was then beginning,' he writes in the 'Advertisement' to his poem *Guilt and Sorrow*,[1] 'and which many thought would be brought to a speedy close by the irresistible arms of Great Britain being added to those of the Allies, I was assured in my own mind would be of long continuance, and productive of distress and misery beyond all possible calculation.' He goes on to assert that the poor 'more than other classes' are subject to the calamities 'consequent upon war'. *Guilt and Sorrow* enforces this truth and indicts the vices of the penal law.

The poem brings together on the waste of Salisbury Plain two outcasts, both victims of the War of American Independence. One is a sailor, who had been seized by the press-gang: a man naturally kind-hearted, but long inured to the violence of war. Returning to England on his discharge, and intending to rejoin his family, he is defrauded of his savings, and in a moment of desperation robs and kills a traveller. The other is a woman whose husband, forced by unemployment to enlist, crosses to America with his family and perishes there, with his children, 'by sword and ravenous plague'. The destitute widow returns to England. Taking refuge from a storm, these two meet in a deserted building on the Plain. The woman's story is relieved by many tender

[1] *P.W.* i, pp. 94–95.

memories and some feeling for Nature: detached from its setting it became 'The Female Vagrant' of *Lyrical Ballads*. But the Sailor's narrative moves only pity and horror. Though his instincts of kindness are unimpaired, he has no peace of mind until he gives himself up to the Law, which inflicts the supreme penalty. When Wordsworth first published the poem in 1842, he changed the last stanza, dismissing the original ending as an 'intolerable thought'.

Guilt and Sorrow has none of the intellectual power of *The Borderers*, though it partially anticipates that tragedy. The Sailor, like Oswald, is 'betrayed into a great crime', but he is incapable of Oswald's strong mental reaction. He is almost totally passive after his one act of violence, and his stricken imagination transforms all that meets his eye into tokens of his dreadful fate. There is a brooding power in the controlled simplicity of the style, and Wordsworth himself considered that the poem has a continuous hold on the mind 'effected by the identity of moral interest that places the two personages upon the same footing in the reader's sympathies'. But the conception of the Sailor, compared with the image in *The Prelude* of the Discharged Soldier, which lay somewhere in the recesses of Wordsworth's memory, is almost a poetic blasphemy. The poem has, indeed, an important place in the development of his mind and art, but he rightly considered it 'addressed to coarse sympathies'. He had yet to discover that poetic excitement can be aroused without recourse to 'violent stimulants'.

Guilt and Sorrow was finished in 1793–4. A temporary relief of political anxiety came with the death of Robespierre in 1794, to be followed by a still darker period of philosophical despair. To this time belonged the composition of *The Borderers* (1796–7): it not only expressed the poet's perplexities, but greatly relieved them. Before considering this tragedy, we must return for a time to *The Prelude*.

Residence in England did little towards lightening Wordsworth's distress in the course of the Revolution. Indeed, there was now the added grief that his own country was at war with the champions of Liberty: the description of his divided loyalties is one of the most poignant passages of *The Prelude*. Foreign attacks favoured the extremists in France: 'beset with foes The goaded land waxed mad'. It is hard to believe that he was living in the civil order of his own country, as one reads the passage of mounting intensity on the rise of a few merciless men to supreme power and the ceaseless work of the guillotine, particularly as we contemplate the darkness of spirit in which the poet lived through the horror:

> Most melancholy at that time, O Friend!
> Were my day-thoughts, — my nights were miserable;
> Through months, through years, long after the last beat
> Of those atrocities, the hour of sleep
> To me came rarely charged with natural gifts,
> Such ghastly visions had I of despair
> And tyranny, and implements of death; . . .[1]

One would suppose him to have witnessed the actual events which he describes. His fevered imagination usurps even 'the mighty world of eye and ear'

But that imagination had also its own stubborn strength, which was his salvation. It gave him an insight into the moral causes of national convulsions. He saw that the evils in France lay not in popular government as such, but were a legacy from generations of tyranny and ignorance — 'a reservoir of guilt'. There is no taint of insular superiority in his attitude. He is not judging a nation: he is groping in the darkness which surrounds human society. But he knew the quality of his own mind, and it is with the courage of conviction that he dares to compare himself with the 'ancient Prophets, borne aloft in visions':

> So did some portions of that spirit fall
> On me, to uphold me through those evil times,
> And in their rage and dog-day heat I found
> Something to glory in, as just and fit,
> And in the order of sublimest laws; . . .[2]

And with a determination to draw strength from every possible source, he found comfort in the records of those victims of the Terror who had given 'fair examples'

---

[1] *The Prelude*, x. 397–403.   [2] Ibid. 410–14 (1805).

> Of fortitude, and energy, and love,
> And human nature faithful to itself
> Under worst trials . . .[1]

The fall of Robespierre and the end of the Reign of Terror revived the hopes of an earlier time, but the relief was short-lived. A few months later, the invasion of Holland by the French turned a war of self-defence into one of aggression. Liberty, as Wordsworth believed in it, was 'doomed'. It was the final destruction of his hopes for man through revolutionary politics, and his mind was left in a dangerous state of vacuum. He already had some acquaintance with Godwin's *Enquiry concerning Political Justice*, which was published in 1793, but the time had now arrived (1794–5) for Godwin to become his infallible guide. Wordsworth does not discuss *Political Justice* in *The Prelude*, but we can well understand its irresistible appeal. A system of political thought not subject to the unpredictable ways of men, not dependent upon national character, not bound up with the emotions, and therefore superior to pity, not founded on creed or tradition, not variable from one region to another — such is what Wordsworth craved for at this time; and Godwin seemed to supply it. The hopes of Man were to be 'abstracted out of his feelings' and 'fix'd thenceforth For ever in a purer element'. At the same time Man was made arbiter of his political fate by dealing pragmatically with every situation on its merits, unhampered by principle:

> How glorious! in self-knowledge and self-rule,
> To look through all the frailties of the world,
> And, with a resolute mastery shaking off
> Infirmities of nature, time, and place,
> Build social upon personal Liberty,
> Which, to the blind restraints of general laws
> Superior, magisterially adopts
> One guide, the light of circumstances, flashed
> Upon an independent intellect.[2]

For a man of Wordsworth's deep instinctive belief in the reality of goodness and justice the decision to judge questions of weight

---

[1] Ibid. 447–9.
[2] *The Prelude*, xi. 236–44. Cf. *The Borderers*, 1493–6.

by some opportunistic standard would have been spiritual suicide. And this he at length discovered. No passage in *The Prelude* strikes harder than the thirteen lines[1] on his frenzied attempt to capture, by analysis, the essential being of his soul:

> endlessly perplexed
> With impulse, motive, right and wrong, the ground
> Of obligation, what the rule and whence
> The sanction; . . .

with the final result that he

> Yielded up moral questions in despair.

V

His tragedy, *The Borderers*, is an introduction to his answer to these perplexities. The answer itself is the entire body of his subsequent poetry. By writing the tragedy, Wordsworth attained a degree of self-knowledge which, with the help of his sister Dorothy and of Coleridge, enabled him to enter upon his characteristic work, marked, in Coleridge's words, by 'unity of interest' and 'homogeneity of character'. *The Borderers* was begun in 1796 and finished in the following year. Wordsworth was then living at Racedown in Dorset, with Dorothy, and could concentrate his entire mind on the work. He wrote an introductory essay on it, dealing with his observations of human nature during the French Revolution and these are the basis of the tragedy. The dramatic action is secondary, and the essence of the work lies in the ethical and psychological problems embodied in the two main characters, Oswald and Marmaduke. *The Borderers* could not possibly succeed as a stage-play and Swinburne thought it a dramatic monstrosity. Outwardly it is modelled on *Othello*: in both works an unscrupulous 'friend' aims at the total ruin of an unsuspicious benefactor. But whereas Shakespeare with consummate skill long diverts our enquiry as to Iago's motives, if any, the reasons for Oswald's plot to deceive Mortimer cry out for an answer, which is delayed until the fourth Act. Up to that point the action has no visible principle of cohesion.

---

[1] *The Prelude*, xi. 293–305.

Critics of *The Borderers* have dealt much on its relation with
Godwinism. Oswald himself upholds the view that action should
be governed by pure calculation without regard to pity or the
other natural emotions, and Marmaduke becomes his pupil.
Marmaduke is the leader of the Borderers, a band dedicated to
enforcing the elements of order on the confines of England and
Scotland in the reign of Henry III. Oswald, who once owed his life
to Marmaduke, exercises a strong influence upon him, but is
distrusted by the rest of the Band. His attack on the happiness of
his chief begins in the invention of a hideous calumny against the
blind and aged Herbert — a former Crusader — father of Idonea,
whom Marmaduke loves. Herbert, according to Oswald, is an
impostor who abuses Idonea's trust to sell her to the lustful
purposes of the vicious Lord Clifford. This tissue of lies is presented
with manipulated 'evidence' cunningly devised to convince
Marmaduke's mind. The chief has himself the enthusiasm and
instability of revolutionary times: with good natural feelings, he
is emancipated from tradition and highly amenable to 'reason'.
In his contest with Oswald over the treatment due to Herbert for
his 'villainy', Marmaduke at first upholds compassion as being to
man 'as natural as life', but at last, under the pressure of Oswald's
'evidence' goes to the extreme of ruthlessness:

> Now for the corner-stone of my philosophy:
> I would not give a denier for the man
> Who, on such provocation as this earth
> Yields, could not chuck his babe beneath the chin,
> And send it with a fillip to its grave.[1]

This was the kind of 'transition in soul' known at times in the
Revolutionary Tribunals of 1792–3, where the sacrifice of natural
feeling to 'patriotism' was often greeted with rapturous applause.
   Wordsworth's prefatory Essay on *The Borderers* brilliantly
illuminates his conception of Oswald as a character of the
Revolution. He is, we are told 'a young man of great intellectual
powers yet without any solid principles of genuine benevolence.
His master passions are pride and the love of distinction. He has
deeply imbibed a spirit of enterprise in a tumultuous age. He goes

---

[1] *The Borderers*, 1240–4.

into the world and is betrayed into a great crime. . . . His feelings
are interested in making him a moral sceptic, and as his scepticism
increases he is raised in his own esteem. . . . The recovery of his
original importance and the exhibition of his own powers are
therefore in his mind almost identified with the extinction of those
powerful feelings which attend the recollection of his guilt. . . .
I have introduced him deliberately prosecuting the destruction of
an amiable young man by the most atrocious means, and with a
pertinacity, as it should seem, not to be accounted for but on the
supposition of the most malignant injuries. No such injuries
however appear to have been sustained. What then are his
motives?' After a short comparison of Oswald with Iago, Wordsworth proceeds: 'in a course of criminal conduct every fresh step
that we make appears a justification of the one which preceded it,
it seems to bring again the moment of liberty and choice; it
banishes the idea of repentance, and seems to set remorse at
defiance. Every time we plan a fresh accumulation of our guilt we
have restored to us something like that original state of mind, that
perturbed pleasure, which first made the crime attractive. . . . The
general moral intended to be impressed by the delineation of such
a character is obvious — it is to shew the dangerous use which
may be made of reason when a man has committed a great crime.'[1]

Long before the action of the play begins, Oswald had been
betrayed, by a plot, into causing the death of an innocent man by
exposing him without help on a barren island. Marmaduke, by
Oswald's contrivance, is beguiled into a similar crime: he abandons
Herbert to the elements on a wild moor. It is the difference
between the behaviour of the two men on realizing what they have
done that constitutes, for Wordsworth, the deeper meaning of the
tragedy. Oswald resolves to escape from the moral 'slavery' of
remorse:

> Three nights
> Did constant meditation dry my blood;
> Three sleepless nights I passed in sounding on,
> Through words and things, a dim and perilous way;
> And, whereso'er I turned me, I beheld
> A slavery compared to which the dungeon

[1] *P.W.* i, pp. 345–8.

And clanking chains are perfect liberty.
You understand me — I was comforted;
I saw that every possible shape of action
Might lead to good — I saw it and burst forth,
Thirsting for some of those exploits that fill
The earth for sure redemption of lost peace.[1]

His advice to the conscience-stricken is given in these words:

Remorse —
It cannot live with thought; think on, think on,
And it will die.[2]

Marmaduke refuses to buy this false freedom which leads to moral enslavement. He accepts the doom of expiation and becomes a wanderer over the earth, awaiting the release of death. *The Borderers* is not just about Wordsworth and Godwinism, but about Godwinism as related to the instinct of self-justification after wrong-doing.

Wordsworth was called upon to accept his share of responsibility for the ruin of Annette Vallon's life. He did so, and thus resembles Marmaduke in his relation with Herbert. Now the original name for Marmaduke in the tragedy was 'Mortimer', and it has been pointed out[3] that Wordsworth used this name as a pseudonym in one of his early poems. But the poet's personal connexion with *The Borderers* is not confined to the part of Marmaduke. Oswald also reflects important features of his character. The most impassioned speeches in the play are spoken by him. An ambition like Oswald's to enlarge 'Man's intellectual empire' belonged at this time to the poet. Again, Oswald's unshakeable confidence reflects the stubborn spirit with which Wordsworth was to face the abuse of the reviewers:

I felt that merit has no surer test
Than obloquy; that, if we wish to serve
The world in substance, not deceive by show,
We must become obnoxious to its hate, . . .[4]

Mortimer stops short of repentance, which would necessarily be the work of time, but he submits to contrition. The action of *The*

---

[1] *The Borderers*, 1772–83.   [2] Ibid. 1560–2.
[3] By J. R. MacGillivray (*P.W.* i, p. 344).   [4] *The Borderers*, 1827–30.

Borderers morally subordinates Oswald (and Godwin) to Mortimer in the crucial contrast of their attitude to remorse, and by writing the tragedy Wordsworth released himself from the terrific strain of the revolutionary years. Political and moral philosophy might continue to attract him, but only so far as they left intact the supreme truth that 'Man's heart is a holy thing'.

CHAPTER III

The First Lyrical Ballads

THE barren habit of moral analysis was shaken off 'entirely and for ever', and Wordsworth became, in his own phrase, 'a sensitive being, a creative soul'. The deliverance was aided by changed circumstances which partly enter into the subject-matter of his contributions to the first *Lyrical Ballads* (1798). That he was now peacefully settled in rural life, the master of his own time, with the companionship of his sister and a boy called 'Edward', the poems themselves inform us. The world of large cities is seldom alluded to and then only as a memory, and if there is an undercurrent of sadness, a sense of 'what man has made of man', it is heard as from a distance. The poet's daily contacts are limited to the small incidents, scenes, and interests of village life. From the style of the poems he might seem to have lived outside the literary world, since he is content mainly with the simple metres of older times such as are used in hymn-books and popular verse, though there is an occasional hint of wider reading. The diction is conspicuously unadorned — at times familiar and homely. There is no sign that the poet's life is deeply rooted in the place where he is dwelling. Such might be the impressions of the first *Lyrical Ballads*, viewed separately and externally.

But when they are taken together and seen as forming a little world of their own, the effect is greatly different. From all sides the poet is invaded by joy. He sees it in the budding twigs; he hears it in the songs of the blackbird and the thrush. His power of feeling and perception is rejuvenated and he invites us to share the miracle. He describes an old thorn-tree with an intensity which sets ordinary associations at defiance, but we can never forget the tree or the mossy mound beside it. When we come to the end of *The Idiot Boy* and are told the poet's words, 'I never wrote anything with so much glee', we easily believe him. If at times he partly fails, he succeeds in the vital thing he aims at: he may keep us waiting in *Simon Lee* for the point of the story, but once known, it remains fixed in our minds. For many readers of Wordsworth such impressions may lie far back in the past, but they revive when the *Ballads* are re-read. There is the zest of life in their pages.

Joyous receptivity of eye and ear is more than a vital experience in these poems — it is a philosophical faith. Wordsworth had found a teacher whose systematic thought was the moral physic his condition required. This was David Hartley, who supplanted Godwin in his admiration, and helped to revive those instincts which *Political Justice* was starving to death. Hartley, author of *Observations on Man, his Frame, Duty, and Expectations* (1749)[1] taught that the sensations of pleasure and pain, operating through, and purified by, a series of associations, finally produce 'theopathy', i.e. the 'sympathetic passive feeling excited by the contemplation of God'. It was a philosophy which strongly appealed to Coleridge, though but for a time. On Wordsworth it acted as an antidote to Godwin. For whereas Godwin's influence had tended to break his contact with the fruitful memories of his past, Hartley's teaching gave them a theoretical sanction. The beginnings of the 'cheerful faith' of *Tintern Abbey* are evident in the well-known stanzas of *Expostulation and Reply*:

> The eye — it cannot choose but see;
> We cannot bid the ear be still;
> Our bodies feel, where'er they be,
> Against or with our will.
>
> Nor less I deem that there are Powers
> Which of themselves our minds impress;
> That we can feed this mind of ours
> In a wise passiveness.

This, though untheological in language, is essentially a poetic version of 'theopathy'. It is also an epitome of Wordsworth's visionary experiences of adolescence reborn in a new medium of thought and a new simplicity of expression.

[1] See Arthur Beatty, *William Wordsworth: his Doctrine and Art in their Historical Relations* (University of Wisconsin Press, 1922).

The first *Lyrical Ballads* reflect a vital phase in Wordsworth's poetic life, but they must be read in the context of his entire work. Some of them place a one-sided emphasis on certain points of his teaching. If in 1798 he felt that he had had enough of science and of art, enough of books and moral philosophy, this was only a stage in a nearly completed convalescence. In a few years he was to call books 'a substantial world, both pure and good', and his reasoned love of them can be read at large in the Fifth Book of *The Prelude*. For the time being he was in a mood for 'spontaneous wisdom breathed by health', but his permanent attitude was to welcome insight into moral good and evil wherever he could find it — from his own meditation, from his travels or, later, from ancient philosophy. Many of these early poems, for all their blithe spontaneity, are of a transitional character.

Wordsworth himself stated that the majority of the first *Ballads* were to be considered as experiments. We feel this especially when he deals with human passions, characters, and incidents. From the two pathetic poems, *The Mad Mother* (the title of which was changed to *Her Eyes are Wild* in 1815) and *The Complaint of a Forsaken Indian Woman* it is hard for the modern reader to dissociate a sense of the poignancy of Annette's situation after William's departure for England. In both poems imaginative insight is at issue with emotional oppression. Their wildness of tone is in strong contrast with the restraint which was soon to become a feature of Wordsworth's pathos and a source of its power. In some of the poems there is too large an element of Hartleian psychology. This is so in *Goody Blake and Harry Gill*, the story of an old woman's curse, which afflicts a hard-hearted neighbour with perpetual cold. The incident, Wordsworth informs us, really happened, and it seems to have attracted him as an illustration of the theory of association. 'For Hartley a simple idea and a sensation are almost identical, the difference normally being that an idea is fainter than its corresponding sensation. But what if the idea were impressed upon the mind with great force? Might it not become, as with Harry Gill's feeling of cold, almost as permanent and vivid as a real sensation?'[1] Wordsworth humanizes

[1] From the Introduction to *Lyrical Ballads*, ed. R. L. Brett and A. R. Jones, p. xxxv (Methuen, 1963).

the story to the utmost, but nothing can dispel the oddity of it in metrical form. Much the same is true of the *Anecdote for Fathers*. It certainly illustrates 'the manner in which we associate ideas in a state of excitement', but it is hard to go all the way with the poet in his evident feeling that this trait of 'simple childhood' gives a glimpse into 'the mystery of man'. These two pieces lie outside the central 'unity' of his poetry. It is otherwise with *We are Seven*, a true-born offspring of genius, closely related to his other pictures of childhood and a precursor of the Immortality *Ode*.

Three other poems on men and women have the distinctive Wordsworthian character, but are still experimental. *The Last of the Flock* is a little poem on the educative power of ownership when the affections are called forth by the care of living creatures, like the flock of this south-country shepherd. It is a poem of somewhat embittered pathos — a mere sketch compared with a fully developed pastoral picture, such as *Michael*. *Simon Lee* is a poem on which Wordsworth bestowed great pains in later years, altering the text and order of the first seven stanzas again and again. The last five stanzas are — to use the poet's own word — 'inevitable': but, 'in 1798 contrasted traits of youth and age jostle each other'[1] in the first half of the poem. Finally these were sorted out, and the transition in Simon from vigour to decrepitude was marked by the phrase 'But oh, the heavy change!' In the original version of the story the difference in style between the two parts is so strong that it is hard to believe the narrator can be the same person: there is an unintentional flippancy in the opening stanzas quite at variance with the faultless tone of the last five. Within a year or two Wordsworth had ceased to involve himself in this kind of difficulty. *The Thorn* is another poem of 'two speakers'. A certain thorn-tree on the Quantock Hills which had passed unnoticed in bright weather attracted the poet's attention in a storm and he invented the tale to make the tree 'permanently impressive' as the storm had made it to him.[2] He succeeded in his object, but by a method which seems open to some objection. Martha Ray, a deserted mother who haunts the site of the thorn-tree, the little pond beside it and the supposed

[1] T. Hutchinson; quoted by de Selincourt, *P.W.* iv, p. 413.
[2] Fenwick Notes.

grave of her child, is like a 'supertragic' figure conceived in adolescence, as Book VIII of *The Prelude* records. Wordsworth shifts the responsibility for the story to a hypothetical narrator, 'a superstitious man moderately imaginative, of slow faculties and deep feelings', as Coleridge calls him. The poet unleashed the whole force of his imagination to work its will on the tree and the mossy mound, and seldom have natural objects been described with such disturbing power. But here again the two speakers — or rather, the two minds — are imperfectly harmonized. Miss Darbishire praises the poem for 'its fusion of the elements, the human passion and the natural scene, so that each expresses itself in and through the other'.[1] But we must also accept the distinction drawn by Coleridge: 'The passages exclusively appropriate to the supposed narrator are felt by many unprejudiced and unsophisticated hearts, as sudden and unpleasant sinkings from the height to which the poet had previously lifted them, and to which he again re-elevates both himself and his reader.'[2] Many readers, I think, will not be ashamed to rank, on this question, with the unprejudiced and unsophisticated hearts.

There is no conflict of styles in *The Idiot Boy*. The human situation, however, is in strong contrast with that of the other poems, being neither serious nor pathetic, though the story is one of maternal love. *The Idiot Boy* was Wordsworth's discovery of his lighter style, which was to be further illustrated in poems like *The Farmer of Tilsbury Vale* and *The Waggoner*, and in part of *The Prelude*. Coleridge's description of the Mother as 'an impersonation of an instinct abandoned by judgement' is surely too harsh. There is more truth in Professor J. F. Danby's view of the poem as 'a comedy of the passions'.[3] Betty Foy's forgetfulness of her sick neighbour when at last she arrives at midnight at the doctor's door is a trait of genuine comedy: any 'folly' on her part is subordinate to her passions of anxiety and relief. Touches of parody are consistent with the character of the poem: it has the agitation and rapid movement — though not of

---

[1] Helen Darbishire, *The Poet Wordsworth* (O.U.P., 1950), pp. 43–44.

[2] *Biographia Literaria* (Shawcross edn.), xvii.

[3] J. F. Danby, *The Simple Wordsworth* (Routledge & Kegan Paul, 1960).

course the macabre power — of Bürger's *Lenore*, the most popular ballad of the age, which is recalled in the phrase:

> All like a silent horseman-ghost;

and the line:

> Und aussen, horch! ging's trapp trapp trapp

is echoed in

> She lifts the knocker, rap, rap, rap.

The Idiot Boy, a poem of wonderfully transparent emotions, was said by its author to have been composed 'almost extempore': it could not have been written otherwise.

Tintern Abbey was added as an after-thought to the other poems of the volume. It is a panoramic vision of the power of a remembered landscape working under the surface in a mind perplexed with five years of inward conflict; and, by implication, a record of the creative instinct triumphing over the forces of disintegration. The setting of the meditation is a harmonious landscape in which earth, sky, and the signs of human life are blended in complete repose. The poem moves quietly through unquiet memories, then with gathering power traces the stages of its author's communion with Nature to its culmination. His passion breaks free from restraint in the concluding address to Dorothy, in whose eyes he can read the record of his earlier self. *Tintern Abbey* has an unchallengeable place among Wordsworth's greater poems, but whether it gives a perfectly proportioned view of his general teaching may be questioned. The middle part of the poem has two centres, one describing what he *has* felt (ll. 66–102); the other, what he feels at the time of writing (ll. 102–11). Almost until the end of his life Wordsworth recognized his poetical dependence upon 'nature and the language of the sense', but in 1798, with his recovery from sceptical despair dominant in his mind, it seemed to be something more — the 'soul of all [his] moral being'. The writing of *The Prelude*, in 1799 and in 1804–5 enabled him to see his 'recovery' in a truer relation with his whole poetic history. By 1802 he was nearing the recognition that 'mortal life' hears 'voices of two different natures', not of the senses only. But this too he had known in the past:

> I have felt
> A presence that disturbs me with the joy
> Of elevated thoughts; . . .

In *Tintern Abbey* he is so overwhelmed with the present joy of recovering his 'genial spirits' that he does not fully foresee the revival of his past as a living power in the future. Without the language of the sense he could not have been a poet at all, but something else was needed to stir 'awakenings to noble aspiration'. He admitted later that the description of himself as 'a worshipper of Nature' (l. 152) was 'a passionate expression uttered incautiously'.[1]

Yet the poem remains a landmark in literature. The word-music alone would give it the highest distinction. Drawn from the depths of the poet's experience, independent of any literary model, flowing spontaneously, and obedient to the demands of impassioned imagination, it places its author among the few great masters of blank verse. The poem is also a manifesto of the height to which inspiration from Nature might attain. In *Tintern Abbey* Wordsworth was the spokesman of a new spirit in poetry; a fact fervently recognized by the poets of the next generation.

[1] Wordsworth to Mrs. Clarkson. *The Correspondence of Henry Crabb Robinson with the Wordsworth Circle (1808–1866)*, ed. Edith J. Morley (Oxford, Clarendon Press, 1927), vol. i, pp. 78–79.

CHAPTER IV

The Second Lyrical Ballads

'HOME AT GRASMERE' — PASTORALS — ELEGIES

religio loci — CHARACTER PIECES

I

WHATEVER the reception of the first *Lyrical Ballads* by the public, Wordsworth was himself encouraged to proceed to the composition of further poems for a new edition of the volume. But much of his thought at Alfoxden had been given to the planning of larger schemes. It was there that he conceived the idea of a *magnum opus* to be called *The Recluse*; there too that he wrote *The Ruined Cottage*, later embodied in *The Excursion*, as well as the earliest form of *Peter Bell*, a poem much altered before its publication in 1819. In the same years he planned his future as a Poet of Nature. The scheme was modified and enriched in course of time, but its foundation remained. The new *Lyrical Ballads* are not 'experiments', but poems inspired by firmly held beliefs about the human mind and the function of poetry.

It has long been recognized that a kind of philosophical system can be extracted from Wordsworth's poetry — at least from what was written between 1798 and 1814 — and the task has been carried out in Norman Lacey's *Wordsworth's View of Nature and its Ethical Consequences*.[1] But Wordsworth's 'philosophy' loses much of its power in any but its own poetic form. With all the comprehensiveness of his imagination, his mind was not markedly speculative. As he insisted, the spirit of his philosophical passages is more important than the letter. 'Nature' is of course a favourite word with him, but it is used in many different ways — abstract and concrete, subjective and objective, and sometimes with apparent inconsistency. Thus, within a hundred lines, the

---

[1] (Cambridge, 1948).

D

Wanderer can denounce the 'outrage done to nature' caused by
the Industrial Revolution and exult in the 'dominion over nature
gained'.[1] The context is everything. We must not scent a theory
each time the word 'Nature' is used.

Wordsworth's poetry of Nature has both an objective and a
subjective basis. It is founded, objectively, on a large and ever
growing intimacy with earth, air, and sky, and with the plants and
animal life of the rural areas where he dwelt. Chapters might be
written on his flowers and trees; his rocks, crags, and mountains;
his clouds and streams; on his animals, especially the sheep and
dogs of the fells; his birds, from the wren to the eagle; and on the
nightly sky where men may see the unimpaired perfection of the
Creation. Subjectively, his Nature poetry is based on the psychological discovery formulated by Coleridge:

> we receive but what we give,
> And in our life alone does Nature live.

These lines occur in *Dejection: an Ode*, but for Wordsworth this
truth was chiefly associated with the joyously creative life at
Alfoxden and his first years at Grasmere. Once in a MS. passage
written in the winter or spring of 1797–8 his enthusiasm for this
process rose to such a height that intercourse with Nature seemed
to open up a boundless prospect:

> Thus disciplined
> All things shall live in us and we shall live
> In all things that surround us. This I deem
> Our tendency, and thus shall every day
> Enlarge our sphere of pleasure and of power,
> For thus the senses and the intellect
> Shall each to each supply a mutual aid,
> Invigorate and sharpen and refine
> Each other with a power that knows no bound,
> And forms and feelings acting thus, and thus
> Reacting, they shall each acquire
> A living spirit and a character
> Till then unfelt, and each be multiplied
> With a variety that knows no end.[2]

[1] *The Excursion*, VIII. 153, 211.   [2] *P.W.* v, p. 402.

Wordsworth did not print these lines, nor did he confine himself
to developing the aesthetic enjoyment which they promise. Had
he done so he would never have made that exploration of the spirit
of man which is his greater glory. But another passage in the same
draft shows that he was endeavouring to extend his 'natural joy'
to the baffling sphere of human relations. He profoundly honours
the human heart in the first *Lyrical Ballads*: but there was a time
at Alfoxden when his enthusiasm soared higher and he envisaged
the attainment of a truly Christian charity (though not so called)
by natural means. A passage to this effect was incorporated —
almost unchanged — in *The Excursion*,[1] and it is quoted in a letter
by Coleridge of April 1798. The man, says Wordsworth, who
communes with 'the Forms of nature ... with understanding
heart' will 'feel the joy of the pure principle of love so deeply',
that he will 'seek for objects of a kindred love' in mankind:

> Accordingly he by degrees perceives
> His feelings of aversion softened down;
> A holy tenderness pervade his frame. . . .
>   he looks round
> And seeks for good; and finds the good he seeks:
> Until abhorrence and contempt are things
> He only knows by name; . . .

Wordsworth never uttered these lines in his own person but the
aspiration they express is felt in some of the best poems written
at Grasmere in 1800. Never before had he been so entirely at one
with his environment as when he settled at Dove Cottage in 1799.
Never again was he so favourably disposed towards his neighbours,
or so confident of finding in them the sympathetic depth of soul
he craved for, as when under the sway of the feelings described in
the lines 'Home at Grasmere'. Human existence was for a while
transfigured in his imagination by the emotional stability and the
surrounding grandeur which were his portion at Dove Cottage.

II

The group of poems which Wordsworth added to the second
Lyrical Ballads had been begun in Germany at Goslar in 1799,

---

[1] IV. 1207–29.

a place he hated — but the companionship of Dorothy, and the creative power of memory, combined to encourage that flow of inspiration which continued at Grasmere. In Germany, with his thoughts concentrated on his childhood, he wrote some of the best passages of *The Prelude* and also — partly in a mood of home-sickness — five of the 'Lucy' poems: 'Strange fits of passion have I known', 'I travelled among unknown men',[1] 'She dwelt among the untrodden ways', 'Three years she grew in sun and shower', 'A slumber did my spirit seal'. Others also of the 1799–1800 poems are reflectively elegiac and a number are called pastorals. Thomas Hutchinson[2] describes the work written in 1800 at Dove Cottage as including 'many pastorals', and the additions to the *Lyrical Ballads* in the reissue of 1802 were entitled *Pastoral and other Poems*. In calling poems like *Michael* by this title, Wordsworth evidently meant to give the type itself a higher rank in poetry, just as he had enlarged the scope and raised the status of the ballad. The best of his Pastorals belong to poetry considered as 'the most philosophic of all writing'. They were in no sense 'juvenilia' or 'virtuoso' pieces like the Pastorals of Pope. They were to be genuine pictures of rural life and manners, and yet, in their total effect, meditations 'On man, the heart of man, and human life'. In the pastoral group, however, room was found for compositions of a lighter kind, the best of which — unjustly despised for its extreme simplicity — is *The Pet Lamb*. Its charm has been acknowledged by many good critics, including Pater, and it well deserves the praise he gave to Wordsworth's pastorals, the first reading of which 'is like a day spent in a new country'.

The outstanding Pastoral in the whole of Wordsworth's poetry is *Michael*, written towards the end of 1800; but it is almost equalled by *The Brothers*, which belongs to the earlier part of the same year. It is remarkable that two poems so unlike anything else in the English language should also be so distinct from each other. The use of dialogue in *The Brothers* is not merely a concession to the precedent of the Virgilian eclogue, for the poem is

---

[1] De Selincourt thinks that 'this poem was not written, as Wordsworth stated, in Germany in 1799, but some time after his return'.

[2] Editor of the Oxford 'Wordsworth'.

genuinely, though quietly, dramatic. The irony of the situation, in which one speaker in the dialogue knows his interlocutor but the other does not, produces a growing tension which captures and holds the reader's interest. Leonard has returned from sea to his native Ennerdale, wishing to settle with his younger brother whom he has not seen for years, but the sight of a new grave in the churchyard (where head-stones are not used) has aroused the fear that he may have come too late. The two brothers, as children, had learned the force of human affection from the kindness of their grandfather, but apart from him had been alone in the world. In conversation with 'the homely priest of Ennerdale', who does not recognize the newcomer, Leonard is torn between desire and fear to know the truth about the grave and dares not break the suspense. At length, the news that James, the younger of the two, had after his brother's departure developed the habit of sleep-walking in which he seemed to be searching for an absent person, produces so strong an emotion that Leonard no longer resists the truth which he already knows by instinct, and simply asks the question:

> But this Youth,
> How did he die at last ?[1]

It only remains for the Priest to tell how James had evidently fallen in his sleep from the surface of the Pillar Rock (that 'aery summit crowned with heath') where he had remained alone after climbing thither with some companions. No other poem by Wordsworth depicts more convincingly the strength to which the affections may grow in a sparse population where life is hardy and simple and memories are long. *The Brothers* is, indeed, as Wordsworth classified it, a 'poem of the affections'. It is a masterly poem of the mountains in their twofold power to deepen the domestic emotions and to tranquillize the mind. In Leonard the first influence prevails, the second in the Priest:

> We have no need of names and epitaphs;
> We talk about the dead by our fire-sides.
> And then, for our immortal part! *we* want
> No symbols, Sir, to tell us that plain tale:

[1] *The Brothers*, ll. 355–6.

The thought of death sits easy on the man
Who has been born and dies among the mountains.[1]

In *Michael*, Wordsworth again traces the disappointment of a
great affection, but with closer reliance on the sympathies of the
reader. There is no dramatic situation to heighten the interest,
nothing to correspond to the narrative value of James's sleep-
walking and fall. The story 'homely and rude' is offered to the 'few
natural hearts' to whom it may appeal and who will be the poet's
'second self' when he is gone. Of all Wordsworth's longer narrative
poems it is the one most completely impregnated with his spirit.
His 'thought and love' penetrate everywhere. He also grasped the
social sources of the equality and dignity in the life he describes.
'Towards the head of these Dales', he says in his *Guide to the
Lakes*, 'was found a perfect Republic of Shepherds and Agri-
culturists . . . Neither high-born nobleman, knight, nor esquire
was there; but many of these humble sons of the hills had a
consciousness that the land, which they walked over and tilled,
had for more than five hundred years been possessed by men of
their name and blood.' Michael's 'consciousness of the land' and
his sense therein of the 'pleasure which there is in life itself' are
conveyed to us through Wordsworth's minute knowledge of
pastoral manners which enables him to give us a living picture of
the Shepherd's life on the hills, by the fireside, at table — a life
'Of hardship, skill or courage, joy or fear'. The shepherd's calling
in its impressive surroundings had, from early days, laid strong
hold on the poet's affections and these extend to the homeliest
details of Michael's life. Everything in the story is involved, from
the intense attachment of the shepherd to his wife and son, his
flock and lands, down to the late-burning cottage lamp, a 'public
symbol' of the life lived by the thrifty pair. Michael is the human
centre on whom the poet's love of the region is focused, and from
whom it is reflected over the whole range of pastoral life. Though
full of homely realism, the poem is kept above the level of prose
by the vitalizing presence of its rhythm, itself the living expression
of the author's love of his theme.

Michael is a 'heroic pastoral'. During his long years of childless-

[1] Ibid., ll. 178–83.

ness, the old shepherd had been sustained by the simple pleasures of his strenuous life. With the birth of Luke, his heart seemed 'born again' and all his instincts of life and love were centred in the child of his old age. With the loss of this son, not by death but by disgrace, he is robbed of his hopes but not broken in soul, for his love has grown to be an independent spiritual power. This is the sense of the famous paragraph beginning

There is a comfort in the strength of love. . . .

From this emotional climax, the tension is slackened until the narrative comes harmoniously to rest. *Michael* is classical in its forcible simplicity and grasp of essential human nature.

III

The poems of 1799 and 1800 which I have called by the name of 'elegies' are all concerned with the thought of death and its impact on the imagination. They are more properly 'elegiac meditations' and do not arise from the immediate effect of a near personal loss. The Lucy poems, whether based on fact or on imagination, deal with a grief which has been distanced by time; *The Two April Mornings* and *The Fountain* are on the bereavements suffered by the poet's old friend and teacher; *Matthew* comes nearest to an elegy in the strict sense of the word. All these poems, however, are bound together by a strong similarity of style, the simple words being charged with an extraordinary force. Behind them lie the poet's thoughts on the ultimate things of life, and these are the substance of the poetry. Why is it that Wordsworth's meditations on the death of Lucy, of Matthew's children, and of Matthew himself, have their unique and unforgettable power?

We must note, in the first place, the finality with which the fact of death is accepted: 'she is in her grave'; 'Matthew is in his grave'; 'Six feet in earth my Emma lay'. There is no hint in these poems of the Christian hope of a future life, though there probably remained in the poet's mind a background of Christian belief; to which, however, at this time he seldom refers.[1] That the true

---

[1] The last stanza of *Ruth* is a rare instance.

home of the soul is infinity he does not doubt, though this is for
him a natural, not a religious truth:

> Dust as we are, the immortal spirit grows
> Like harmony in music.[1]

The pulses of the poet's life beat strongly at this time, and his
faith in the interpretative power of joy was at its height: an
endless vista of imaginative experiences from the reciprocal
activity of nature and his own mind seemed to stretch before
him. But moods of melancholy reaction were bound to recur, and,
if Coleridge is right, it was in one of these that he 'fancied the
moment in which his sister would die' and so composed the
'sublime epitaph': 'A slumber did my spirit seal'. Between two
realities there was a gulf which his mind could not pass: the
mortality of man and the reality of the oneness of the soul with
the immortality of Nature, as he had felt it in his adolescence.

About 1800 Wordsworth's philosophy was to have no philosophy, but to live by the heart's imaginations and insights. He
had discarded the teaching of Godwin; the teaching of Hartley
had served its purpose, and he had not yet found a new support
in the law of Duty. But his intuition of immortal being enabled
him to meet the thought of death, if not the reality — of which
he was spared the experience in these years — with a rock-like
steadfastness of the soul. The strongest passages in these 'elegies'
give the impression of passionate emotion subdued to a state of
perfect calm. But natural firmness has its limits; and once — at
the end of *Matthew* — there is an irrepressible cry against the apparent acquiescence of Nature in the extinction of a human spirit:

> Thou soul of God's best earthly mould!
> Thou happy Soul! and can it be
> That these two words of glittering gold
> Are all that must remain of thee?

IV

Hart-Leap Well combines the characters of pastoral and elegy
with a third element — the feeling of a *religio loci*. Wordsworth's

---

[1] *The Prelude*, I. 340–1.

sense of 'the souls of lonely places' is a conspicuous feature of his poetry of nature, especially in his work of 1799–1800 and 1803, the year of his first tour in Scotland. In this season of his mature imagination the sense of a local spirit or presence was the means either of some enlarged sympathy with human beings or of a quasi-religious reverential emotion. The process thus assumes two forms: recognition of a *genius loci* and of a *religio loci*. In some of Wordsworth's greatest passages the spirit of a lonely region is embodied in a human figure — the Genius of Solitude. The basis of the imaginative effect of the situation is stated in its simplest form in a passage from Dorothy's record of 'A Tour made in Scotland': 'While we were walking forward, the road leading us over the top of a brow, we stopped suddenly at the sound of a half-articulate Gaelic hooting from the field close to us. It came from a little boy, whom we could see on the hill between us and the lake, wrapped up in a grey plaid. He was probably calling home the cattle for the night. His appearance was in the highest degree moving to the imagination: mists were on the hillsides, darkness shutting in upon the huge avenue of mountains, torrents roaring, no house in sight to which the child might belong.'[1] Some of Wordsworth's most beautiful lyrics are the sublimation of a situation like this. The Highland Girl, at Inversneyd, in the poem addressed to her, forms a single being with her environment,

> the cabin small,
> The lake, the bay, the waterfall, . . .[2]

but it is in *Lucy Gray; or, Solitude* (1799) that such poetry has its finest flower. The four lines spoken by Lucy herself give the poem its distinctive character. Her father has told her to take the lantern and light her mother home from the town before the impending snow-storm; and she replies,

> 'That, Father! will I gladly do:
> 'Tis scarcely afternoon —
> The minster-clock has just struck two,
> And yonder is the moon!'[3]

This stanza, besides illustrating the child's conflicting trust and fear, helps the poet's purpose 'to exhibit poetically entire *solitude*',

[1] Sunday 28 August.   [2] ll. 76–77.   [3] ll. 17–20.

for he has shown Lucy 'observing the day-moon, which no town or village girl would ever notice'.[1] Of all the 'spirits' of lonely places in Wordsworth's poetry, none fills the role with such magic and sweetness as Lucy, who, as some maintain, still trips o'er rough and smooth, singing her solitary song, inseparable from 'the lonesome wild'.

The *religio loci* is a feeling endowed by imagination with mythical or animistic form. Thus, in *Nutting* (1800), the 'virgin' array of clustering hazel-nuts is invested with a kind of sentient life:

> the shady nook
> Of hazels, and the green and mossy bower,
> Deformed and sullied, patiently gave up
> Their quiet being: . . .

and the poem ends with a plea for tenderness from the 'dearest Maiden':

> with gentle hand
> Touch — for there is a spirit in the woods.

That some men are saved only by consternation at the results of their own wantonness was an abiding conviction with Wordsworth, and was the theme of *Peter Bell. Hart-Leap Well*, another imaginative poem working to ethical ends is, like *Nutting*, imbued with the sense of a *religio loci* which begets a feeling of reverence for the 'unoffending' life of Nature. More precisely, it is concerned with two local presences: that of the deserted palace of pleasure built to commemorate the conclusion of an ancient 'blood-sport', and the desolation brooding over the spot where the hunted hart leaped desperately to its death. A ruin may be noble, but not the mansion of Sir Walter. Ruskin expresses the same thought in relation to a ruin in Italy. 'No vestiges are here of sacred hearth or sweet homestead, left lonely through vicissitudes of fate, and heaven-sent sorrow. Nothing is here but the vain apparellings of pride sunk into dishonour, and vain appanages of delight now no more delightsome.'[2] *Hart-Leap Well*, like much of Wordsworth's teaching, looks forward to the time when the delights of violent

[1] Crabb Robinson 'recording in his Diary a conversation with Wordsworth'. (*P.W.* i, p. 360).

[2] Ruskin, *Cambridge Inaugural Address* from *Life, Letters and Works* ed. Cook and Wedderburn, xvi, pp. 194–7.

excitement involving indifference to the suffering of sentient
creatures shall have given place to the pleasures of a 'milder day'.
By sensitive attention to the processes of growth and decay and
to the memorials which time both preserves and obliterates, the
shepherd who tells the story and the poet who hears it, may each
arrive at a common 'Ehrfurcht vor dem Leben' learned from
Nature:

> 'One lesson, Shepherd, let us two divide,
> Taught both by what she shows, and what conceals;
> Never to blend our pleasure or our pride
> With sorrow of the meanest thing that feels.'[1]

The sense of locality and its kinship with the human spirit was an
abundant source of future inspiration to Wordsworth. It kept
pace with the widening of his intellectual and moral range and
the enrichment of his poetic style.

In his Preface to the *Lyrical Ballads* of 1800 Wordsworth
asserts that it had also been his general purpose 'to attempt to
sketch characters under the influence of less impassioned feelings'.
Specimens of such writing are *The Two Thieves* and *The Farmer of
Tilsbury Vale*, which will be noticed in the chapter called 'The
Lighter Muse'. In the group called *Poems on the Naming of
Places* he combines 'impassioned feelings' with character sketches
of intimate friends. All seven poems are associated with the
neighbourhood of Dove Cottage, and perpetuate some of 'the best
and happiest moments' of the poet's year. Each of the poems
associates a particular part of the Grasmere landscape with a
member of the two small family groups which (with Coleridge)
formed the Wordsworth circle at that time. With great delicacy
the poet discriminates the peculiar quality of his relations with
each different person. Dorothy Wordsworth, Mary Hutchinson,
Joanna Hutchinson, John Wordsworth, form, with the poet
himself, the original group; and forty-five years later Wordsworth
recaptured enough of the original mood and style to write a fitting
epilogue in the joint honour of Mary Hutchinson (Wordsworth)
and her sister, Sara. One of the poems is a slight but charming
character-sketch of Joanna Hutchinson, 'that wild-hearted Maid',

---

[1] *Hartleap Well*, ll. 177–80.

who was unprepared for the ways of the poet and on beholding his
'ravishment' at a sight of a beautiful rock broke out in a laugh
which awoke the echoes of surrounding hills. Among the unforgettable passages is the beautiful tribute to Dorothy in iii.
14–17, but the best piece of sustained writing is the poem on the
Fir-Grove path[1] associated with the poet's brother John. It
reveals some of the more secret meanings of the phrase 'Home at
Grasmere'.[2] The affinity between the near relatives is beautifully
suggested in their independent discovery of the same fir-grove as a
favourite haunt:

> He had surveyed it with a finer eye,
> A heart more wakeful; and had worn the track
> By pacing here, unwearied and alone,
> In that habitual restlessness of foot
> That haunts the Sailor measuring o'er and o'er
> His short domain upon the vessel's deck,
> While she pursues her course through the dreary sea.

One cannot read *The Brothers* without relating it to the bereavement which Wordsworth was to suffer five years later in the death
of John, and 'The Fir-Grove Path'[3] adds the details of portraiture
which make these two poems in combination a finer memorial
than the elegy which was written by the poet when overwhelmed
by his loss. One poem of an earlier date (1797) may be added to
the best 'character pieces' of the volume: this is *The Old Cumberland Beggar*, written before the author had fully formulated his
conception of poetry. It is devoted to 'a worthy purpose', for the
Beggar is represented as the unconscious means of touching those
springs of human kindness, without which life on earth could not
be endured. Even the poorest, says the poet, are not satisfied in
fulfilling the basic demands of morality and custom:

> of the poor man ask, the abject poor;
> Go, and demand of him, if there be here

---

[1] *Poems on the Naming of Places*, vi. 60–66.
[2] Cf.   Hidden was Grasmere's vale from sight,
       Our home and his, his heart's delight,
       His quiet heart's selected home.
               Elegiac Verses (on John Wordsworth)
[3] M. Arnold's title for this poem.

In this cold abstinence from evil deeds,
And these inevitable charities,
Wherewith to satisfy the human soul?
No — man is dear to man; the poorest poor
Long for some moments in a weary life
When they can know and feel that they have been,
Themselves, the fathers and the dealers-out
Of some small blessings; have been kind to such
As needed kindness, for this single cause,
That we have all of us one human heart.[1]

In some Catholic countries the beggar is still invested with a kind of sanctity. The saying 'homo homini lupus' is proved every day. But are there not moments known to us all, when the heart is warmed and we can say with the poet, 'man is dear to man'? If so, the poetry of Nature has a valid manifestation in this early piece.

The two main types of poetry in the second *Lyrical Ballads* — the elegies and kindred poems in ballad form, and the local poems inspired by 'thought and love', in keeping with the austerity of the poet's life at Dove Cottage — are harmonized by their common spirit of Doric simplicity and strength. The rudimentary art required for the forms of verse employed was to Wordsworth as if it had been no art at all, but purely spontaneous. The scope for such elemental poetry was limited, and the emotional strain of writing it was severe. The following year, 1801, was almost entirely barren of original work. The soil of the poet's mind needed rest and fertilization.

[1] *The Old Cumberland Beggar*, ll. 142–53.

CHAPTER V

The Expansion of Wordsworth's Mind and Art, 1801-4

I N tracing the expansion of Wordsworth's poetic outlook during the years 1801–4, we shall again concentrate on the minor poems. It must be remembered that during these years Wordsworth had several long poems on hand — *The Prelude*, begun in earnest when he was in Goslar; *The Excursion*, which developed out of an amalgam of *The Ruined Cottage* and *The Pedlar*; and the 'Yorkshire Wolds' poem, afterwards named *Peter Bell*. *The Prelude* was a completed work by 1805, though retouched at intervals during the remainder of the poet's life; *The Excursion* was alternately resumed and put aside until its publication in 1814; and *Peter Bell*, though begun at Alfoxden, was not published until 1819. The history of the composition of each of these poems is in itself an important critical study, but does not much illustrate the general development of Wordsworth's mind and art. On the other hand, the minor poems, placed in chronological order, show a well-marked series of intellectual and aesthetic phases. *The Prelude* and *The Excursion* will be considered as belonging to the years 1805 and 1814 respectively, while *Peter Bell* will be discussed with other of the longer narrative poems.

About the end of 1800 one phase of Wordsworth's poetic art came decisively to an end. The second edition of *Lyrical Ballads* came out in January 1801, and for about a year the output of shorter poems almost ceased. When he again began to compose freely in 1802 there was, indeed, no spectacular change of subject or style, but a certain increased freedom in both respects. This change has, in my opinion, been insufficiently noticed, chiefly because the writers who have endeavoured to view Wordsworth's achievement as a whole have seen it too much in its biographical setting. Now Wordsworth's comparative silence in 1801 can hardly have a biographical explanation. There are signs, indeed, that he was feeling less settled in his residence in Grasmere, and thoughts of his marriage, which took place in the following year, must have been stirring in his mind. But the slackening of his impulse to compose cannot be wholly attributed to these causes. Can his relative silence be explained on 'internal' evidence — by reference to the poetry itself?

In part, at least, it certainly can. The poetry of 1800 was inspired by an intense imaginative sympathy with the home life of the Lakeland people as seen from Grasmere:

> Here may the heart
> Breathe in the air of fellow-suffering
> Dreadless, as in a kind of fresher breeze
> Of her own native element, . . .[1]

In this mood, and when almost every day brought a new beauty to the dale, Wordsworth could read men's lives and destinies in the light of their affections for hearth and home. But such a plan could not yield a great variety of results. The poet was relying on his own heart and observation, almost discarding the help of other men's books. The passions of genuine pastoral life might be deep, but they could not vary much from home to home, or dale to dale. Nor was Wordsworth prepared to create a factitious variety by novelties of poetic style. By the end of 1800 the vein of pastoral poetry was virtually worked out. The second year at Grasmere could not continue on the same lines, and a pause was necessary for collecting new experiences.

No poetry can flourish without some kind of literary stimulus, though the *Lyrical Ballads* had been an outstanding example of relative independence. The simplest stanza forms had sufficed. But it does not follow that Wordsworth was uninterested in stanza forms as such: his experimental use of an exotic stanza form in *Ellen Irwin* proves the contrary. In 1801 he began the search, soon to be carried further, for other new forms of verse. He also had recourse to literary stimulus in his modernization of three Chaucerian poems in the same year. No student of poetry will deny the importance of these matters, though there is naturally a higher

---

[1] *The Recluse*, Book First — 'Home at Grasmere' ll. 367–70.

interest in other new sources of inspiration found — to use Words-worth's own words — in 'heart-experience' and 'soul-illumination'.

Wordsworth's rediscovery of the sonnet-form was an important event in his poetic history. He had written a few sonnets in early youth, but the reading to him by Dorothy of Milton's Sonnets on 21 May 1802 gave him a new idea of the possibilities of that form. He was 'singularly struck with the style of harmony, and the gravity, and republican austerity of those compositions', and he wrote three sonnets on the same afternoon. Although from his critical comments one would suppose he preferred the 'Miltonic' or unitary form of sonnet without break at the eighth line, he admitted that the Italian model, whether with one pause or two (one at the fourth line), would 'often be found excellent'. In his own practice, all three styles are found, with perhaps a slight preference for the 'Miltonic' variety. Apparently, Wordsworth had some thought of returning to the sonnet before the reading of Milton, for three months before, he had published his early sonnet 'Calm is all nature', in the *Morning Post* as if to test how a poem of his in that form would be received. What Milton revealed to him was the fitness of the form for pronouncements on great public issues in the grand style, and one of the three sonnets written that afternoon was the earliest of the *Poems Dedicated to National Independence and Liberty*.

Another aspect of Wordsworth's poetic 'expansion' appears in his Chaucerian modernizations of 1801, of *The Prioress's Tale* and twenty-four stanzas from *Troilus and Cressida*.[1] Some critics dismiss these pieces lightly as if they were merely intended 'to prove to the world that the language of daily intercourse common to men was a satisfactory medium for poetic expression'.[2] But the modernizations have a substantial interest and value. For one thing, they were early essays in the 'rhyme royal' stanza which he was to use again in *Laodamia*. More important is the evident care which he took in the selection of these two pieces from the whole body of Chaucer's work. Wordsworth really entered into the spirit

[1] He also modernized *The Cuckoo and the Nightingale*, then supposed to be the work of Chaucer.

[2] Harper, *William Wordsworth, his Life, Works and Influence*, 2nd ed. (John Murray, 1923), II. 5.

of *The Prioress's Tale* and was probably one of the first persons to appreciate the delicacy of its human touches, while reprobating the 'fierce bigotry' of its anti-Semitism. His selection of the particular passage from Book v of *Troilus and Cressida* agrees with his preference for poetry in which the feeling gives interest to the situation rather than the converse, for he has taken the pathetic description of Troilus's grief outside Cressida's deserted home, not the more dramatically contrived passage, a little further on, in which Troilus waits with Pandarus at the city-gate for her return to Troy. No doubt the changes necessary to modernize the language were unusually few in the chosen pieces, but they have been effected with great judgement, and Wordsworth has even in a measure become Chaucer's collaborator. These modernizations were an event in the history of Wordsworth's imagination: they helped to release it from the pastoral spell remaining from the previous year.

Before returning to the main course of Wordsworth's 'expansion' in 1802, it is necessary to notice how the choice or structure of stanza forms continued to play a part in the poetic invention of the years under review. One of the few writers who have dealt critically with Wordsworth's versification is W. P. Ker,[1] who says truly: 'Wordsworth likes building stanzas', and it is equally true that he found some prompting to his invention in the stanzas of other poets. The most striking instance of this, next to his borrowing of the 'Miltonic' sonnet, is his adoption of stanza-forms from Ben Jonson and Drayton, whose poems he was reading with Dorothy in February–March 1802. A stanza used by Jonson in *Underwoods, Eupheme*, Song i, is the origin of the stanza in three poems *To the Daisy*[2] (though Wordsworth, unlike Jonson, uses double rhymes in lines 4 and 8), while the slightly different stanza of Drayton's *Nymphidia* is the model used in *The Green Linnet*. From both of these borrowed measures Wordsworth draws a fuller and more varied music than their originators. For *Resolution and Independence* (1802) he adopts the rhyme royal, ending with an Alexandrine instead of a heroic line. It has been suggested that he is here following the lead of Milton or Chatterton, but he was

---

[1] W. P. Ker, *Form and Style in Poetry* (Macmillan, 1928; 2nd ed. 1966).
[2] 'Bright Flower!', 'In youth from rock to rock', 'With little here'.

in a mood to invent variations for himself. He continued from time to time to adopt stanzas for their special associations. In his three poems on Burns he uses the stanza which is, more than any other, associated with Burns himself, the six-lined measure of Provençal origin familiar to us in the *Address to the Deil*, *To a Mouse*, etc. For his *Ode to Duty* he uses an uncommon stanza to which Gray's *Hymn to Adversity* had given somewhat sombre associations.

In 1802 and after, Wordsworth was experimenting in verse with considerable freedom, though not with uniform success. He needed a regular metrical pattern. The poem *To a Sky-Lark*,[1] in a kind of free verse, was as its author himself admits treated 'contemptuously' by Coleridge.[2] The first lines have a spirited upward *élan*, but the poem has no strength of wing to sustain it and it flutters heavily to the ground. *The Redbreast Chasing a Butterfly* is an example of Wordsworth's failure to vary iambic with trisyllabic feet in pleasing proportions. He is at his best as an 'iambic' poet, and as Coleridge saw, his greatest passages are produced when he relies on 'the music of his own thoughts'.[3]

As a 'builder' of stanzas Wordsworth had by 1801 discovered a source for effects closely consonant with his special mode of imagination and feeling. W. P. Ker alludes to a 'very beautiful variety' of stanzas used by Wordsworth, consisting of four iambic lines of 8886 syllables — a mixture, as Ker calls it, of 'Long Metre' and 'Common Metre'.[4] Readers may be pardoned if they do not at once perceive how an abstract stanza pattern can be called 'very beautiful', but a consideration of a few poems will illustrate the point which Ker has in mind. The four poems to be discussed are on the family affections — a characteristic source of Wordsworth's poetry. The stanza-form used in the *Elegiac Verses* on John Wordsworth opens with the four-line arrangement mentioned by Ker, and the third stanza begins as follows:

> Here did we stop; and here looked round
> While each into himself descends,

[1] 'Up with me!' Hutchinson and de Selincourt both suggest 1802 as the date of this poem.
[2] *P.W.* ii, p. 491.   [3] *Biographia Literaria*, ch. xviii.
[4] Ker, *Form and Style in Poetry*, p. 229.

> For that last thought of parting Friends
> That is not to be found.

The vital point here is obviously the last line — short to the ear
and plain to the heart. If it were as long as the rest we should have
an 'In Memoriam' stanza, which might have a plaintive beauty of
its own, but would want the strong directness which Wordsworth
achieves. In three poems on his early affection for 'Emmeline'
(Dorothy) Wordsworth applies this metrical device in a longer
stanza. The poems are: *The Sparrow's Nest* and two poems
entitled *To a Butterfly*. The 'soul' of the poem is in each instance
in the concluding short line, and these three pieces are classic
examples of the power with which a metrical pattern — consonant
with the individuality of a particular poet — can heighten the
emotional power of simple words. To dismember any of these
poems for the purpose of quotation would be an outrage, and the
reader is asked to verify these statements for himself. 'Eights'
and 'sixes' were familiar to English ears even before the time of
Bottom and Quince, but Wordsworth's art in handling this
contrast in line-length seems perennially fresh, like the best of his
poetry itself.

Wordsworth's nature poems of 1802, though not numerous,
differ significantly from those of the pastoral year. In 1800,
Nature is shown chiefly in a series of localized scenes, beautiful in
themselves and made still more so by their association with human
affections. But some of the best nature poems of 1802 are on
common flowers which may grow anywhere and whose full charm
is missed until a poet perceives it.

> Bright Flower! whose home is everywhere,

is the opening line of one of the poems to the Daisy, and this
thought is repeated later:

> Thou wander'st the wide world about.

All three of the Daisy poems are charming elaborations of the idea
that the beauty of the flower is as much made as found — 'my own
delights I make' — this being possible from the sympathy between
the habits of the flower and the moods or fancies of the poet. The
reading of Chaucer prompts Wordsworth to call the flower 'the

Poet's darling', but at the same time it is an 'unassuming common-
place of Nature'. The Small Celandine is also 'unassuming'[1] and
indeed has been 'all unheard of' until 'found out'[1] by the poet and
given its right place in his calendar. Ruskin has criticized Wordsworth for praising a flower which is defective in beauty, but his
remarks show him forgetful of his own principle that the 'aesthetic'
is inferior to the 'theoretic'[2] faculty.

The feeling of change or impending change is strongly marked
in the poems which belong to the earlier half of 1802. There is the
change which arises from the unfolding of the poet's imagination,
as it grows in strength and deepens in insight. At the same time
there was the realization that the uninterrupted companionship
with his sister at Grasmere was approaching its end. This change
is announced in the stanzas (modified Spenserian) called *A Fare-*
well (29 May 1802). As the poem looks forward to the arrival of
Wordsworth's bride as the new mistress of Dove Cottage, it
clothes the immediate future in a cheerful light, yet an emotional
crisis lay under the surface. The private intimacy between William
and Dorothy, so happy in itself, so rich in its poetic results, could
not be ended without pain to both, even when the destroyer was
so welcome an intruder as Mary Hutchinson. For some time before
the composition of *A Farewell*, Wordsworth's mind had been
dwelling on the change, and the thought of it had given the
recollections of his childhood with Dorothy a bitter sweetness of
intense poignancy. These conflicting emotions lie behind the
poems of this time. *The Sparrow's Nest*, written in 1801, is an
early member of the group which includes the two poems *To a*
Butterfly, composed in the March and April of 1802. But the
vividness of his recollections of childhood could be, in another
light, a source of unmixed rejoicing, and this is the theme of the
poem *To the Cuckoo* (written 23–26 March 1802),[3] less than a

[1] The references are to the poem entitled *To the Small Celandine*
beginning 'Pansies, lilies, kingcups, daisies'.

[2] 'Relating to the moral perception of beauty. Used in this sense by
Ruskin.' (*O.E.D.*)

[3] The dates of these pieces prove that they are literally poems of
imagination, not of experience. The cuckoo is not heard in Westmorland as early as March, nor are butterflies yet abroad.

fortnight after the first Butterfly poem. The sound of the cuckoo's cry can restore the 'golden time' of childhood and its 'visionary hours', just as the sight of the rainbow can make his heart leap up as in boyhood (26 March 1802).

But the Rainbow poem is not an expression of pure exhilaration. If — as some of Wordsworth's best critics have believed — it is the 'timely utterance' mentioned in the Immortality *Ode*, it is closely linked with that regret for the departure of a once known glory from the earth, of which Wordsworth was sensible in the early months of 1802. The completed *Ode* records both loss and gain; whereas the first four strophes — all that was written of the *Ode* in 1802 — merely lament the declining power of what Coleridge in his contemporary *Dejection* calls his 'genial spirits'. Up to this time, Wordsworth's natural genius had been his good genius, and the human representative of his natural genius had been his sister. Time had led him to the threshold of two great changes, the inner one and the domestic one. He was tenacious of the past, and where his heart was deeply concerned, change or loss was painful, even tragic. In 1802 he could not foresee how he would end the *Ode*, which was in fact completed in not less than two years:[1] but between May and July he was composing *Resolution and Independence* which marks a great advance in the evolution of his interpretation of life, and is in its way as effective a sequel to the first four strophes of the *Ode* as the actual concluding ones, though of course it has not the same lyrical splendour.

In the poetry of both Wordsworth and Coleridge the word 'genial' is so pregnant with meaning, and often so vital to the sense of a passage, that its full significance must be grasped. The information given by the Oxford Dictionary is surprisingly brief. The definition of 'genial' under the relevant heading is simply: 'pertaining to "genius" or natural disposition', and the quotations do little beyond calling attention to the fact that the phrase 'genial spirits' is usually reminiscent of a passage in *Samson Agonistes*. 'Genial spirits' occurs in *Tintern Abbey* and Coleridge's *Dejection*; 'genial faith' in *Resolution and Independence*, and the idea is often present in different words. The belief that

[1] De Selincourt thinks in 1804. For a long time 1806 was the accepted date.

poetry is the 'spontaneous overflow of powerful feelings' is the same as the belief that it is 'genial', and is another form of the half-truth that the 'artless' is superior to the 'artful'. Milton called his verse 'unpremeditated' and there are few poets who do not prefer to emphasize this side of the truth. The belief in the 'genial' nature of poetry arises from the fact that the first consciousness of poetic power is often felt in the 'genial' season of childhood. Wordsworth's belief in his 'genius' was another side of his passion for liberty, his trust in impulse, and his impatience of constraint. The crisis in his poetic life was the inevitable weakening, with time, of his 'genial spirits'. It is amazing that it should have been delayed so late as 1802, and should have lasted so long. Its traces are evident in *Resolution and Independence*, in the Immortality *Ode*, in the *Elegiac Stanzas on a Picture of Peele Castle*, in the *Ode to Duty*, and even in so late a poem as *Laodamia*. Wordsworth had immense powers of resistance to the inevitable, and the struggle released some of his deepest spiritual forces. He is never greater than in his effort to transcend the conscious loss or weakening of his 'genial spirits'. But the struggle was tremendous and it wore out his vital forces. Many critics who have speculated on the reasons for his fluctuations in poetic power have misunderstood the temperament of the man himself. Among his contemporaries De Quincey alone goes to the heart of the matter: his remarks on the 'self-consuming style of thought' in Dorothy as well as her brother should never be forgotten. 'And', continues De Quincey, 'strangers invariably supposed them fifteen to twenty years older than they were'.[1] The poets who remain in full activity until advanced old age are men of a different type. Goethe in his 'ivory tower' could go on writing equably until the end, so could Bridges, 'fortunatus nimium'. But in Wordsworth the forces of decay and renewal were always in conflict.

The work on Chaucer revived Wordsworth's inclination for narrative poetry, and he spent much of the early part of 1802 on improving *The Pedlar*.[2] But shorter compositions also claimed

[1] *Reminiscences of the English Lake Poets* Everyman edn., p. 107. De Quincey adds that, in view of Wordsworth's long life, 'it is plain that the premature expression of decay does not argue any real decay'.

[2] See especially Dorothy Wordsworth's *Journal* for February 1802.

much of his time. The chief completed narrative poem of the year was *Resolution and Independence*, which took two months to write (3 May — 4 July); two shorter ones are *Beggars*, and *Alice Fell*, both composed in March of the same year. As we are considering Wordsworth's poetry in the light of its expansion after the 'home' or pastoral epoch, we must note that the subjects of all three of these poems are deprived of the benefits of a true home and its associations. The beggars are 'joyous Vagrants'; Alice Fell, though she 'belongs' in some sense to Durham, is 'fatherless and motherless' and appears only as a waif in the night; while the Leech-Gatherer houses 'with God's good help, by choice or chance'. The actual meeting with the Beggars and the Leech-Gatherer took place some two years before the poems about them were written: both incidents therefore had to wait long for the mood which was destined to endow them with poetic life.

The imaginative greatness of *Resolution and Independence* cannot be missed. It also shows how an apparent self-contradiction in Wordsworth's attitude to life was really a stage in his poetic development. A similar contrast appears in the poem *Beggars* of 1802, and the *Sequel, composed many years after* (1817). He was right when he exulted in the useless beauty of nature's 'weeds' in the earlier poem; right also in his self-searching reflections at a later season:

> They met me in a genial hour,
> When universal nature breathed
> As with the breath of one sweet flower, —
> A time to overrule the power
> Of discontent, and check the birth
> Of thoughts with better thoughts at strife,
> The most familiar bane of life
> Since parting Innocence bequeathed
> Mortality to Earth!

So too the 'genial faith' of his youth had been right in its season. Needful things had come to him unsought. The 'marvellous boy' likewise had had his hour of pride, and Burns had followed the plough 'in glory and in joy': their subsequent fate cannot destroy the past. But 'genial faith' may deteriorate into wilful blindness: it must withdraw before a fuller revelation. That the fuller light was entering Wordsworth's consciousness with awe and mystery is beautifully suggested by the aspect of the Leech-Gatherer, at once sublime and visionary, a dream-like figure sent from some far region. It is forced upon the poet's mind that the old man's moral greatness does not originate in Nature but has another Source. This realization flashes out in the poet's appeal to God in the last lines of the poem. *Resolution and Independence* is like an outstanding peak in a chain of heights: it looks backwards to *Tintern Abbey* and forwards to the Immortality *Ode*, *Peele Castle*, the *Ode to Duty*, and the 'Mountain Echo'.

Soon after writing *Resolution and Independence* Wordsworth visited France in order to meet Annette Vallon for the last time before his marriage with Mary Hutchinson. The serenity of the sonnet 'It is a beauteous evening', written after a walk with his young daughter on Calais sands, proves that Wordsworth's emotions, mixed as they must have been, were not of a nature to prevent his taking an intense interest in the land he left ten years before. His mind was reawakened to public concerns after its long concentration on his inner life and a small circle of friends. Always stimulated by travel, he saw familiar sights with new eyes. His route lay through London; and a few weeks later he wrote the finest poem ever inspired by a view over the whole city. In Calais he felt acutely the contrast in mood between the two festivals he had witnessed in that town: the rapture at the Festival of the Federation on the first anniversary (1790) of the Fall of the Bastille, and the hollow rejoicings in 1802 on the birthday of the First Consul. The spontaneous rebirth of hope he had witnessed in 1790 was still a vital memory, but for its sequel he looked elsewhere than to the actions of the French people. Hope survived partly in his own 'genial spirits', and for its fulfilment he still trusted, though with many misgivings, to the future destiny of man. In 1790

> A homeless sound of joy was in the Sky;
> The antiquated Earth, as one might say,
> Beat like the heart of Man: songs, garlands, play,
> Banners, and happy faces, far and nigh!
> And now, sole register that these things were,
> Two solitary greetings have I heard,
> '*Good-morrow, Citizen!*' a hollow word,

As if a dead Man spake it! Yet despair
I feel not: happy am I as a Bird:
Fair seasons yet will come, and hopes as fair.[1] (1802)

In the sonnets, as in most of Wordsworth's poetry at this time, we shall find a concentration of spiritual energy and a clearer insight emerging from his inward conflict.

Wordsworth's 'hopes' originated partly in the spirit of the time, but the belief that the destruction of 'priestcraft' and 'tyranny' would set humanity free to follow the path to its own 'perfection' never took deep root in his mind. His passionate exultation in the opening phases of the French Revolution was in the main an outburst of the instinctive enthusiasm of youth, and its vision was the reign of 'virtuous Liberty' such as the Roman patriots had died for. Wordsworth's passion for Liberty, though derived partly from books, had been 'genial' like his passion for Nature. Both emotions were now being tempered into something firmer and tougher by time and experience.

It was only with the greatest reluctance that Wordsworth ceased to identify the cause of Liberty with the energy and generous spirit of the French nation. He had a high appreciation of the Latin mind and character, as he was to show in his attitude to Spain and his sense of the greatness of Italian poetry and art. But his spiritual allegiance was now shifting from Revolutionary France to the England of Shakespeare and Milton, of Daniel and Herbert. In some of his first patriotic sonnets, such as 'I grieved for Buonaparté' and 'Fair Star of Evening', one feels his regret for the growing alienation from France. But his tone soon becomes more decided. He has been blamed for the harshness of his sonnet on the 'perpetual emptiness' and 'unceasing change' in the character and actions of the French people, but he is no less severe to the servile worship of success in his own countrymen who 'crowd to bend the knee' to the 'new-born Majesty' of the First Consul:

Shame on you, feeble Heads, to slavery prone![2]

The cause of true Liberty was now paramount. The new Republic

[1] *P.W.* iii, p. 110. 'Jones! when from Calais', etc.: the version of 1807.
[2] *Calais, August, 1802. P.W.* iii, p. 109.

had already been guilty of crimes against the liberty of other
states, and by frankly facing the facts Wordsworth was stirred to
a militant mood which released the full vigour of his mind. His
imagination took a wider flight and brought into view the historic
achievements of Liberty in medieval Europe and its unfulfilled
aspirations in the New World. In stateliness and majesty the
sonnet *On the Extinction of the Venetian Republic* is unsurpassed
in his poetry, and the ending of the Toussaint sonnet suffices to
make it one of the great poems in the English language.

Within a few weeks Wordsworth had become a writer of
splendid sonnets, and when he returned to England at the end of
August he continued the series in exhortations to his own country.
If 'Sept. 3rd, 1802' is the correct date for the composition of
'Westminster Bridge', it looks as if he was now recalling his
feelings of 31 July on the way to France in their relation to his
task of reviving the 'plain living and high thinking' of the past.
The city as he had beheld it from the Bridge in the early morning
was a London reabsorbed into the rural life of Middlesex — a
'mighty heart' but as passive as a sleeping village. It was a scene
to arouse the deepest feelings of a 'lover or a child'. On relanding
in England at the end of August, his prevailing emotion had been
a new affection for the familiar sights of the country, 'the cock
that crows, the smoke that curls, that sound of bells',[1] but the
wealth and commerce of London 'oppressed' him, and he contrasted with shame the devotion of its Puritan citizens to 'the
good old cause', with the worldliness of the present generation.
This conflict of emotions wrought up his power of composition to
its highest pitch and was the source of the great sonnets begun
in the early autumn of 1802: 'Inland, within a hollow vale I stood',
'O Friend! I know not which way I must look', 'Milton! thou
should'st be living at this hour', 'Great men have been among us',
'When I have borne in memory', and the sonnet which closes
with the passage beginning 'We must be free or die'. One or two
may belong to the following year, but their spirit is still the same,
and all breathe the conviction that the destiny of Man hangs in
this time of crisis on the historic virtues of the poet's countrymen.
There is a strong emphasis throughout on the relation of 'house-

[1] *Composed in the Valley, near Dover.*

hold laws' to 'pure religion': 'manners', the sum-total of the 'unremembered acts' of obscure men, are ranked with 'virtue, freedom, power'. The dedicated austerity of these sonnets helps to make them 'in their simplicity sublime'.

The spirit of the sonnets written in 1803, when war with France had been renewed after the Peace of Amiens, differs little from that of the 1802 sonnets. Some of them, however, are more war-like. There was in 1803 an acute fear of invasion and Wordsworth himself, at Grasmere, joined the local volunteer force. The eloquent *Lines on the Expected Invasion* (1803) show his patriotism still drawing strength from seventeenth century memories: men who would have sided with the Royalists Falkland and Montrose are summoned, in the national peril, to forget their differences with those who would have joined the Republicans Pym and Milton. At intervals in 1803 the flow of great sonnets continued. 'They are', says A. V. Dicey, 'the finest war songs ever composed by a patriot to stir up the valour and nobility of his country; they might be termed the psalms of England, and like the Psalter they combine penitence for past errors with confidence in final victory based on the belief in the final triumph of righteousness.'[1] A distinction must be drawn between the purely militant sonnets and those in which the poet trembles to think that the cause of Liberty should be entrusted to a country in dire need of repentance. The sonnet *To the Men of Kent* is a spirited war poem, but there are some of far rarer value which it is amazing that a poet should have dared to write in such a year of peril as 1803. It would be a better time, says Wordsworth, addressing his country:

> But for thy trespasses . . .
> But worse, more ignorant in love and hate,
> Far — far more abject, is thine Enemy:
> Therefore the wise pray for thee, though the freight
> Of thy offences be a heavy weight:
> Oh grief that Earth's best hopes rest all with Thee![2]

The sonnets became rarer as the fear of invasion waned. The crisis of Napoleon's victory at Jena in 1806 produced what is

---

[1] *The Statesmanship of Wordsworth* (Oxford, Clarendon Press, 1917), p. 84.

[2] *Poems dedicated to Liberty*, I. xxxi.

perhaps the finest of the militant sonnets. In the succeeding years of the struggle with Napoleon,. Wordsworth's thoughts were directed as much to Spain and the insurgent Germans as to his own country: some of the most intimate feeling therefore disappears from his war poetry, though many of these later sonnets have a greatness of their own.

Wordsworth's sonnets dedicated to Liberty,[1] regarded as a whole, reflect the same movements of his mind as we have observed in *Resolution and Independence*. The 'genial mood', though still strong, is confronted by the more sober aspiration towards a higher spiritual life. Liberty is seen to be, not the free gift of Nature as it had appeared when the poet surveyed the great scene of human affairs in the fervour of youth,[2] but to be won at the cost of ceaseless effort, vigilance, and virtue: 'By the soul Only, the Nations shall be great and free.' He was beginning to weigh the causes of national greatness and decline in the light of a widening view of history. Venice and Switzerland had been the subjects of two great sonnets: Spain, Germany, and Italy were later to engage his anxious hopes. There is a change in Wordsworth's poetic style with this enlargement of view. The basic purity of diction is strengthened by Biblical and Puritan phrases (e.g. 'sufficient for the day', 'a reed that's shaken by the wind', 'the good old cause') and a slight but ennobling archaism.[3] His great effort is to teach the virtues of magnanimity and 'cheerful godliness'.

The shorter poems which Wordsworth wrote in 1803–4, apart from the sonnets, were not numerous, but they were very varied; some are unique examples of a particular style, and several show Wordsworth's mastery of the lyric at its height. His mind was partly diverted from public anxieties by a two months' tour in Scotland, and the new scenes were the occasion of his largest

---

[1] *Sonnets dedicated to Liberty* (1807).

[2] Cf. *French Revolution, as it appeared to Enthusiasts at its Commencement* (1804).

[3] Cf., for example, these two lines as Wordsworth wrote them:

> Two solitary greetings have I heard,
>   'Good-morrow Citizen!' a hollow word, etc.

with what their effect would be if the greeting were altered to 'Good-morning', the usual contemporary form.

body of verse during the year. The international situation improved somewhat with the return of Pitt to power in 1804 and that year was one of Wordsworth's most productive periods, but his mind was largely given to work on *The Prelude*, which was completed in the following year. The years 1803 and 1804 were more remarkable for the quality of the shorter poems than for their volume.

Some of these poems belong in spirit to an earlier time. *The Green Linnet* is a charming addition to the Grasmere poems, with the extra grace of Drayton's fairy-like stanza. *The Affliction of Margaret* was conceived with the searching insight into maternal grief which belongs to several of the first *Lyrical Ballads*, but its execution has the added strength and splendour of later years.[1] On the other hand, *Yew Trees*, though dated 1803 by Wordsworth, is thought by de Selincourt to have been written later, and the evidence of style perhaps supports this view. No finer poem, surely, was ever inspired by a *religio loci*. The warlike memories, the majestic aspect, the solemn associations, the unconquerable life of the 'fraternal four' are conveyed in some of the most splendid verse and diction in the English language. The concluding lines summon up mythically the primeval emotions which will continue to haunt the mind of man as long as he confronts the power of time, death, hope, and silence.

During the tour in Scotland Wordsworth was on the alert for the stimulus of novelty. In the Lowlands he was deeply and painfully impressed by the sight of Burns's grave, and the outcome was a set of three poems, left unfinished at the time. Shortly before, Wordsworth had depicted Burns as the poet who had followed the plough in glory and in joy, and the right sequel to this conception had yet to be written. He was troubled in spirit by the memory of a great poet who had lived so intensely and perhaps too long by the 'genial spirits' of youth.

Another of the poems, *Yarrow Unvisited*, commemorates a decision *not* to visit one of the most alluring Lowland regions, and the partly gentle, partly jaunty refusal to indulge his sister on this point, supported by a poet's respect for his own imagination,

[1] It was dated 1804 by Wordsworth. De Selincourt thinks that 'a slightly earlier date' is probable.

> We have a vision of our own;
> Ah! why should we undo it?

has a half-Scottish flavour which makes it a delightful piece of Border minstrelsy. It is no wonder that this spring-like ballad was followed by two successors in the moods of summer and autumn. But Wordsworth was not really in a Lowland mood on this tour: his heart was in the Highlands. He found a wild sublimity in the people, often solitary and apparently homeless amid their 'visionary' mountains. Strangeness, not intimacy, is the note of the Highland poems, and the sound of Gaelic speech was no small addition to the poet's enjoyment. The song of the solitary reaper is in an unknown tongue; the Highland girl of Inversneyd has but 'few words of English speech'. Wordsworth was even at pains to discover an authentic cry in Gaelic for the blind Highland boy on his voyage to the sea. It is a daring adventure, but the boy was following an 'inward light'. To leave the security of home for the hazards of the unknown is part of man's spiritual destiny. The poem which best sums up the spirit of the tour is the little piece *Stepping Westward*. The courteous greeting of the 'two well-dressed women' on the shore of Loch Katrine brought the spiritual meaning of his wanderings to Wordsworth's consciousness. The '*wildish* destiny' of travelling as the 'guests of chance' with little care for 'home or shelter' was really a '*heavenly* destiny', and, the poet continues:

> The echo of the voice enwrought
> A human sweetness with the thought
> Of travelling through the world that lay
> Before me in my endless way.

Part of the spirit of the poem is reproduced in the beautiful lines of the following year, 'She was a phantom of delight', Mary Wordsworth herself being 'A Traveller between life and death'.

This period of Wordsworth's life also produced two of his supremely beautiful lyrics, 'I wandered lonely as a cloud' (1804) and *The Solitary Reaper* (1805). Any attempt to characterize the quality of two such well-known poems would be superfluous. But each contains one or two features of general critical interest. Poets of all ages have sought to suggest the unity of a complicated scene within the compass of a few words, and this has seldom been done with such energy and vividness as in the lines (added in 1815):

> Continuous as the stars that shine
> And twinkle on the milky way,
> They stretched in never-ending line
> Along the margin of a bay:
> Ten thousand saw I at a glance,
> Tossing their heads in sprightly dance.

In *The Solitary Reaper* it is to be noticed how completely the reader's imagination is captivated by the first stanza so that he accepts without question the daring comparison of the girl's voice to the cry of the cuckoo in the Hebrides and the song of a nightingale in Arabia. It is curious also how so Wordsworthian a poem should owe a considerable verbal debt — acknowledged by the poet — to Thomas Wilkinson's *Tours of the British Mountains*. Wilkinson was a man after Wordsworth's own heart. He is remembered by the poet's lines addressed to his spade, of which Mrs. Moorman has courageously said that they have perhaps met with more ridicule than they deserve.[1] It is a pleasing thought that this man of Quaker habits — 'too pure to be refined' — whom Wordsworth describes with a plainness like his own, should have written the words which suggested one of the most glamorous of his friend's poems. 'Passed a Female', writes this traveller, 'who was reaping alone, she sung in Erse as she bended over her sickle, the sweetest human voice I ever heard. Her strains were tenderly melancholy, and felt delicious long after they were heard no more.'

Some further aspects of these 'Memorials' of the Tour in Scotland will be noticed in the chapter on the Poetry of Travel.

[1] Moorman, *Wordsworth, Early Years*, p. 519.

CHAPTER VI

Four Aspects of The Prelude

1. A POEM OF WORDSWORTH'S EARLY MATURITY

THE key-passage to the unity of *The Prelude* occurs near the beginning of Book VI:

> Four years and thirty, told this very week,
> Have I been now a sojourner on earth,
> And yet the morning gladness is not gone . . .[1]

The statement seems, at first, a little surprising, since two years earlier Wordsworth had deplored his loss of the 'visionary gleam' in the opening stanzas of the Immortality *Ode*. Though most of *The Prelude* was written in 1804–5, the first two books were probably finished by 1799. The stream of inspiration, we are told, stopped for years before it was heard again in the spring of 1804: still, it was evidently flowing from the same source. There is a continuous vitality in the whole *Prelude*: the poet seems verily upheld by 'morning gladness' even in recalling his most tragic years. Several deaths are recorded, including that of his father, which was remembered vividly, and yet his thoughts are almost exclusively bent on the things of life; as if at the age of thirty-four he could revive 'the feeling of immortality in youth'. But the power of renewal which the composition of the poem carried with it lasted only until the beginning of 1805, when the death of the poet's brother, John, left the sense of irretrievable loss as described in the *Peele Castle* poem. For these reasons *The Prelude*, especially the version of 1799–1805, must be regarded as a work of Wordsworth's *early* maturity.

No better short description of it could be imagined than the one given by Coleridge in his Lines 'To a Gentleman, Composed after his Recitation of a Poem on the Growth of an Individual Mind':[2]

[1] *The Prelude*, VI. 61–63 (1805).
[2] Coleridge, *Poetical Works*, pp. 176–8.

a linked lay of Truth,
Of Truth profound a sweet continuous lay;

and after touching on the development of the theme from child-hood's 'smiles spontaneous and mysterious fears' to 'the Social Sense distending wide', Coleridge continues:

Then (last strain)
Of Duty, chosen Laws controlling choice,
Action and joy!

And he sums up the whole work as 'that Lay more than historic, that prophetic Lay'. Few writers have recognized duty as one of the themes of *The Prelude*, nor indeed could it have been, had the poem been composed a few years earlier: but 1804, when most of it was written, was also the year of the *Ode to Duty*, and Coleridge's description is strictly accurate. Moreover, the poem not only links the Wordsworth of 1804 with his earliest memories, it is also 'prophetic'. On this note it ends:

What we have loved,
Others will love; and we may teach them how.[1]

These words express the consistent aspiration of his life.

The Prelude is a poem of two themes. The main theme is the course by which the liberty of the poet's life fostered the full, but not unhindered, development of his imagination; the counter-theme is the turning of his mind from a negative to a positive conception of Liberty, which is also the subject of the *Ode to Duty*. Naturally, the main theme is more prominent at first — the counter-theme emerges gradually. In the record of the poet's schooldays there are no scruples about the uses of liberty, which is the simple absence of restraint upon his intercourse with Nature — a blessed negation. So too, in the discussion of books, it is the reading of the holidays, free as to time, unfettered as to choice, that is gratefully remembered. In his first year at Cambridge, Wordsworth was never roused to that enthusiasm for learning which would have been its own discipline:

Youth should be aw'd, possess'd, as with a sense
Religious, of what holy joy there is

[1] *The Prelude*, XIII. 444–5 (1805).

> In knowledge, if it be sincerely sought
> For its own sake, . . .[1]

As it was, he constantly felt the irksomeness of authority.

During his second and third years at Cambridge however, 'the weight of too much liberty' began to be felt, and he rebukes

> that overlove
> Of freedom planted in me from the very first
> And indolence, by force of which I turn'd
> From regulations even of my own, . . .[2]

On the eve of setting out for France, he realized that the scheme was 'an open slight of College cares and study',[3] as well as ungrateful to those who had his worldly interests at heart. This compunction, however, could not avail against the intuition that his own education must be on a larger scale and of longer duration than that of other men. Most university students by the end of their course have achieved some sort of working reconciliation between inclination and duty. This resolution of opposites was delayed for Wordsworth; partly by a need, felt by many great poets, for prolonged preparation, partly by the apparent sanction, on an immense scale, to negative liberty which the early phases of the French Revolution exhibited before his eyes.

The admiration which Wordsworth shared with Beaupuy for Roman Republican virtue must have tended to strengthen his respect for the claims of duty. But the times made peculiar demands. Much of the old regime remained to be destroyed, and on the eve of Great Britain's declaration of war on France in 1793, Wordsworth still felt

> That throwing off oppression must be work
> As well of license as of liberty.[4]

Under the surface, however, the beginnings of his permanent philosophy were forming in his mind. He saw that human action was not so free as he had supposed. Just as the 'weight of ages' had been felt to hang over London as he first entered the city, so the ferocities of the Paris streets were seen as the issue of an evil

---

[1] Ibid. III. 396–9 (1805). [2] Ibid. VI. 44–47 (1805).
[3] Ibid. 342–3 (1805). [4] Ibid. X. 747–8 (1805).

legacy from the past. Wordsworth recognized this with something of the insight of the Hebrew Prophets: it was 'in the order of sublimest laws'.[1] There was thus a limit to human freedom in the constancy of a divine moral order. He clearly announces this counter-movement in his unfolding record: 'juvenile errors are my theme'.[2] The outcome was that he recognized the fallacy of founding a political system on 'abstract rights'. All the enormities in France had been wrought 'beneath [the] innocent authority'[3] of Liberty. So too, the negations of his private life were leading straight to the moral opportunism of which he writes with fierce sarcasm, quoting a well-known passage from his own tragedy, *The Borderers*, on 'the freedom of the individual mind', which acknowledges but 'one guide':

> the light of circumstances, flash'd
> Upon an independent intellect.[4]

The Prelude brings the narrative of Wordsworth's life only down to 1798. For some time after, the question of Liberty, personal and political, was shelved in the absorbing interest of the new poetry. The renewal of war in 1803, after the Peace of Amiens, brought to a head Wordsworth's indignation against French aggression, first felt as far back as 1794. As champion of national liberty and independence he discovered a positive and concrete Liberty which, albeit narrower than the boundless ideal of his first enthusiasm, was precisely what the times demanded. By enrolling himself in 1803 in the local Volunteers to resist invasion he verified the truths which he had dimly perceived years before. He became

> A moral agent, judging between good
> And evil, not as for the mind's delight
> But for her safety, . . .
> And through dislike and most offensive pain
> Was to the truth conducted; of this faith
> Never forsaken, that by acting well
> And understanding, I should learn to love
> The end of life and every thing we know.[5]

---

[1] Ibid. 414 (1805).   [2] Ibid. 638 (1805).   [3] Ibid. 351–2 (1805).
[4] Ibid. 829–30 (1805).   [5] Ibid. viii. 667–76 (1805).

This is the mature ethical outlook which is expressed in the *Ode to Duty*. Wordsworth makes no claim to any original discovery: these are 'things common to all'. But here, as elsewhere, it is his peculiar power to make us see common things in a new light — in ethics no less than in nature. *The Prelude* describes the travail through which he passed to attain this power. Against the recognition of Duty were ranged the insistent demands of his genius for its free development as well as the shattering experiences which seemed for a time to threaten the survival of his moral being. *The Prelude*, as its counter-theme, traces the greater part of this ethical evolution, though it does not include its later stages. It is therefore important to recognize, with Coleridge, that the growth of his mind, after Books I and II, is recorded from the standpoint of the mature position which he reached some years later, at the age of thirty-four.

The Prelude is also the record of Wordsworth's outgrowing of much immaturity and error in the art of poetry. By the time when he was about twenty his communion with Nature had attained its full development, but his mind had hardly begun to penetrate the real passions or social relations of men. Hence the chief labour of acquiring an original style lay all before him. The development of his literary art and taste is only a subordinate topic in *The Prelude*, and it is not consecutively traced, but when the parts are put together they are seen to fit into the stages of the larger scheme.

At an early age — thirteen or less,[1] he tells us — Wordsworth began to feel a conscious pleasure in 'words in tuneful order' *'for their own sakes'*. His first attempts at verse-writing followed, to be condemned, naturally, in due course:

> I was a better judge of thoughts than words,
> Misled in estimating words, not only
> By common inexperience of youth,
> But by the trade in classic niceties,
> The dangerous craft of culling term and phrase
> From languages that want the living voice
> To carry meaning to the natural heart; . . .[2]

---

[1] Ibid. v. 575–6 (1805). Altered to 'twice five years' in 1850.
[2] Ibid. VI. 106–12 (1850).

This is mainly an indictment of the practice of writing classical verse as a school-exercise, but it also condemns his use of second-hand, 'gradus', diction in his early descriptive poems. Two other adolescent faults are recalled: an inclination to indulge in melancholy sentiment, when he was extravagantly happy, as described in the *Ode to Lycoris*, and a tendency to treat human sorrows with 'wilful Fancy', i.e. to exaggerate the tragic into the 'super-tragic'. The Book entitled 'Cambridge and the Alps' is a rewriting in Wordsworth's mature style of the very faulty *Descriptive Sketches* (1793). It may seem strange, at first sight, that the great central passages on Imagination, and the Simplon Pass, should appear as early as Book VI of *The Prelude*. But their position is right and significant. Nature still stood higher than man in Wordsworth's interest and affection until he was twenty-two or twenty-three.[1] His capacity for feeling the sublime unity of a visionary scene had reached its culmination, but to describe the experience was still beyond him. One line and a half were indeed borrowed from *Descriptive Sketches* for the *Prelude* passage on the Simplon Pass, but for many years after 1793 he could not have compassed the sustained power of rhythm and diction of the great verse-paragraph. The description of the 'super-tragic' tendency follows in Book VIII, where Wordsworth, in tracing the extension of his love of Nature to the love of Man, dwells on the difficulties of attaining 'truth's golden mean'.[2] On one rare occasion, when he was seventeen, his feelings in the presence of Nature expressed themselves,

> In a pure stream of words fresh from the heart.

He paraphrases these early lines in *The Prelude* (VIII 468–75) and in their original form 'Dear native regions . . .', they still stand first in his *Collected Poems*.

One other deviation from the true path of imaginative inter-course with Nature is described. This was the violation of one of Wordsworth's strongest mature beliefs — that Nature must not be merely seen or heard by the senses, but felt by the soul. At the time when the moral world was under his 'microscopic' examina-tion, the natural world likewise came under the sole dominion of

----

[1] 23 in 1805, 22 in 1850.   [2] *The Prelude*, VIII. 382.

the eye — the eye not of the poet, but of a connoisseur in the picturesque, absorbed in 'superficial things', in 'meagre novelties of colour and proportion'.[1] For the true poet, the eye is an organ of the soul, not its master. Uncontrolled, 'it is the most despotic of our senses'[2] as Wordsworth knew to his cost, in spite of Nature's efforts to keep the balance between them. Time confirmed this conviction: he often returned to it, and at the age of seventy-six wrote an indignant sonnet[3] on the popular craving to indulge the eye with new pleasures at the expense of intellectual exertion.

2. STRUCTURE

The blank verse of *The Prelude* owes more to inspiration than to art and is of unequal quality. The verse of *The Excursion*, being partly modelled on Milton, is more sustained but has less natural character. The verse of *The Prelude* fluctuates with the varying vividness of the poet's memories and strength of emotion. He cared little for the independent beauty of rhythm and diction by which Milton unfailingly raised his style above the level of prose. Wordsworth wrote best when he wrote on impulse, and the planning of his long poem was therefore of crucial importance.

The chief scope for the exercise of his deliberate art lay in the structure of the work. He had to choose and arrange his material so that his mind spontaneously took a poetic course. More accurately, as poetic a course as possible; for as de Selincourt says, *The Prelude* 'cannot be judged solely by poetic canons': 'it is the frank autobiography of a great man'. But the autobiographical element has often been studied to some neglect of its other features. Though it was begun as a semi-private poem, not to be published before the completion of *The Recluse*, Wordsworth spared no effort in the essential parts of his task. Once he had decided to write the history of his own mind, whether in five, thirteen, or fourteen books, he was prepared to tax his powers to the utmost. His statement that poetry is the spontaneous overflow of powerful feelings is not a complete truth, as he afterwards admitted, but it has a special application to the writing of *The*

---

[1] Ibid. XII. 116–18.   [2] Ibid. 129.
[3] *Illustrated Books and Newspapers.*

Prelude. The past was receding, and the mood for composition must be seized. The inspired parts stand out in greater contrast to the rest than in *The Excursion*, where the urgency to write was not so pressing. The inequality of *The Prelude* in style should be frankly recognized, that its uniquely great qualities may stand out in clearer relief.

By the test of spontaneity we can go a long way towards distinguishing, and understanding the distinction, between the best and the less good books of the poem. The first two books are at once the most spontaneous and the widest in appeal: they set a standard for judging the rest of the work. The opening of the first book is a fine example of poetic strategy. In the first fifty-four lines (1805) the poet is rejoicing in his liberation from a 'City's walls' and in his possession of creative energy to 'consecrate' this newly won liberty. What he felt at the time he poured out 'in measur'd strains':

> poetic numbers came
> Spontaneously, . . .[1]

As if unwilling to lose the impulse, he continues with the record of a loitering journey of two days towards 'one sweet vale' which will be his home. His thoughts are turned towards 'some work of glory'. Arrived at his destination, he considers what subject he shall choose. He reviews several possible 'arguments' of a heroic kind, including the unheralded fame of one who

> Suffer'd in silence for the love of truth; . . .[2]

approaching by degrees the theme of *The Recluse*:

> some philosophic Song
> Of Truth that cherishes our daily life;
> With meditations passionate from deep
> Recesses in man's heart, . . .[3]

But he is still baffled, and begins to blame his failure in the stewardship of talent. Was it for this purpose that the Derwent murmured past his father's house, bringing him in childhood

> A knowledge, a dim earnest, of the calm
> That Nature breathes among the hills and groves?[4]

---

[1] *The Prelude*, i. 60–61 (1805).   [2] Ibid. 204 (1805).
[3] Ibid. 230–3 (1805).   [4] Ibid. 284–5 (1805).

That is enough: he has struck gold and a mine lies at his feet. With no epic invocation, but in his own original manner he has, like Dante, conditioned the reader's mind to accompany him to another world. Moreover, the initiative seems to lie with Nature: the theme, not the poet, has taken the decisive step. Hence the spontaneity of the whole first book. In Book II the boy is a conscious agent in the quest of beauty, and the narrative proceeds with gathering power to a splendid conclusion. Clearly the scheme of Book I cannot be repeated: it is Book II which provides the ideal pattern for the further stages of the poem, and for the special powers of the poet.

Two groups of books in *The Prelude* are devoted to its two main divisions. The first four books trace the growth of the poet's mind up to two decisive experiences in his first university vacation. The process is not regular, for the third book describes a slowing-down in his poetic growth, due to an infection of worldliness from the Cambridge of his day. This worldliness is overcome in the fourth book, and the end of the first stage of the poem is reached as the author recognizes his setting apart as 'a dedicated spirit'. Three books of this group are perfectly spontaneous, dictated by a natural inspiration. Books IX–XIV form the second connected group. They trace Wordsworth's adherence to the cause of Man as proclaimed at the outset of the French Revolution; his discovery that this faith was largely illusory; and his final attainment of a new hope, based on the permanent elements in human nature. These books are severed, except in a few passages, from the primary sources of inspiration in which the poem opens, but they exhibit the wider range of Wordsworth's poetic powers. Moral and intellectual enthusiasm; personal affection and admiration; contacts with living history; soaring hopes for mankind; the drama of the Revolution, whether in glory or terror — these things also touch him to poetic utterance. Stirred either by 'a vital breeze' or 'a tempest, a redundant energy' his verse moves forward to the goal assigned for each book. When possible, he orders his material to heighten this impression. For instance, by dividing the original tenth book into two, he makes the first resulting book a thrilling narrative, half personal, half historical, beginning with the September Massacres and ending with the Fall of

Robespierre. But several books of *The Prelude* lie outside its main currents. They are often on topics of less vital concern to the poet, less centred on what is universal in his love of Nature, or fundamental in his relations with Man. His style is affected by this difference; and several critical questions thus present themselves. These books, which we have now to consider, are III, V, VI, VII, and VIII.

It was necessary to the scheme of Books I–IV that Book III ('Residence in Cambridge') should end in something of an anti-climax, for Book IV was by contrast to record the poet's recovery of a purpose in life. The first year at Cambridge, as the summary tells us, was passed in 'submissive idleness', and its chief impression was 'an aching and a barren sense of gay confusion'. The book is a medley of recollections — some trivial or amusing, some on wayward but profitable reading, varied by a tribute to the historic greatness of the university. The important passage on his quest for 'universal things' in the flat Cambridgeshire landscape does not come as the culmination of the book but near its opening, and is out of tune with the dissatisfied conclusion. Yet in spite of this inconsistency, the total effect of the book is pleasing. It reveals the poet in a very human light and is, on the whole, in his lighter vein.[1] This mood is continued in the opening of the next book.

Book V ('Books') is 'static' in relation to the main course of *The Prelude* and has partly the character of an essay. For Wordsworth, the normal child is something of a natural poet, whose instinct and enthusiasm are his best guides. His own imagination was first nourished on fairy-tales; later by 'good books, though few'. The book opens with the dream of an 'Arab phantom' (who is also a 'semi-Quixote'), bent on preserving the two great lights of the human mind — 'geometric Truth' (Reason) and Poetry (Imagination) from imminent destruction.[2] Here Wordsworth is on his own ground, but when he enters a contemporary controversy on children's education, the pulse of poetry beats feebly. He attacks the condemnation of fairy-tales by the disciples of Rousseau, admitting this is a 'transitory theme'. His satirical description of the paragon child, 'a miracle of scientific lore', is not absorbed

[1] See pp. 168, 169.   [2] See pp. 8, 9.

into the current of the poetry. Its chief service to *The Prelude* is
to throw into relief the exquisite idyll of childhood — the lines on
the boy of Winander. It is the power of the opening dream and
the subtle observation of children absorbed in their own discoveries which create the best poetry of this book.

Books VI, VII, and VIII fill the interval between the two main
parts of *The Prelude* and lie outside the more stressful periods of
the poet's history. The first of the three, 'Cambridge and the
Alps' contains some of the best poetry in all the books and is
concerned wholly with 'genial' themes. The poet's right to liberty
was taken perhaps too much for granted but its fruits were
splendid. Soon the book becomes the greatest of Wordsworth's
many achievements in travel-poetry. First there are recollections
of visits to Dovedale and 'hidden tracts' of his native region, with
Dorothy as his companion. These are followed by a rewriting of
Descriptive Sketches in what the poet justly calls 'a more melodious
song'. Never again did he know such radiant hope as in this tour
through France of 1790. There, however, his emotion and
sympathies were active, not his reason. The best poetry of the
Book is reserved for an occasion on which his total mind rose to
recognize its counterpart in Nature. His imagination was
summoned from its 'Abyss' to encounter the sublimity of the
Alpine scenery:

> In such strength
> Of usurpation, when the light of sense
> Goes out, but with a flash that has revealed
> The invisible world, doth greatness make abode.
> There harbours; whether we be young or old,
> Our destiny, our being's heart and home,
> Is with infinitude, and only there; . . .[1]

Immediately follow the magnificent lines on the Simplon Pass in
which the visible and the invisible worlds are merged in a single
revelation. Any sequel to these passages, one would suppose, must
be an anti-climax, and Wordsworth does not wholly escape this
danger, though he still has some fine scenes — Locarno and
Como — to describe. But his real reserve of strength is his high
confidence in the mind's independent greatness:

[1] *The Prelude*, VI. 599–605.

> Not rich one moment to be poor for ever;
> Not prostrate, overborne, as if the mind
> Herself were nothing, a mere pensioner
> On outward forms — did we in presence stand
> Of that magnificent region.[1]

In 'Residence in London' (Book VII), the 'external' quality of the capital is so handled that it harmonizes as well as possible with the general spirit of the poem. Though Wordsworth was out of his usual element he resisted 'ungenial' domination. The Book opens with his romantic expectations before visiting London and closes with the well-founded assertion that the Spirit of Nature was upon him there.[2] If London did not lay 'strong hold on his affections' it at least gave him patriotic pride as the metropolis and it broadened his imagination. In time, his memories of common street-scenes began to form the background of some highly characteristic poems. There were the companion pieces on rural exiles in thoroughfare or market: *The Reverie of Poor Susan* and *The Farmer of Tilsbury Vale*. Some years later, he wrote three poems, *Power of Music*, *Star-Gazers*, and *Stray Pleasures*, on the natural instincts of humble people breaking out in Oxford Street or Leicester Square or on a Thames-side floating mill. No reader who enters into the spirit of this book need feel surprise that the City remained permanently in the background of Wordsworth's thoughts.

'Retrospect' (Book VIII) is the least satisfying of all the books, for much of it reverts to the past without greatly enriching the main narrative. The sub-title is 'Love of Nature leading to Love of Man', i.e. the power of a cherished environment to inspire affection for the persons associated with it. Wordsworth had already given illustrations of this process in the *Lyrical Ballads*, and a large part of the book traverses the same ground, with a disquisition on pastoral poetry, which might have been useful in another place. He recalls his school-boy rambles, when a shepherd and his sheep might suddenly appear through thick fog, impressively magnified. This is a good anthology piece, but placed in this part of *The Prelude*, it tends to exaggerate the importance of a particular memory. Twice already Wordsworth has described

---

[1] Ibid. 735–9.   [2] Ibid. VII. 766.

stages of his advance in 'human-heartedness' beyond the time of childhood — in the opening part of Book IV and in several passages of 'Residence in London'. It is perhaps a relief when at l. 476 the poet exclaims:

> Enough of humble arguments; recal,
> My Song! those high emotions which thy voice
> Has heretofore made known; . . .

He now enters on a reappraisal of what Cambridge and London had contributed to his preparation for the larger and sterner business of life. Hitherto his mind had been stimulated by impressions of Nature 'fitted' to itself: now he was about to receive a wider revelation. The strength of the book lies in this weighty concluding passage. After a lingering course in Books V, VII, and VIII, the current of the poem again gathers impetus in Book IX.

De Selincourt remarks that *The Prelude* 'has something of epic structure'. It also has something, or rather much, of the epic spirit. The poet begins his work in the faith that the history of his mind contains matter to sustain his verse through a long poem at a high and serious level. Though resorting occasionally to a lighter tone, he is on the whole triumphantly justified. Through the two chief divisions of his work his verse is responsive to his sustaining confidence. In the 'static' parts, where the impulse is more variable, he is more liable to mischance. The continuity of the record from one book to another is also best preserved in the two main divisions, except in Book IX ('Residence in France') where the interpolated story of 'Vaudracour and Julia' (whether in full, or reduced to a few lines) indicates a hiatus in the main record which cannot be denied or filled. Some readers have wished that Wordsworth had entirely passed over this episode, which contributes an unsolved enigma to the poem, but second thoughts will decide that the break in continuity bears witness to his integrity. He could not tell all, nor could he pretend that there was nothing to tell.[1]

The strongly-marked character of Wordsworth's mind prevents

---

[1] On p. 573 of his edition of *The Prelude*, de Selincourt discusses this question with an insight and breadth of view which cannot be overpraised.

any danger of serious inconsistency between the beginning of the poem and its close. The poet himself occasionally reminds us of its continuity. For instance, the news of Robespierre's death reaches him on the sea-shore which he had once visited on a riding expedition in his school-days, and the memory is recalled by a quotation from the earlier book, as if the joyous exultation of the past was itself revived. Again, Book XII concludes with two illustrations of 'imaginative power' drawn from memories of childhood which, by thus bringing the narrative back to its starting point, strengthen the impression of the poem's fundamental unity.

The Prelude was written mainly in two periods separated by about five years. Wordsworth's thought was always developing and a certain change took place in the interval. It is de Selincourt's view that 'when Wordsworth wrote *The Prelude* he had in nothing swerved from the faith that inspired the *Lines composed a few miles above Tintern Abbey*'. But at least the implications of that faith may have been more fully realized: there is certainly some change in the terms in which it is expressed. Coleridge's description of his friend as a 'semi-atheist' may be consistent with *Tintern Abbey*, but cannot be so with *Resolution and Independence* or the *Ode to Duty*. It is true that when the first *Prelude* was finished in 1805, Wordsworth was some distance from the orthodox Christianity which is traceable in certain passages of the 1850 version, but there is an element of Theism in 1805 which would not have appeared if the poem had been finished in 1799. This change makes *The Prelude* more central to the poet's work as a whole than if it had been perfectly consistent. In one sense, it is impossible to say that either the first *Prelude* or the last is the 'true' poem. Both versions, with all the MS. variations which lie between, reflect some stage in the growth of his mind. Further points on the relation between the two versions will be discussed in the last section of this chapter.

3. THE CLOSING BOOKS (XI–XIV)

The last four books of *The Prelude* have not found much favour with Wordsworth's biographers. De Selincourt complains that 'the narrative, up to this point clear and consecutive, becomes involved and wavering'; the author 'goes backwards and forwards, so that the progress of events is not easy to trace'. But readers interested primarily in the growth of the poet's mind will rejoice in the concentration of these final books on that subject. Book XI deals with the poet's afterthoughts on the Revolution and his despair in the non-fulfilment of its promises. Books XII and XIII, on his 'restoration', are concerned, respectively, with the relations of his imagination to Nature, and to Man. The last book (XIV) gives a picture of Imagination in operation and looks forward to the parallel efforts in poetry of Wordsworth himself and of Coleridge. Two points, however, must be noticed. If it is true, as I have suggested, that the answer to Wordsworth's philosophical despair is the whole body of his poetry from 1797 onwards, an account of his 'restoration' given as early as 1804–5 could not be complete. Secondly, *The Prelude*, being addressed to Coleridge, refers only to those poems with which Coleridge was closely associated, i.e., the first *Lyrical Ballads*. Thus there is no specific reference to any of the poems written between 1799 and 1804, which are among the most eloquent in illustrating the growth of their author's mind.

Most of the important points in Books XI and XII — the latter of which insists that the true appreciation of Nature requires participation by the total personality — are discussed in other parts of this study. Reference, however, must be made to the two vivid memories, 'spots of time' from his childhood, recorded in Book XII, illustrating how 'outward sense' is the 'obedient servant' of the mind — an anticipation of the final passage of *The Prelude*. Book XIII opens some new areas of thought. In expounding the relations of Wordsworth's restored imagination to Man, three aspects of the subject, sometimes merging one with the other, are brought into view. Man is considered as an individual; as needing an elemental culture; and as part of the Cosmos. Only as an individual can he truly be an object of 'pure imagination and of love'. The generalizations of politician and economist are discounted in advance: the interest of poetic imagination is on the man whom we behold with our own eyes. Here is the principle often noticed in Wordsworth's poems on

single objects in nature extended to the human sphere. Just as the
individual flower or tree is sublimated into something of higher
meaning or beauty than its ordinary self so certain men and
women, under the illuminating light of imagination, may reveal
an unsuspected nobility of nature. In cities this transformation is
more rare and difficult: it was chiefly on 'the lonely roads', the
poet tells us, that he 'saw into the depth of human souls, Souls
that appear to have no depth at all'. To readers of the poems
written between 1800 and 1804, this is simply a generalized statement of what they know already. They remember the persons
described in the best of the Grasmere poems, or those met in the
wilder parts of Scotland. Another great poet of rural life has
made precisely the same observation. 'The thought of Pascal's
was brought home to him: A mesure qu'on a plus d'esprit, on
trouve qu'il y a plus d'hommes originaux. Les gens du commun
ne trouvent pas de différence entre les hommes.' And among the
varieties of rural character described by Hardy is one which was
particularly dear to Wordsworth — the 'mutely Miltonic':

> Others, too,
> There are among the walks of homely life
> Still higher, men for contemplation framed,
> Shy, and unpractis'd in the strife of phrase,
> Meek men, whose very souls perhaps would sink
> Beneath them, summon'd to such intercourse:
> Theirs is the language of the heavens, the power,
> The thought, the image, and the silent joy; . . .[1]

Others, also worthy of the poet's song, are not the product of
Nature alone, but also of nurture. They have been

> Not unexalted by religious hope,
> Not uninformed by books, good books though few,
> In Nature's presence: . . .[2]

These are somewhat frigid words compared with the fervent
language on the sources of spiritual strength in lives like those of
the Leech-Gatherer or the Matron of Jedborough. But it is
significant that the poet's meaning is expressed as a general truth.
The quotation is taken from a passage, printed for the first time

---

[1] *The Prelude*, XII. 264–71 (1805).   [2] Ibid. 242–4 (1805).

in the Postscript to Wordsworth's volume of 1835. Little alter-
ation was necessary to correspond with changes in his thought
during thirty years. The passage, he says, 'turns upon the individual dignity which humbleness of social condition does not
preclude, but frequently promotes.' The change of one word,
however, points to a strengthening of conviction: the phrase
'religious hope' (1805) becomes 'religious faith'.

Thirdly, Wordsworth relates his discovery of these outstanding
individuals — 'souls of God's best earthly mould' — to his more
sober hopes for the future of the race which replaced the unbounded confidence of his youth. Rare though such men and
women are in proportion to the whole population — perhaps
'one only in ten thousand' — 'what one is,' asks the poet, 'why
may not millions be?' We may well ask on what foundation this
sanguine belief is based. Wordsworth supports it by the memory
of a vision which seemed to him a second-sight revelation —
granted through the power of Imagination to perceive 'objects
unseen before'. The poet was walking over Salisbury Plain in the
summer of 1793. He had been gloomily impressed by the naval
preparations off the Isle of Wight, and the vast monotonous
aspect of the Plain with its pre-historic monuments combined to
produce to his inner eye a vision penetrating far into the past
and future of the race. First he had a glimpse of life in the dawn
of human history:

> Multitudes of men, and, here and there
> A single Briton clothed in wolf-skin vest;[1]

then, after darkness had fallen:

> The Desert visible by dismal flames,[2]

and all the horrors of human sacrifices; thirdly, as in a waking
dream, a sight full of charm:

> long-bearded teachers, with white wands
> Uplifted, pointing to the starry sky,[3]

with music to sway their motions. The interpretation of the
visions evidently is that Man, while doomed to pass through great
tribulation, does really achieve some vast gradual progress, to

[1] Ibid. XIII. 321–2.   [2] Ibid. 330.   [3] Ibid. 345–6.

which the aspirations of a chosen few contribute by their message
of confident hope. That there is an element of 'cosmic optimism'
in Wordsworth's thought at this time is confirmed by his use of a
phrase like 'the unreasoning progress of the world'[1] in another
part of *The Prelude*. But in *The Excursion* there is a change,
though not, it is true, signified by the poet speaking in his own
person. The retrospective view into the remote past and its
contrast with the present reappear near the end of the later
poem. But the white-bearded teachers have gone, and the Pastor
attributes the 'marvellous advance' to 'the true and only God'
and the Christian faith.[2]

In Book XIV Wordsworth takes leave of his subject briefly, but
as if viewed from a commanding eminence. He begins with the
description of an ascent of Snowdon by night and of the panoramic view which broke on his vision at sunrise. The prospect, at
once immensely varied and yet a unity, is likened to a complex
poetic theme moulded by the power of imagination. Wordsworth
seems to be writing here in a kind of sympathetic collaboration
with Coleridge. The whole book is in large measure a tribute to the
friends most closely associated with Wordsworth's poetic enter-
prises. Dorothy is the object of heart-felt gratitude, so is Raisley
Calvert, the giver of the legacy which made the poet independent.
Looking to the future, Wordsworth joins himself with Coleridge
in the aspiration that both may prove Prophets of Nature. Having
regard to the total course of Wordsworth's poetry one is tempted
to prefer the humbler hope quoted earlier:

> what we have loved,
> Others will love, and we will teach them how[3]

— a promise faithfully fulfilled. But *The Prelude*, for good or ill,
has the limitations of its date, and the bolder aspiration is in
accord with the faith and hope of his 'early maturity'. His
intellectual growth did not cease with the completion of *The
Prelude* in 1805.

4. STYLE

When the 1805 version of *The Prelude* was first published in 1926,
a number of readers were inclined to regard it as the authentic

[1] Ibid. v. 359.   [2] *The Excursion*, IX. 720–2.   [3] 'may' (1805).

text of the poem. Subsequent changes were assumed in general to mark a decline both in poetic power and political wisdom from the glorious prime of the author: he had disfigured his master-piece with 'pompous phrase-making' and 'pietistic embroidery' and the unsullied form was now recovered. This view, though based chiefly on the dogma of Wordsworth's poetic fall from grace after 1807 is not without some foundation, but at present it is still the other side of the truth that needs to be emphasized.

The poem as it stood in 1805 was not supposed to be ready for publication. When Wordsworth wrote to Sir George Beaumont on 8 June 1805, 'I finished my work about a fortnight ago', he was referring to the more creative and arduous part of composi-tion. His most pressing task had been to get his thoughts on to paper in metrical lines. Had he decided to publish in his lifetime, many alterations would have been made in much the same way in any year between 1805 and 1850. A change such as the one from

<blockquote>Beneath the gloomy hills I homeward went   I. 448 (1805)</blockquote>

to

<blockquote>Beneath the gloomy hills homeward I went   I. 421 (1850)</blockquote>

is almost inevitable. The change from

<blockquote>The solid Mountains were as bright as clouds   IV. 333 (1805)</blockquote>

to

<blockquote>The solid Mountains shone, bright as the clouds,   IV. 327 (1850)</blockquote>

and the change from

<blockquote>the great Sea meanwhile

Was at safe distance to   x. 529–30 (1805)

the great Sea meanwhile

Heaved at safe distance,   x. 566–7 (1850)</blockquote>

are equally simple and welcome. The reader of the 1805 version will quickly recognize the passages which need such amendment and will usually find it made.

A change of more critical interest is the reduction in the number of geographical terms. Wordsworth loved the place-

names of the Lake District, but too liberal a use of them might
have interfered with the poetic generalization of his life-story.
Accordingly we find various place-names and phrases deleted
from the 1805 version: e.g. Cockermouth (I. 287), Patterdale
(I. 376), 'the flat Plains of Huntingdon' (III. 2), 'the Heights of
Kendal' (IV. 2), 'Blencathra's rugged sides' (VII. 8), 'Coker's stream'
(VII. 345), Cambridge (IX. 227) — not all of which, indeed, are very
suitable for verse. Hawkshead is not named in either version: it is
'that beloved vale' or 'that sweet valley'. Wordsworth, however,
desires to satisfy the reader that there was a basis of fact to every
flight of imagination, and on one occasion, when he could not
quote the evidence, he honestly admits the fault:

> that rural castle, name now slipped
> From my remembrance.[1]

Throughout the poem he has to hold the balance between the
particular and the general, and these rival claims vary with
circumstances. After his return from France the history of his
mind was narrowed down to an intense internal drama in which
details of time and place were of small account. Such geographical
names as occur in Books XII–XIV, e.g. 'Sarum's Plain', 'Snowdon',
relate mostly to incidents already in the past at the time of which
he is writing.

In revising *The Prelude*, Wordsworth sometimes made a needless
change in the simplicity of the original text, but this fault has
been somewhat exaggerated. 'The sole stylistic error of his later
version', says de Selincourt, 'lies in a too generous concession to
the vulgar taste for poetical ornament.' But this criticism must be
accepted with caution: some later elaborations are harmless;
some are improvements. For instance, an undergraduate seen by
Wordsworth as he first entered Cambridge by coach was gazed at
until left 'a hundred yards behind': later, 'an arrow's flight behind'.
Our poet was so often ridiculed for his mathematical precision
that surely this mild concession to 'vulgar taste' may be pardoned.
On the other hand, there was no need to alter the simplicity of the
line describing a beautiful 'cottage-child':

> As ever sate upon a Mother's knee

[1] *The Prelude*, IX. 483–4 (1805, 1850).

to the more emotional:

> As ever clung around a mother's neck;[1]

nor was it an improvement to replace a plain allusion to 'Doctor Young' by a periphrasis of two lines:

> the Bard
> Whose genius spangled o'er a gloomy theme
> With fancies thick as his inspiring stars.[2]

These examples are from what I have called the 'static' Books — the less spontaneous parts of the poem. Certain additions here and there in the other Books make the 1850 *Prelude* in some ways a more interesting and beautiful poem than the original version. For instance, by elaborating the nondescript

> Bidding then
> A farewell to the City left behind[3]

into

> casting then
> A backward glance upon the curling cloud
> Of city smoke, by distance ruralised,[4]

he has given a touch of pleasure to readers who still care for the picturesque, at the same time adding a new word to the vocabulary of description. Equally graphic is the transforming line added to the account of his return to Hawkshead from Cambridge:

> I overlook'd the bed of Windermere,   (both versions)
> Like a vast river, stretching in the sun.[5]   (1850 only)

It is now generally known that the two magical lines which follow the memory of Roubiliac's Newton at Trinity College are a later addition, as is also the beautiful line on the Cumberland landscape in autumn:

> Clothed in the sunshine of the withering fern.[6]

Without denying Wordsworth's power of handling abstract arguments in severe simplicity and yet unprosaically, we must admit that he was, in his own words, 'too reckless of mild grace'.[7]

---

[1] Ibid. vii. 370 (1805) to ibid. 340 (1850).
[2] Ibid. 564–6.   [3] Ibid. i. 97–98 (1805).   [4] Ibid. 87–89 (1850).
[5] Ibid. iv. 6.   [6] Ibid. vi. 11.   [7] Ibid. xiv. 248.

The revision of *The Prelude* has helped to supply what was wanting, and the 'rock with torrents roaring' has had its crevices sparingly planted with flowers.

Further comparison of the two versions leads us back to the aspect of *The Prelude* as a work of Wordsworth's early maturity. Later modifications in the text in the direction of conformity with Christian doctrine raise questions of great difficulty which cannot be separated from the religious convictions of the critic. Every thoughtful reader of Wordsworth is bound to be something of a theologian. It appears to me that Wordsworth meant to leave *The Prelude* substantially true to the state of his mind in 1805, and that in general he did so. The seriousness with which he regarded his responsibility as a teacher, however, caused him on occasion to break this rule. He could not forget that he had been condemned 'for not distinguishing between Nature as the work of God and God himself'. There are passages, especially in Book II of *The Prelude* (1805) which, taken by themselves, might give rise to this misconception. He there sums up his early intercourse with Nature in a form which might have appeared in *Tintern Abbey*:

> Wonder not
> If such my transports were; for in all things now
> I saw one life, and felt that it was joy.[1]

This passage was expanded as follows in 1850:

> Wonder not
> If high the transport, great the joy I felt,
> Communing in this sort through earth and heaven
> With every form of creature, as it looked
> Towards the Uncreated with a countenance
> Of adoration, with an eye of love.[2]

This marked distinction between the Creator and the creation harmonizes with the growing Theism of Wordsworth's outlook in 1804–5 as compared with that of 1799. If he wished to interpret an early experience in the light of his later thought, assuredly he was right to do so. The new lines are a good poetic passage and

---

[1] Ibid. II. 428–30. (1805).   [2] Ibid. 409–14 (1850).

do not seriously offend chronology. But this cannot be said of all the changes. For instance, the phrase added to the description of Man as the crown 'of all visible natures',

> though born
> Of dust, and kindred to the worm; . . .[1]

accords with *The Excursion*, but not with *The Prelude*. The poet's hard struggle for the grace of humility belongs to the period of the later poem.

Generally speaking, the omission of passages from the 1805 version of *The Prelude* was a gain. The poet wisely curtailed Book VIII by two hundred lines. The omission of seventeen lines from Book XI (121–137) was another improvement. There is one exception, however, which is too interesting to be overlooked. Some strongly worded lines are omitted from a passage in Book IV in which Wordsworth is sitting in judgement on the tendency to worldliness in his first year at Cambridge and its injury to true 'religious dignity of mind'. If this is 'wanting' or 'extinguished',

> Man, a creature great and good,
> Seems but a pageant plaything with vile claws
> And this great frame of breathing elements
> A senseless Idol.[2]

This passage was retained — with modifications — until a late revision of *The Prelude*. Why Wordsworth finally dropped it is open to conjecture, but to doubt that religion had a fundamental place in his conception of Man and Nature is fatal to any profound understanding of his poetry.

[1] Ibid. VIII. 487–8.　　[2] Ibid. IV. 301–4 (1805).

CHAPTER VII

Paulo majora canamus

THE 'Immortality' Ode which closes the second of Wordsworth's two volumes published in 1807 is headed by the
quotation chosen as the title of this chapter and was clearly
intended to be the culminating poem of the collection. Few
readers will question Wordsworth's rightness of judgement in
giving the *Ode* this pride of place. The amplitude of its scope
and the spell of its style give it an irresistible appeal: it infallibly
touches the reader's imagination to spiritual issues. Even those
who object to it on philosophical grounds seldom question its
success as poetry. But are there no other poems in the two volumes
which attain to something of the same greatness? Wordsworth's
arrangement of the contents suggests the answer. Of the three
poems which immediately precede the *Ode* in the original collection, two may certainly make this claim: the *Song, at the Feast of
Brougham Castle* and *Elegiac Stanzas, Suggested by a Picture of
Peele Castle*; and the third (*Lines, Composed at Grasmere*)[1] may be
included with them in spite of its brevity. The same distinction
might apply to certain other poems (e.g. the *Ode to Duty*) in
different parts of the two volumes. It will be the task of the
present chapter to discuss this group of greater poems.

The date of the 'Immortality' *Ode* has occasioned a good deal of
discussion. Its composition in two periods of the poet's life,
separated by two or three years, is certain; but whereas Wordsworth himself assigned the poem to the years 1803–6, de Selincourt
dates it as 1802–4. That the *Ode* was begun in 1802 seems clear,
since there are 'deliberate reminiscences' of lines 40 and 9 in
Coleridge's *Dejection*, written on 4 April of that year.[2] His own
Ode, Wordsworth says, was completed 'two years at least' after its

[1] i.e. 'Loud is the Vale!', etc.

[2] *P.W.* iv, p. 464. The reference is to lines 136 and 295 in the earliest
and afterwards abandoned form of *Dejection: an Ode*.

inception. De Selincourt, basing his views on certain facts connected with Coleridge's knowledge and use of the poem, then existing only in manuscript, infers that it must have been completed within the first quarter of 1804, and that it was included in the MS. poems of Wordsworth, which Coleridge took with him when he left England for Malta in April 1804. De Selincourt's conclusions are summarized in the sentence: 'It was begun in March 1802; it seems to have been finished in March 1804.' In that case the *Ode* is not connected with the poet's grief at the death of his brother John on 5 February 1805, and lines 197–9 do not contain the personal allusion sometimes attributed to them.[1] After the shock of his great loss, Wordsworth was never the same man again, and it is important to recognize that the change in his view of life recorded in the *Elegiac Stanzas on a Picture of Peele Castle* had not taken place when the 'Immortality' *Ode* was written.

Many readers regard the *Ode* as a philosophical poem on Wordsworth's changing attitude to Nature. Such in one sense it undeniably is, and it is the poet himself who relates his reflections to 'the philosophic mind'. But the *Ode* appears to be more broadly based in common experience than is admitted in this view. Though Wordsworth's intercourse with Nature was deeper than that of most persons, it differed from theirs only in degree, and many readers of the *Ode* recognize it as a true mirror of certain phases in their intellectual history. The poet himself passes from 'I' in the earlier stanzas (1–4) to 'we' in the middle passages, and the change is readily accepted. No doubt Wordsworth's poem on the Three Ages of Man contains more of its author's individuality than the impersonal speech on the Seven Ages of Man in *As You Like It*, and yet the *Ode* is as much a poem on mankind as on the poet himself. This, of course, is a feature of most great lyrical poems, but in the present instance the point needs special emphasis. It is chiefly this aspect of the *Ode* that I shall attempt to bring into prominence in the following remarks.

[1] For further reasons for concluding that 'the date of the Ode must be put back at least to January 1805', see de Selincourt's notes: iv, pp. 464–5.

There are two main obstacles to regarding the *Ode* in this broader aspect. It will be said by some objectors: Does not the *Ode* require its readers to believe in the pre-existence of the soul? Although Wordsworth has thrown off here and there some passing speculations on the truth of this doctrine, it had no fixed place among his convictions. It is adopted in the poem rather as a description than as an explanation of the mysteries of childhood. His own words are explicit. 'A pre-existent state', he says, 'has entered into the popular creeds of many nations; and, among all persons acquainted with classic literature, is known as one ingredient in Platonic philosophy . . . I took hold of the notion of pre-existence as having sufficient foundation in humanity for authorizing me to make for my purpose the best use of it I could as a poet.'[1] It is easy to recall similar instances of the adoption within the limits of a single poem of some belief or theory for its imaginative effect. Marvell does this in *The Garden*, Coleridge in *The Ancient Mariner*, and neither poet is accused of false teaching. There is no reason why Wordsworth should not use a similar licence in his *Ode*, especially when he makes it clear that he is doing so.

Secondly, we must not allow certain references to philosophy to restrict our interpretation of the *Ode*. They do not affect its basic character. Coleridge's objection to a particular passage in which the child is apostrophized as a 'Philosopher' need not, I think, be taken very seriously. A child can be called a philosopher in humorous or imaginative exaggeration. It is, however, misleading to regard Wordsworth's 'solipsism' as determining the general character of the poem. The poet's own comments have perhaps tended to emphasize the uniqueness of the *Ode* at the expense of its wider application. 'I was often unable', he said, speaking of his childhood in a note dictated to Miss Fenwick, 'to think of external things as having external existence, and I communed with all that I saw as something not apart from, but inherent in, my own immaterial nature. Many times while going to school have I grasped at a wall or tree to recall myself from this abyss of idealism to the reality.' Wordsworth was somewhat sceptical about the appeal of the *Ode*. 'This poem rests entirely upon two

[1] Fenwick Note.

recollections of childhood', he wrote to Mrs. Clarkson,[1] 'one that of a splendour in the objects of sense which is passed away, and the other an indisposition to bend to the law of death as applying to our own particular case. A Reader who has not a vivid re-collection of these feelings having existed in his mind in Childhood cannot understand that poem.' But in the *Ode*, as in all his genuine poetry, Wordsworth was a man speaking to men. The dream-world in which he passed his early years was, it is true, unusually intense and long-enduring, and when at length he emerged from it into a continuous consciousness of 'reality' (the 'sense-world'), it was like the birth into a new existence: the earth and every common sight wore the glory and the freshness of a dream. But numbers of other men have similar recollections of childhood, even if these are removed by many gradations from what Wordsworth describes. Poets especially have sometimes alluded to trances and visions of their own which correspond to Wordsworth's 'idealism', and these in like manner were the basis of their future 'genius' or poetic power. If they have said com-paratively little about them, it is because they did not possess his compelling reasons, as described in *The Prelude*, for linking his mature mind with his childhood.

It may indeed seem strange that the world should have had to wait so long for such a poem. Wordsworth's generation had been prepared by Rousseau and his successors to regard childhood with a new seriousness, but anticipations of the main thought of the *Ode* are easily found at an earlier date. A kind of pre-Wordsworthian tradition may be traced back at least as far as the early seventeenth century. There is a character-sketch of 'A Childe' in Earle's *Microcosmographie* (1628) which comes peculiarly close to the spirit of the *Ode* (stanzas 5, 6, and 7): 'We laugh at his foolish sports, but his game is our earnest: and his drums, rattles and hobby horses but the emblems, and mocking (i.e. imitation) of man's business. His father . . . sighs to see what innocence he has outlived. The elder he grows, he is a stair lower from God. . . . Could he put off his body with his little coat, he had got eternity without a burthen, and exchang'd but one Heaven for another'. The parallel between Vaughan's poem, *The Retreate*, and

[1] December 1814.

the *Ode* has often been noticed. Not less remarkable are various passages in the verse and prose of Thomas Traherne. Like Wordsworth, Traherne, with the same unworldly love of the world, wishes to arouse men's minds from 'the lethargy of custom' to become aware of the common beauty of the earth. 'These hidden pleasures', he writes, 'because they are great, common, and simple, are not understood.'[1] He, too, had his great moments when he saw in nature 'The types and symbols of eternity'. The world, he says, 'hath not only represented [God's] infinity and eternity which we thought impossible to be represented by a body, but His beauty also, His wisdom, goodness, love, and blessedness'.[2] In a better known passage, Traherne describes his recollection of seeing all things apparelled in celestial light. 'Certainly, Adam in Paradise had not more sweet and curious apprehensions of the world, than I when I was a child.'[3] Such parallels would confirm Wordsworth's trust that his poetry was rooted in the enduring elements of human nature.

At one time Wordsworth believed that the great questions about the human soul are answered by man's right relation to nature. But this position had been gradually undermined by the temporal changes which are the precursors of death. The soaring terms in which he apostrophizes the feeling of immortality in the child reflect the intensity with which his imagination was impregnated by the life of nature. This intensity returned to him in seasons of inspiration beyond the age of thirty: it was still a potent, though gradually weakening, force for several years longer. No recent writer of comparable power in our literature has recorded a similar experience in his own life so clearly as Ruskin. 'These feelings', he says (describing his 'continual perception of Sanctity in the whole of nature'), 'remained in their full intensity till I was eighteen or twenty, and then, as the reflective and practical power increased, and the "cares of the world" gained upon me, faded gradually away, in the manner described by Wordsworth in his *Intimations of Immortality*.'[4] Ruskin's

[1] Thomas Traherne, *Centuries of Meditations*, ed. B. Dobell (Dobell, 1908), ii, p. 16.
[2] Ibid., p. 21.   [3] Ibid. iii, p. i.
[4] *Modern Painters*, vol. III, pp. 365–8 (Allen & Unwin, 1913).

experience, it will be perceived, did not last long enough to make him a poet.

Stanzas v–xi of the *Ode* give the answer, as far as poetry can give it, to the question with which stanza iv concludes:

> Whither is fled the visionary gleam?
> Where is it now, the glory and the dream?

The answer is itself the general contrast between the first and second parts of the *Ode*. In the first part, the centre and source of the poet's life is external nature; in the second it is the whole range of his deepest inward experience. With the gradual loss of illumination from nature, he will have recourse to the lights of his own higher being — faith and philosophy. The summary of the entire change is in the last four lines in which the 'meanest flower' owes its link with the soul not to itself but to 'the human heart' that transforms it. This conclusion is the final answer to the question in stanza iv and the true culmination of the whole poem.

Few poets have succeeded more than once or twice in the difficult form of the 'free Pindaric' ode, and never did Wordsworth repeat the splendid success of this poem. The main flaw in execution is the rhythmic looseness in part of stanza iv. But if the joyous cadences of ll. 42–49 are too uncontrolled, the failure is redeemed by the contrasting return, in ll. 51–57, to the tone of fateful melancholy. The diction has the impassioned sobriety proper to a poem of this depth and range. Was *Hamlet* in the poet's mind as he wrote this ode? In any case, 'prison-house' (l. 67), 'a guilty Thing' (l. 148), and 'heart of hearts' (l. 190),[1] are all expressions from that tragedy. Wordsworth was taxing his invention and ransacking his memory for the aptest and most forceful language possible, and it is not surprising that Shakespeare should have supplied some of it.

If de Selincourt is right in supposing that the *Ode* was completed by March 1804, the composition of it must have done something towards restoring for a time 'the glory and the dream' of Nature which seemed to be passing away. The 'timely utterance' of the lines on the Rainbow had relieved the 'thought of grief' in stanza

---

[1] 'Prison-house', *Hamlet*, I. v. 14. 'A guilty thing', ibid. i. 149. 'Heart of heart', ibid. III. ii. 73.

iii,[1] and the writing of the whole *Ode* seems to have had a like effect on a larger scale, for there is a remarkable buoyancy in the lines of *The Prelude* already quoted,[2] written in the week of his thirty-fourth birthday (7 April 1804).

The spirit of creative reminiscence in which *The Prelude* was composed must have done much to check the sense of change and 'passing being' which was invading Wordsworth's mind at this time. It seems probable that the *Ode to Duty* belongs to this same epoch.[3] Wordsworth himself dated it 1805, but there are strong reasons for thinking that it was among the poems in manuscript which Coleridge took abroad with him in April 1804. If that is so, it is nearly contemporary with the 'Immortality' *Ode*, with which it has close spiritual affinities. There is, however, an important contrast: the 'Immortality' *Ode* is a poem of transition, linking together past and present, while the *Ode to Duty*, with its new illumination, looks mainly towards the future. *Duty* is the final repudiation of negative liberty — in other words, unbounded personal liberty. Wordsworth had been moving in this direction ever since the years of his 'recovery', and by 1803 a statement of his new position was becoming imperative. As the champion of national independence and liberty, he had by implication already renounced his claim to complete personal liberty. His patriotic sonnets and his enrolment in the Grasmere Volunteers were outward expressions of this principle. But it is highly probable that in a nature so profoundly ethical as Wordsworth's, conversion from an adolescent enthusiasm for Liberty to a mature allegiance to Duty would have taken place without the shock of a European war. Even a mind so aloof from politics as Goethe's had, by a natural evolution, reached a similar conclusion:

Und das Gesetz nur kann uns Freiheit geben.

In the purely aesthetic sphere of verse-expression Wordsworth was also feeling 'the weight of too much liberty'. But public affairs were growing to be the breath of his nostrils. His *Ode to Duty* is closely linked with the extraordinary spirit of patriotism which

[1] H. W. Garrod, *Wordsworth, Lectures & Essays* (O.U.P., 1927), p. 113.
[2] See p. 66.
[3] *T.L.S.* Correspondence column, 30 May and 20 June 1935.

animated so many among the rank and file of his countrymen at
this time. His own impression of the national temper is given in
the sonnet *October, 1803*, written under the threat of invasion:

> tens of thousands, thinking on the affray,
> Men unto whom sufficient for the day
> And minds not stinted or untilled are given,
> Sound, healthy, children of the God of heaven,
> Are cheerful as the rising sun in May.

Methodism, Evangelicalism, the personal example of Pitt — all
were playing their part in producing a genuine national revival.
Many religious men were dedicated to great public causes, and
Thomas Clarkson, the abolitionist, well earned from Wordsworth
the title of 'Duty's intrepid liegeman'. Nelson accurately gauged
the temper of his countrymen when he appealed to their sense of
Duty in his famous signal.

The form and style of the *Ode* corresponded to a change of
temper in the poet. There was a certain buoyancy in his adoption
of the stanza-form from so joyless a poem as Gray's *Hymn to
Adversity*. He was, however, not to imitate Gray, but to surpass
him on his own ground, the joy of Duty being nearer to Heaven
than its discipline. The final form of the *Ode* was not attained
without many attempts, and the changes made between 1807
and 1845 are not all improvements. For instance, the latest
version:

> And oft, when in my heart was heard
> Thy timely mandate, I deferred
> The task, in smoother walks to stray (1845)

is tame beside the spirited lines:

> Resolved that nothing e'er should press
> Upon my present happiness
> I shov'd unwelcome tasks away. (1807)

But Wordsworth was surely right in cancelling what was originally
stanza vi, in which he seems to be striving to make the best of
both worlds — 'to feel past doubt', as he says, that his 'sub-
missiveness was choice'.[1] The great stanza beginning 'Stern

---

[1] De Selincourt, however, considers this stanza 'a valuable link in the
thought'.

Lawgiver!' and the last, which follows it, remained the same in wording from 1807 onwards. I have called the *Ode to Duty* a poem of 'completed change'. It is so in relation to his past, but the adjustment of Duty and Law to other values was to remain a problem for the rest of the poet's life. This appears, impressively, in the various endings of *Laodamia*. All commentators have noticed the Miltonic echoes in this *Ode*, but these do not constitute its really important feature, which is the last stanza but one. It is by the magnificent expansion of the poet's inward vision to a view of the Universe which includes the 'unalterable law' of the stars that the *Ode* is connected with the great poetry of the world.

In the year following the composition of the two odes Wordsworth experienced the greatest emotional shock he had known since his settlement at Grasmere. This was the death by drowning of his brother John on 5 February 1805. The poet could remember his mother's death when he was eight, and his father's death when he was thirteen, but the intense family affection of his adult age was concentrated on his own generation — particularly on Dorothy, and on John, the sailor and 'silent poet'. The overwhelming sorrow for his brother's death was a turning-point in Wordsworth's religious life. He now felt, as never before, the necessity for the Christian hope of immortality. 'Would it not be blasphemy', he wrote to Sir George Beaumont, 'to say that, upon the supposition of the thinking principle being destroyed by death, however inferior we may be to the great Cause and Ruler of things, we have more of love in our nature than He has? The thought is monstrous; and yet how to get rid of it, except upon the supposition of another and better world, I do not see'. To Wordsworth the death of his brother became an intimation of immortality, and from this time the doctrines of Christianity begin to permeate his thought.

When the first extremity of grief had subsided, Wordsworth began to seek relief in 'the sad mechanic exercise' of verse-writing. He had already written the beautiful lines on John Wordsworth included among *Poems on the Naming of Places*. He now wrote three further poems, to his memory: *To the Daisy* ('Sweet Flower! belike one day to have A place upon thy Poet's grave'), *Elegiac Verses*, and *Elegiac Stanzas, suggested by a Picture of Peele Castle,*

in a Storm. The first two of these new poems were not included
in the volumes of 1807, and the *Elegiac Verses* did not appear
until 1842. De Selincourt thinks the latter poem was withheld
from publication so long 'because of its intimate personal
character'. It seems to me more likely that Wordsworth thought
the verses scarcely worthy of the occasion. There are beautiful
lines, and the pathos of the brothers' last parting near Grisedale
Tarn cannot be forgotten. But the poem does not sufficiently
mark his brother's death as an epoch in his own life. This is
precisely what the *Peele Castle* poem succeeds in doing. It is a
sequel to the 'Immortality' *Ode*, but the past and the present are
shown in sharper contrast. Before his brother's death, he would —
had he been a painter — have expressed his deepest thoughts by
depicting the Castle in such peace as he once saw it during 'four
summer weeks', adding the visionary gleam of imagination, 'the
light that never was, on sea or land'. But now all is changed.
The picture of the storm-beaten Castle is the true portrayal of
the human situation. 'A power is gone, which nothing can restore'.
John's death brought to a sudden crisis the gradual change in
thought marked by the two odes. Wordsworth's delight in the
illumination from joy in Nature is now exchanged (he tells us) for
an acceptance of sorrow as the central necessity of man's lot. This
is a step further than the voluntary submission to 'law' professed
in the *Ode to Duty* or the decision to live by faith and the philosophic mind at the end of the 'Immortality' *Ode*. But, as usual,
we cannot translate Wordsworth's poetry into abstract language.
The poem preserves an unbroken continuity with its predecessors.
Even if Nature is no longer the soul of Wordsworth's moral being,
he is still, as before, the poet of Nature. Never did he write on it
more beautifully than in the stanzas on the painting he would once
have made 'in the fond illusion' of his heart. And in the last line
the severity of the preceding passage is tempered by a natural or,
it may be, a religious truth:

> Not without hope we suffer and we mourn.

Wordsworth marked the importance he attached to this poem by
using an engraving of Beaumont's painting as the frontispiece to
his *Poems* of 1815.

There are marks of Stoicism in the *Elegiac Stanzas*, and Stoicism, coloured by Christian faith, is also present in the *Character of the Happy Warrior*. Critics who speak slightingly of this poem should surely consider it again. Second-rate or juvenile it is not. It was composed in the December or January after Trafalgar, and the whole country was still mourning the death of its greatest seaman. To William and Dorothy the news of Trafalgar was as much a cause for grief as for rejoicing, as it inevitably renewed some of the emotion which had been felt at the loss of their brother. Wordsworth expressly associated the poem with Nelson,[1] but no features of the 'Character' answer to anything specific either in Nelson's personality or career — even the sea itself is not mentioned. On the other hand, some features of the Warrior whose master-bias leans

> To homefelt pleasures and to gentle scenes,

and who is

> More brave for this, that he hath much to love,

are obviously drawn from the brother whose character appears in the *Poems on the Naming of Places*. But John himself had been in neither of the fighting services, and the features of the portrait derived from military life can only have been suggested by Michel Beaupuy. Parts of the poem are indeed similar in spirit to the beautiful tribute to Beaupuy in *The Prelude*. In associating his most intimate feelings with the memory of Nelson of whom he had no personal knowledge, Wordsworth was following the method which enabled him to write his patriotic sonnets. The 'recluse' of Grasmere, nourishing his thoughts in solitude, with little of the outer world to meet his senses but the mountains and lakes, the winds and waters, saw into the heart of great public events. How conducive this method was to the writing of poetry worthy of the occasion appears in the *Lines, Composed at Grasmere*, as the poet mused on the approaching death of Charles James Fox.

In the *Character of the Happy Warrior* the Stoicism of the *Elegiac Stanzas* is amplified. The military life is the outward form

---

[1] W. to Sir George Beaumont (11 Feb. 1806).

for depicting the warfare of virtue in the world. In the power of virtue to turn painful necessity 'to glorious gain'; in its constant pursuit of perfection ('from well to better, daily self-surpast'); in its indifference to earthly fame ('finds comfort in himself and in his cause') we may recognize the classical features of Stoicism as they are drawn, for instance, in Hume's *Essays*. But the self-sufficiency of the Happy Warrior is tempered by a full measure of tenderness (l. 26) and love (l. 64): he is, too, sustained by Christian hope:

> And, while the mortal mist is gathering, draws
> His breath in confidence of Heaven's applause.

A similar blend of Theistic and Stoical elements appears in the beautiful stanzas which conclude the poem on the death of Fox:

> A Power is passing from the earth
> To breathless Nature's dark abyss;
> But when the great and good depart[1]
> What is it more than this —
>
> That Man, who is from God sent forth,
> Doth yet again to God return? —
> Such ebb and flow must ever be,
> Then wherefore should we mourn?

Wordsworth wrote few sonnets immediately after the Battle of Trafalgar. The deliverance of the country from the threat of invasion ended a phase of his patriotic poetry, and the death of his brother turned his thoughts, for a while, to the timeless questions of man's character and destiny. But the menace from abroad was suddenly revived in a new and terrible form. The sweeping victory of Napoleon over Prussia at Jena in October 1806 opened the way to incalculable perils, and this at a time when the nation had lost its greatest leaders, Pitt, Nelson, and Fox. Wordsworth reacted in a magnificent sonnet of defiance and warning — warning like that at the end of *King John*, and defiance as spirited as words can express. A few months later he saw, with prophetic insight, that the victory of Napoleon was bound to create a national spirit

[1] But when the Mighty pass away (1807).

in Germany which might renew the hopes of Europe. Hope as 'a paramount duty' was to become the main theme of Wordsworth's patriotic writings up to the final victory. It is true that the sonnet, *A Prophecy, February 1807* ('High deeds, O Germans, are to come from you!') is more remarkable for its foresight than its poetry, but a few other sonnets of this time are of the highest order. One of these ('Two Voices are there') was considered by Wordsworth to be the best he had written; another, nobly conceived and expressed, is the one *To Thomas Clarkson, on the final passing of the Bill for the Abolition of the Slave Trade, March, 1807.*

It was the purpose of Wordsworth during these years to rouse the mind and spirit of his countrymen to the highest possible level. While he was heart and soul with national resistance to an invader, he never forgot how soon the passions of war degenerate into savagery. During a visit to Sir George Beaumont at Coleorton in the early part of 1807, he wrote his great poem on the hollowness of the aggressor's glory — the *Song at the Feast of Brougham Castle.* Among the 'Poems of the Imagination' it is placed immediately after *Hart-Leap Well*, both poems being concerned with 'the coming of the milder day'. Wordsworth was not vying with Scott when he wrote the *Song*, but it is true that his thoughts were turning to the romance of local history. This, indeed, was almost non-existent in the Lake District, but the land on its eastern borders was steeped in it, and Wordsworth was never indifferent to memorials of 'the invincible knights of old'. 'This whole neighbourhood abounds in interesting traditions and vestiges of antiquity', he wrote.[1] His choice of the historical setting for the Brougham Castle poem was partly determined, no doubt, by its association with Sir George Beaumont, a former member of whose family, Sir John Beaumont, had written a poem, *Bosworth Field.* In Wordsworth's poem several moods are harmonized to produce a deeply satisfying effect. Its main *motif* is the inferiority of aggressive war, as a school of virtue, to peace, but it is the opposite view that is urged in the stirring song of 'the impassioned minstrel'. The occasion was the restoration of Henry, Lord Clifford, to his estates after the Battle of Bosworth. The victory of the Yorkists at Towton had ruined his family, and for

[1] Note on *Hart's-horn Tree* (*P.W.* iii, p. 535).

twenty years he had lived in obscurity. The Minstrel recalls the flight of Clifford's mother with the young boy after the defeat; describes the years he spent in hiding, disguised as a shepherd among the northern fells of the Lake District; recalls the legendary powers over bird and beast ascribed to the young noble; and ends by summoning him to repeat the deeds of his ancestors by carrying war into Scotland or France. But Clifford has outlived the moods of ferocity and revenge in his exile and prefers to end his days in the unexciting practice of well-doing among his people.

The poem is intensely characteristic of Wordsworth at this stage of his career. He has turned his reviving interest in northern history to brilliant account in this denunciation of militarism at the height of Napoleon's power. In the midst of his patriotic poems he never forgets his steadfast principle:

> 'Tis not in battles that from youth we train
> The Governor who must be wise and good.

To every detail of his *Song* the Minstrel gives a romantic colouring: the forlorn birth of the child (in a stave of elegiac cadence); the return of hope as the young boy throws himself into the life of the mountain shepherd; the sounding names of his haunts among the hill-recesses; his native nobility and magical powers; and finally, the spirited appeal to his supposed instincts of warlike aggression. It may be felt that the Minstrel's *Song* is more poetic than martial, but the impression is not injurious. Literary it certainly is; for example, the line,

> [He] hath buried deep his book,

is an evident link with Prospero, the exile and magician finally restored to his rights. As in some of his earlier poems, Wordsworth has dared to lay a strain on his reader's patience for the sake of a strong contrast in the conclusion, and in this work no apology is offered or required. On the 'consecration' of one stanza in particular depends the poetic and ethical effect of the whole composition. To quote this stanza out of its context, as is sometimes done, detracts from Wordsworth's art. It is the rightly balanced relation of the parts that constitutes the poem's beauty.

Two short poems call for notice in this place. The lines, 'Yes,

it was the mountain echo', (1806) do not attain that distinction of
style which marks the other poems discussed in this chapter, but
they are a landmark in the evolution of Wordsworth's thought.
No longer are the senses linked with our moral being: on the
contrary, man is represented as hearing 'voices of two different
natures':

> Have not *we* too? — yes, we have
> Answers, and we know not whence;
> Echoes from beyond the grave,
> Recognised intelligence!
>
> Such within ourselves we hear
> Oft-times, ours though sent from far;
> Listen, ponder, hold them dear;
> For of God, — of God they are.

The second of these stanzas is only one degree less theistic than in
the final version of 1836.[1]

The poem *Fidelity* has a kinship with the 'Mountain Echo' lines
in its clear recognition of a Power transcending the limits of
nature. The fidelity of Charles Gough's dog who remained by his
master's body for three months without visible means of sub-
sistence made a deep impression in the neighbourhood. Scott also
wrote a poem on the event. Wordsworth reported that the sentiment in the last four lines of the last stanza of his poem 'was
uttered by a shepherd with such exactness, that a traveller was
induced to question the man whether he had read them, which he
had not'. Nothing could illustrate more forcibly the true meaning
of 'the real language of men'. *Fidelity* is also remarkable for
ll. 25–28, one of the poet's most evocative descriptions — though
in scarcely more than a score of words.

[1] The first two lines of this stanza then became:

> Such rebounds our inward ear
> Catches sometimes from afar.

CHAPTER VIII

The Excursion:
The Solitary and the Wanderer

An interval of seven years separates the poems of 1807 from the publication of *The Excursion*. During that period Wordsworth had continued his series of sonnets dedicated to Liberty and had written, though not published, *The White Doe of Rylstone*. Both these works evolve from Wordsworth's previous poetry, but *The Excursion* introduces a new didactic note which has damaged its reputation for a large body of readers and tended to conceal its imaginative power. The poem was much read in the decade before the poet's death and for some twenty years later, during which two periods it was twelve times published separately. The importance of Wordsworth's poetry was increasingly recognized, and this work was thought to contain the essence of his teaching. In the latter part of the nineteenth century, *The Prelude* gained in reputation at the expense of *The Excursion*, and its superiority would not now be questioned. There is a finality about *The Excursion* which is really superficial. It is in many respects a poem of transition: but the style had its effect, and — in combination with the poet's personal manner — established for him a reputation for arrogance in the literary world of London. *The Excursion*, however, does not mark the terminus of Wordsworth's thought or poetic invention, and the charge of arrogance was forgotten twenty years later. In time it became apparent that his poetry was not a closed system; nor did he himself represent the 'Egotistical Sublime'. The idea of a great philosophical poem was finally abandoned, and Wordsworth's later years were freed from an incubus.

In a full discussion of *The Excursion* its character as a 'loco-descriptive' poem would assume some importance. It is, as Lamb called it, a 'conversational poem' and its setting in Lakeland is one of its most attractive features. Book II brings the Wanderer and the Poet, who have previously met elsewhere, to the cottage of 'the Solitary', situated on the high ridge between the Great and Little Langdales, beneath the dominating mass of the Langdale Pikes. It is there that the crucial debate of Book IV takes place. The scene is then shifted to Grasmere where the party of three is joined by the Parson, and the second 'conversation piece' takes place in the churchyard of the village. Though the speakers in the dialogues constantly feel the influence of their surroundings, these cannot be much considered in our present attempt to relate *The Excursion* to Wordsworth's work as a whole, but they make a great contribution to the character of the poem, especially at its opening and close.

The story of Margaret — or *The Ruined Cottage* — must also be excluded from the present chapter though it is, in itself, the finest part of the entire poem. It appears in Book I and is recalled for a moment in Book VI,[1] but it has no organic connexion with the general plan, and is introduced mainly to illustrate the character of the Wanderer, who narrates it. His own upbringing and course of life have just been described, and the quality of his mind is felt in the intense sympathy with which he interprets this 'tale of silent suffering'. But *The Ruined Cottage* is too great a work to be considered as part of *The Excursion*: it occupies a central position in Wordsworth's poetry and thought. Other portions of the poem, too, are but loosely connected with its main purpose — the 'correction of despondency', in an imaginary person called 'The Solitary'. He is a character of contemporary rather than of permanent interest; he fades into the background in the latter part of the poem, and his complete moral restoration is left uncertain. He is, however, the cause of poetry in others, and the greatest piece of sustained writing in the entire work, after Book I, is the part called 'Despondency Corrected' (Book IV). This is followed by the Pastor's seventeen 'pictures of life' which bear less specifically on the Solitary's state of mind: collectively, they are an attempt to answer the question whether human nature contains the inherent urge to strive for its own moral amendment. They are short stories of effort, suffering, or error, interpreted by

[1] ll. 1055–61.

Christian hope and charity. In the subsequent discourse of the
Wanderer on the necessity for national education and the
encouragement of emigration, the Solitary speaks no more
than a few lines. *The Excursion* is thus a series of poems, descriptions, and episodes expressing the mind of Wordsworth in
middle life, mainly through the medium of the Wanderer and the
Pastor.

As Wordsworth reminds us, *The Excursion* has 'something of a
dramatic form', but not much is made of the tension between the
speakers. The powerful parts of the poem are personal, not
dramatic. The Solitary's character, history, and present life are
described partly by the Wanderer, partly in the Solitary's own
words. 'I wish', wrote Coleridge to Wordsworth in 1799, 'you
would write a poem, in blank verse, addressed to those, who, in
consequence of the complete failure of the French Revolution,
have thrown up all hopes of the amelioration of mankind, and are
sinking into an almost epicurean selfishness.' Wordsworth has
described in *The Prelude* the impact of the French Revolution on
himself with unsurpassable power, and he could not so effectively
retrace the same story in the life of another. Nor is his own
Solitary, a character based upon observation and memories of
London life in the 1790s, a particularly impressive figure. There
is little in common between the poet whose early life and later
residence in France trained him to take a virile sympathy with
new-born democracy and the dilettante ex-Army chaplain who
embraced the cause of the Revolution in reaction against his
private griefs. The Solitary is a belated 'man of feeling', something of a British Werther, whose sensibility was already old-
fashioned in a poem produced in 1814. He had, it is true, a
historical origin in a certain Mr. Fawcett, 'a preacher at a
dissenting meeting-house at the Old Jewry'. The picture is true to
a contemporary type: there were in the 1790s many English
sympathizers with the Revolution who had never set foot in
France. But the historical features of the Solitary's character,
which may have recommended it to readers of long memory in the
early nineteenth century, tell against its permanent value as
literature. The most powerful part of his story is the description
of his suffering in the death of his daughter and son, followed by

that of their mother: Wordsworth had likewise lost his own children, Catharine and Thomas, within one year.

The Excursion is partly a philosophical poem, and the Solitary is, intellectually, a personified antithesis of the Wanderer. The Solitary's mind and character — sensitive rather than strong — have been broken into fragments by private sorrows and political disillusionments. He ends his own life-story in Book III with the hope that his 'particular current' of the stream of Life will soon reach the 'unfathomable gulf, where all is still'. He has become 'Der Geist, der stets verneint'. The Wanderer's wisdom, on the other hand, springs from a just synthesis of all the mental powers, and the object of his exhortation in Book IV is to show their interdependence. The Solitary supplies an effective stimulus to the other's eloquence. The Wanderer's firm Theistic position enables Wordsworth to give him a more dogmatic tone as spiritual counsellor than he could have then assumed in speaking in his own person.

The Wanderer is a man of the people. Born in Scotland of poor but religious parents, 'among the hills of Atholl . . . on a small hereditary farm', he was brought up under the threefold influence of Nature, of strict and unquestioned family traditions, and the reverential worship of God. His story begins not in an ante-natal state but with his soul-nurture in Covenanting memories. Belief in God took possession of his childish mind:

> thou, who didst wrap the cloud
> Of infancy around us, that thyself
> Therein, with our simplicity awhile
> Might'st hold, on earth, communion undisturbed: . . .[1]

Between the doctrinal religion of his Church and family and the natural religion derived from his solitary duties and childish fears as he tended cattle on the hills there is no conflict but an essential agreement: 'in the mountains did he *feel* his faith'. Wordsworth has adapted one of the culminating passages in Book II of *The Prelude*[2] on his own adolescent love of Nature to the Theistic beliefs of the Scottish peasant:

> In such access of mind, in such high hour
> Of visitation from the living God,

[1] *Excursion*, IV. 83–86.   [2] ll. 418–34 (1805).

Thought was not; in enjoyment it expired.
No thanks he breathed, he proferred no request;
Rapt into still communion that transcends
The imperfect offices of prayer and praise,
His mind was a thanksgiving to the power
That made him; it was blessedness and love![1]

The original of the Wanderer was a 'packman' whom Wordsworth had known at Hawkshead, and his idea that the occupation might encourage a sound working philosophy and enlarged human sympathies was no mere figment of fancy. He quotes from Robert Heron's *Journey in Scotland* in support of his own observations of pedlars and their life: 'As in their peregrinations they have opportunity of contemplating the manners of various men and various cities, they become eminently skilled in the knowledge of the world. *As they wander, each alone, through thinly-inhabited districts, they form habits of reflection and of sublime contemplation.*'[2] Wordsworth himself declared that if he had not been born in a class which gave him a liberal education, he might, 'being strong in body', have taken to that way of life himself. If he has fathered much of his own poetry and eloquence on the Wanderer, he has also drawn strength from his unqualified belief in the possibility of such a life and character.

The attitude of the Wanderer to the Solitary in the Book 'Despondency Corrected', though full of friendliness and sympathy, is not wholly favourable to the poetry, especially in the opening passages. There is a hint of didacticism in the long exhortation to an erring brother. Moreover the speaker is attempting to deliver the quintessence of Wordsworth's thought as already expressed — not discovering truths, but enunciating them. There is therefore a tendency to rhetorical elaboration as compared with the spontaneous simplicity of a first utterance. By degrees, however, the fire and passion of the speaker generate a splendour of their own, and any impression of artifice disappears long before the end of the book.

The spirit and style of the Wanderer's opening passages give little promise of what is to follow. His assertion that belief in God is the one adequate support in the calamities of mortal life has

[1] *Excursion*, I. 211–18.   [2] *P.W.* v, p. 412.

neither the force of sudden illumination, as in Wordsworth at his best, nor is it related to the Christianity in which the Wanderer himself was brought up. It has indeed the note of Deism, and the impression is confirmed by the author's phrase in the original 'Argument': 'ejaculation to the supreme Being'. The assertion of belief in immortality is also a deduction from premises rather than a religious hope. When the Wanderer passes to the political disillusionment suffered by many of his generation, he advocates a patient acceptance of the inevitable. The lessons from Nature for the political thinker are based upon analogies from the lower creation, such as the 'social league' in the ant-world and 'the love of fellowship' prevailing among the 'feathered kinds'. This recalls the didactic manner and the literary style of an earlier generation.

But a new note enters the Wanderer's persuasions as he begins to analyse the peculiar case of his friend's despondency:

> A piteous lot it were to flee from Man —
> Yet not rejoice in Nature.

By pressing this thought to its conclusion, he is led to the heart of the Solitary's spiritual malady:

> Who thinks, and feels,
> And recognizes ever and anon
> The breeze of nature stirring in his soul,
> Why need such man go desperately astray,
> And nurse 'the dreadful appetite of death?'[1]

The disconnexion between 'feeling' associated with the senses and the 'soul' or moral part of man's nature is, the Wanderer suggests, a new malady, unknown among the peoples to whom we trace the birth of our civilization. In the sonnet 'The world is too much with us', Wordsworth asserted the felicity of the 'Pagan suckled in a creed outworn', when compared with the modern man. He saw in the early mythologies that unity of the mental faculties which underlay all that was vital in his own processes of thought. The Wanderer is now launched on the full tide of his eloquence, carried along to the end of his discourse by the mind's 'excursive power'.

If the human mind feels alone in the Universe it is, he implies,

[1] *The Excursion*, IV. 598–602.

through the loss of an instinct hitherto inalienable from the race. The will to live stimulates imagination, through the operation of which men personified the forces they could not control. At least

> Man escaped the doom
> Of destitution; — solitude was not.[1]

Imagination created a mean between Man himself and the inscrutable Universe. The Wanderer dilates on the vitality of the nature religions of Persian, Babylonian, Chaldean, and Greek, not distinguishing clearly between the monotheistic and the polytheistic tendency, but ascribing to all the virtue that in them

> — The imaginative faculty was lord
> Of observations natural; . . .[2]

'Superstition' he declares, is better than 'apathy' — better in being allied to the instinct for life. After a beautiful passage on the mythology of Greece, he meets the Solitary's gibe that he would perhaps like to restore the 'superstitious rites' abolished at the Reformation, by asserting that 'those bewildered Pagans of old time' had at least the basic minimum of religion required to make life endurable:

> Beyond their own poor natures and above
> They looked; were humbly thankful for the good
> Which the warm sun solicited, and earth
> Bestowed; were gladsome, — and their moral sense
> They fortified with reverence for the Gods;
> And they had hopes that overstepped the Grave.[3]

In his praise of the old mythologies Wordsworth was projecting his imagination into an epoch of human history, of which his knowledge was partly speculative. But the passage is at least energetic poetry, and it admirably serves the Wanderer's purpose of rousing the Solitary from his 'apathy'. Wordsworth's enthusiasm is a life-giving power, though needing often to be intellectually controlled by his mature thought. His main principle of retaining the whole of his vital work even if 'incautiously' expressed, was

---

[1] Ibid. 649–50.　　　[2] Ibid. 707–8.
[3] Ibid. 935–40. Wordsworth was indebted to Herodotus and to Pope's Homer in his passage on the ancient religions.

sound, though it left him with a perpetual problem as to the modification of details. The passage from *The Recluse* (composed in 1800), which introduces *The Excursion*, is a case in point. Nowhere has Wordsworth expressed more eloquently the feeling of 'man's unconquerable mind' which he shared with other great figures of Renaissance and Romantic literature. Some of the phrases used, however, especially the allusion to 'Jehovah — with his thunder' caused considerable offence, especially to Blake, and might well give rise to misunderstanding, though the further references to 'empyreal thrones', 'Chaos', and 'Erebus' suggest that the whole passage is a criticism of Milton's cosmology. The imagery of the seventeenth century, Wordsworth implies, is no longer satisfying: even the imagined 'heaven of heavens' is 'but a veil' of magnificent materialism. What is truly startling today, however, is the vista opening to the poet's eye of the imaginative wealth to be expected from the union of the human mind with 'this goodly universe in love and holy passion'. But is it not possible, in the later twentieth century, to see in this bold prospect a prophetic value for our own age, when our material power has extended beyond the wildest dreams of the past? What more urgent need can be conceived than an enlargement in our re-sources of 'love and holy passion'? The great obstacle to our reception of Wordsworth's teaching is its rejection of pride, pomp, and luxury. Its simplicity is the stumbling-block.

There is thus this great advantage in the dramatic form of Wordsworth's philosophical poem: to diagnose the spiritual sickness of the age, it needed an obscure person, outside the intellectual world, but of a comprehensive mind. Some twelve lines of the wisdom of this 'unknown Wanderer' are quoted by Ruskin on the title-pages of *Modern Painters*: the passage deplores a philosophy based upon a relation between the mind of man and the natural world, which limits the infinite complexity of either — in which 'the transcendent universe' is prized

> No more than as a mirror that reflects
> To proud Self-love her own intelligence; . . .[1]

We are thus led back to the seminal season of Wordsworth's life

[1] Ibid. 991–2.

when many of his fundamental ideas came into being. A passage written at Alfoxden and now included in this part of *The Excursion* not only enforced the Wanderer's exhortations but has a powerful application to our own age of fragmented specialization:

> go, demand
> Of mighty Nature, if 'twas ever meant
> That we should pry far off yet be unraised;
> That we should pore, and dwindle as we pore,
> Viewing all objects unremittingly
> In disconnexion dead and spiritless;
> And still dividing, and dividing still,
> Break down all grandeur, still unsatisfied
> With the perverse attempt, while littleness
> May yet become more little; waging thus
> An impious warfare with the very life
> Of our own souls![1]

Inevitably the Wanderer's eloquence has produced an effect on the Solitary, who now asks 'with some impatience in his mien' whether his salvation must be wrought through repentance and Christian faith. The Wanderer answers that the ways of restoration are manifold and various. He is himself no priest. His function is to point out natural remedies:

> The estate of man would be indeed forlorn
> If false conclusions of the reasoning power
> Made the eye blind, and closed the passages
> Through which the ear converses with the heart.[2]

This is the theme of *Tintern Abbey* — an appeal to the mighty world of eye and ear: which, if it saved the poet, may also save the Solitary. So too, the resulting joy in Nature may bear its fruits, as the poet had imagined many years before, in an enlarged charity towards one's fellow-men; and the Wanderer quotes the passage which Coleridge wrote out in a letter of 1798: 'For the Man — who, in this spirit communes with the Forms of nature'.[3] Wordsworth remains consistent with his own past teaching and will not minimize 'the deep power of joy' either in the moral or the intellectual world: 'Science then shall be a precious visitant'.[4]

---

[1] Ibid. 957–68.   [2] Ibid. 1152–5.
[3] Ibid. 1207–29. See p. 37.   [4] Ibid. 1251–2.

But it does not follow that he disbelieved in the necessity or power of Christian conversion in crises of human life to which his own teaching did not extend. Long before, he had begun his great poem of conversion, *Peter Bell*, and five years after the publication of *The Excursion* he gave it to the world.

What conclusions, relative to our special line of approach in this study, are to be drawn from the book 'Despondency Corrected'? It demonstrates the harmonious unity of Wordsworth's previous poetry and its accumulated power when characteristic parts of it are brought to bear on the supreme issue of hope against despair. The Wanderer's opening passages, when not deeply rooted in the poet's experience, fall on the mind coldly, and it is not until feeling and imagination begin to be linked with moral and intellectual issues that the discourse comes fully to life. Then indeed it proceeds with unflagging power. Yet there is hardly any thought in this part of the speech which does not take its origin from some previous poem, whether *Tintern Abbey*, *The Tables Turned*, the *Ode to Duty*, the *Character of the Happy Warrior*, the sonnet 'The World is too much with us', or unpublished passages intended for *The Ruined Cottage*.[1] More impalpably *The Prelude* is always in the background. The systematized exposition of thought from poems for a deliberately didactic purpose which did not belong to their original inspiration is often felt as alien to the true nature of Wordsworth's poetic genius. The difference is reflected in a more literary style, consciously cultivated. This was, however, less regretted by earlier readers who, without knowledge of *The Prelude*, recognized the basically personal character of *The Excursion*. Wordsworth's original power was not exhausted, but some time was to elapse before it recovered something of its true spontaneity.

The return of the Wanderer, after the Pastor's 'pictures', to a central place in *The Excursion* corresponds with a change in the latter part of the poem. For a time it is rooted in Wordsworth's meditation on the state of the country about 1809–12 when, as paymaster of the anti-Napoleonic forces, England was urging on the industrial revolution with feverish energy. As an exhibition of

---

[1] For these, see *P.W.* v, pp. 400–4.

intellectual power, the machinery of the new age moves the
Wanderer to high admiration:

> I exult,
> Casting reserve away, exult to see
> An intellectual mastery exercised
> O'er the blind elements; a purpose given,
> A perseverance fed; almost a soul
> Imparted — to brute matter.[1]

But his fundamental values remain intact. He is painfully impressed by the price paid for 'progress' in the injury to the health
of the workers and the corruption of their manners. 'The old
domestic morals of the land' are to him 'above all price', but
everything is now sacrificed 'to Gain, the master idol of the realm'.
The glimpse we are shown of a new factory ('a many-windowed
fabric huge') and its workers anticipates the vivid descriptions of
the mid-century novelists, Dickens, Disraeli, and Mrs. Gaskell.
In the last book (ix) the Wanderer delivers his prescription for the
evils of the time — large-scale emigration and a system of national
education.[2] Here he rises to a higher strain, opening with a
beautiful passage written in the poet's 'seminal' period, and
basing his thoughts on the great principle of equality in human
rights. No 'modern ingenuity' should have the power to make man
or child 'the senseless member of a vast machine'.[3] In the light of
their common endowments of heart and conscience the in-
equalities between men disappear:

> The primal duties shine aloft — like stars;
> The charities that soothe, and heal, and bless,
> Are scattered at the feet of Man — like flowers.
> The generous inclination, the just rule,
> Kind wishes, and good actions, and pure thoughts —
> No mystery is here! Here is no boon
> For high — yet not for low; for proudly graced —
> Yet not for meek of heart. The smoke ascends
> To heaven as lightly from the cottage-hearth
> As from the haughtiest palace. He, whose soul

[1] *The Excursion*, VIII. 199–204.

[2] In 1870, the year of Forster's Education Act, book ix was published
as an English Classic for Use in Schools.

[3] *The Excursion*, IX. 159.

Ponders this true equality, may walk
The fields of earth with gratitude and hope; . . .[1]

The Wanderer breaks off abruptly: he can obtain no more than a
Pisgah-sight of the future. As the little group to which he has been
speaking move towards the Lake (Grasmere), they are met by the
beautiful sight of a snow-white ram imaged perfectly in a still
pool beneath, and the Pastor's lady (in a whisper) seizes on the
analogy of this reflection with the impression which the
Wanderer's discourse has made upon her:

> 'How pure his spirit! in what vivid hues
> His mind gives back the various forms of things,
> Caught in their fairest, happiest, attitude!
> While he is speaking, I have power to see
> Even as he sees; but when his voice hath ceased,
> Then, with a sigh, sometimes I feel, as now,
> That combinations so serene and bright
> Cannot be lasting in a world like ours,
> Whose highest beauty, beautiful as it is,
> Like that reflected in yon quiet pool,
> Seems but a fleeting sunbeam's gift, whose peace
> The sufferance only of a breath of air.'[2]

The last word is with the Pastor, who addresses the little group
solemnized by the Wanderer's oration and a sunset of unexpected
splendour. The Poet had paid an earlier tribute to the 'State and
Church of England' and the Pastor now reverts to this theme,
drawing a comparison between the sanguinary rites once celebrated in this 'sea-girt isle' and the innocent worship of later
times. This passage resembles the retrospective vision of sacri-
ficial flames on 'Sarum's Plain' near the end of *The Prelude*, but,
as we have noticed, in the later poem it is the Christian faith that
has effected 'this marvellous advance of good from evil'. It is true
that *The Excursion* is not a wholehearted confession of orthodox
Christianity.[3] Something of reserve and long engrained stoicism
prevented Wordsworth from recognizing it as the religion of joy,
as we feel especially when he represents the martyrs as suffering

[1] Ibid. 238–49.   [2] Ibid. 462–73.
[3] See J. S. Lyon, *The Excursion: a Study* (Yale University Press,
1950), pp. 113–19.

with heroic inflexibility rather than in devotion to their Master. He reverences the Church, but is reticent as to the personality of its Founder. 'It seems that in religion, as in other fields of thought, Wordsworth moved slowly, with courageous independence and generally with fidelity to long-term fundamental principles.'[1] It can, however, be no surprise to the attentive reader that some seven years later, he published a series of sonnets on the History of the Christian Church in England. The most abiding impression left by *The Excursion* as a whole is the mind of the Wanderer, the man of the people, who is also the vessel of Wordsworth's austere and sublime culture in his middle years.

[1] Ibid., p. 114.

CHAPTER IX

The Excursion:
The Pastor's 'Pictures'

'MY object', said Wordsworth, writing of his great philosophical poem, 'is to give pictures of Nature, Man and Society.'[1] The seventeen 'pictures' presented by the Pastor to his three listeners in the churchyard at Grasmere are designed to second the Wanderer's efforts to conquer the despondency of the Solitary. Wordsworth's critics have frequently ignored these stories, feeling perhaps with Hazlitt that they are an interruption to the philosophy of the poem. It is true that the Pastor does not give a direct answer to the Solitary's challenging questions: Is religion able to counteract the general weakness of man? How many individual souls have religion and philosophy withdrawn from 'passion's crooked ways'? But he faithfully meets the Wanderer's demand for concrete evidence in place of general arguments:

> Give us, for our abstractions, solid facts;
> For our disputes, plain pictures;

and the seventeen stories, or episodes, are collectively a conclusive answer to the question: Is not life, even among the dwellings of the lovely region in which they are standing, 'fashioned like an ill-constructed tale'? It was the earliest critics who took most pleasure in these stories. Lamb thought them the best part of *The Excursion*.

The Pastor's 'pictures' are not in what has come to be regarded as Wordsworth's most typical manner. They are successors of *The Old Cumberland Beggar* rather than of 'Margaret' or *Michael*. All are stories in whose essential truth Wordsworth himself believed, as a literal rather than a poetic observer. Though the Pastor does

[1] Wordsworth's letter to James Tobin, 6 Mar. 1798.

not touch the darker tragedies of his parish, he ranges over an
ample field of life, making us feel that he faithfully depicts the
general character of his people. As each story is directed, in part,
against the Solitary's defeatist misanthropy, it might seem that
the series must resemble a string of homilies. They are saved by
the high but unobtrusive art with which the tales are arranged,
diversified, and humanized. We should consider them as critics
view *The Canterbury Tales* — in their fitness for the occasion,
their grouping, contrasts, and variety. Wordsworth has conceived
his Pastor in the literary tradition of Chaucer's Parson and
Goldsmith's; in the historical tradition of George Herbert; and
with added local traits suggested by the 'Wonderful Walker',[1] so
called by shepherds of his remote parish in the Duddon Valley.
The manner in which such men, standing in their own church-
yards, would regard the lives of departed parishioners from the
central standpoint of Christianity, is the pattern for the Pastor's
Memorials. He plays his part with admirable consistency. He
knows the topography of his parish with the thoroughness of a
tireless pedestrian. He also understands the struggle for existence
among the fells. He appropriately opens his tales with the
description of a quarryman's wife who carries her lantern to and
fro to light her husband home on winter evenings to their cottage
among the rocks. Equally typical is the manner in which a parson
and his wife 'weather-fend' their bleak dwelling in the hills. The
presence of the churchyard, where the stories are told, hallows
but does not darken them. It is a place consecrated to Death and
Life, 'a mysteriously-united pair'.

The 'Pictures' fall into three distinct groups. The five tales of
the first group are the slightest in substance, being little more
than moral anecdotes in characteristic local settings. But they are
carefully diversified. The quarry-man and his wife, in the first tale,
are among the lowest of the Pastor's flock 'in scale of culture', but
they have adapted their life to the needs of the human heart,
having acquired the graces of contentment, mutual courtesy, and
religious hope. The fifth tale, an anecdote from the eighteenth
century, deals with two men of rank and education. Both of them
disappointed in public life, but of opposed parties, a Jacobite and

[1] The Rev. Robert Walker (1709–1802). See *D.N.B.*

a Hanoverian, they renounced the world and settled in a remote
Lakeland village. Inevitably they met and quarrelled. But by
degrees there grew up between them a genuine, though hardly
halcyon, friendship. The goal of their longer walks was the
Churchyard, and as they entered it,

> One spirit seldom failed to extend its sway
> Over both minds, when they awhile had marked
> The visible quiet of this holy ground, . . .[1]

Foreseeing that they are likely to be buried within the same
precincts, they erect a sundial to their common memory. Two
men 'whom antipathies reconcile', as Lamb says.

The second group of tales is initiated by the Solitary, who
desires stronger fare. He maintains that the great tragedies of
Prometheus and the Theban line have their counterpart in rural
areas where life offers, as elsewhere, examples of 'poor humanity's
afflicted will Struggling in vain with ruthless destiny'. The Pastor
replies, in effect, that the Christian view of tragedy differs from
the pagan, and it is finally agreed that he shall confine himself to
errors which (in human judgement) are not beyond the reach of
divine forgiveness. But he admits that 'the native grandeur of
the human soul' is often shown 'in the perverseness of a selfish
course'.

The first tale of the second group is a vivid sketch, with hardly
any action, of a potentially tragic character — a woman called
Aggy Fisher, who is occasionally mentioned in Dorothy's Journal.
In a few lines Wordsworth draws the picture of a village queen,
commanding not by her beauty but her grandeur of mind and
person. She was later enslaved by two 'degenerate passions' —
weak indulgence to a worthless son and 'unremitting avaricious
thrift'. But nothing could quench her noble thirst for knowledge.
It was her higher nature that impressed the Pastor. As he was
walking by her cottage one spring night when the planet Jupiter
was in the sky, he was roused by her voice and heard her say:

> 'That glorious star
> In its untroubled element will shine

[1] *The Excursion*, VI. 480–2.

> As now it shines, when we are laid in earth
> And safe from all our sorrows.'[1]

Recalling the tone and spirit of these words, he goes on to describe how her ambitious and self-tormenting nature was brought to a state of 'meekness, softened and subdued' by the approach of death. In the valley she is still 'remembered with deep awe'.

The story of Ellen, which follows, is Wordsworth's greatest poem on the theme of a woman's desertion by her lover:

> She loved, and fondly deemed herself beloved.
> — The road is dim, the current unperceived,
> The weakness painful and most pitiful,
> By which a virtuous woman, in pure youth,
> May be delivered to distress and shame.[2]

The character of Ellen, her emotions and actions, have the individuality of unemphatic truth intensely realized. She was not in the usual sense beautiful, but her face had the beauty given by 'gladsome spirits, and benignant looks', and her form and movements 'might have quickened and inspired a Titian's hand'. When her lover's desertion is certain, and before her child is born, she can still find 'a meek resource' 'in lonely reading':

> How thankful for the warmth of summer days,
> When she could slip into the cottage-barn,
> And find a secret oratory there;
> Or, in the garden, under friendly veil
> Of their long twilight, pore upon her book
> By the last lingering help of the open sky
> Until dark night dismissed her to her bed![3]

After the birth of the child, Ellen finds an 'unexpected promise' in her new cares, and for a time she and her widowed mother are comforted. But she cannot long endure to impose this extra burden on her mother's slender means, and she offers her services as a nurse to a neighbouring family. The parents of the foster-child are selfish and cruel, and when her own child falls sick, allow her to make only one visit to see it. The child dies, and Ellen barely obtains leave to attend the funeral, arriving only to find the mourners somewhat impatient to disperse:

[1] Ibid. 763–6.   [2] Ibid. 844–8.   [3] Ibid. 897–903.

'Nay', said she, with commanding look, a spirit
Of anger never seen in her before,
'Nay, ye must wait my time!' and down she sate,
And by the unclosed coffin kept her seat
Weeping and looking, looking on and weeping,
Upon the last sweet slumber of her Child,
Until at length her soul was satisfied.[1]

The story of Ellen's short life is continued to the end with the
same unforced pathos. The high merit of this tale has been more
often recognized than that of any other in the whole group. No
writer could have handled the feelings aroused by the story with a
finer or surer touch.

The unifying principle of the remaining tales is the power of
turning adversity or deprivation to the soul's gain. The theme is
introduced by a charming domestic idyll of a widower with six
daughters, not one of them yet a 'full-blown flower'. Eight years
before the tale begins, the mother had died, but this calamity has
proved a source of unlooked-for good. Within that time the eldest
daughter became an example of cheerful and tireless industry
to the younger children, while the place of a son was taken by
another of the sisters:

a hardy Girl . . .
Who, mounting fearlessly the rocky heights,
Her Father's prompt attendant, does for him
All that a boy could do, but with delight
More keen and prouder daring . . .[2]

Thanks to the gardening fancies of the daughters their home, one
of the 'rudest habitations', blossoms like a rose. The spirit of the
wife and mother survives in the family, and the contrast between
the two generations is faithfully noted by the Pastor:

Mild Man! he is not gay, but they are gay;
And the whole house seems filled with gaiety.[3]

The tale, written in 1800, has all the serious happiness of Wordsworth's 'pastoral year'.

A deaf man and a blind man are the characters in the two
central tales of this last group. The former, deaf from early

[1] Ibid. 976–82.   [2] Ibid. 1157–61.   [3] Ibid. 1186–7.

childhood and never ambitious, cultivated and obtained the grace
of 'pure contentedness'. His 'introverted spirit' was raised by
books above its 'natural elevation' and thus preserved from the
faults to which the deaf are specially liable — suspicion, languor
vain complaint. He died easily at a ripe age, and the poet seems to
indulge the fancy that his spirit, from the grave where it 'lay in
waiting',[1] was endowed with the hearing which had been denied to
the bodily organ while he lived:

> And yon tall pine-tree, whose composing sound
> Was wasted on the good Man's living ear,
> Hath now its own peculiar sanctity;
> And, at the touch of every wandering breeze,
> Murmurs, not idly, o'er his peaceful grave.[2]

The story which follows, of the blind man, is both a counterpart
and a contrast. He triumphed over his defect not passively but
actively, developing the other senses to such a point that the
physical organ of vision seemed superfluous. Thanks to his
sensitiveness of hearing he was as safe, standing at the edge of a
precipice, as a man whose eye could see into the gulf beneath.
His voice as it 'discoursed of natural or moral truth' gave him a
kinship with prophets and poets whom legend or history records
as blind, and especially with that poet whose language is echoed
in the narrative.[3] The original of this 'picture' was a certain
John Gough known to Coleridge, who confirms this account of his
extraordinary powers.

The danger of monotony in a sequence of stories told by the
same narrator is shown once for all in the *Monk's Tale* of Chaucer.
Thanks to the variety of the Pastor's 'Pictures' one might forget
that such danger existed. The hero of the tenth tale seems at first
quite incongruous in his setting. He is a new curate arriving with
his wife and children at the parsonage-house attached to 'Wythe-
burn's modest House of prayer'. A social and ambitious man of the
world who had waited in vain for higher preferment, he had finally
decided to accept this secluded charge. The family's long cross-

---

[1] Cf. *Ode: Intimations of Immortality*, 121–4 (version of 1807).

[2] *The Excursion*, VII. 477–81.

[3] Cf. 'sacred influence' (of light): *Excursion*, VII. 484 and *Paradise Lost*,
II. 1034, and the parallels noted in *P.W.* v, p. 465.

country journey had been a leisurely and at times a comic escapade in which they had been taken for strolling players. Excitement sustained them while they were in motion: but how would this worldly man face the rigours of his mountain-cottage separated by a long and wild tract from the chapel where he was to minister? Without 'saintly zeal', he schooled himself to be satisfied with the narrowest round of duties and pleasures. Though never subdued to perfect harmony with his calling, his life was one in which the Wanderer can trace the hand of Providence:

> a thoughtless Man
> From vice and premature decay preserved
> By useful habits, to a fitter soil
> Transplanted ere too late.[1]

The whole 'picture' of Joseph Sympson's career is as convincing as its details are unexpected, and it has an admirable completeness. Totally different, and of a touching beauty, is the short tale of the prosperous parents of 'seven lusty sons'.[2] When a little daughter was added to their family, their joy and pride and the delight of the grandfather were unbounded. But as soon as the child could walk, with help, in the garden and take note of the Spring flowers, she fell a victim suddenly to the cold of the March winds. The 'dire stroke' was as unlooked for as 'the precious boon itself', and the parents' grief was as deep as their previous joy. But the enlargement of their sympathies brought its own consolations, and when they heard of a sorrow like their own, they could not repress some tears. By the power of time, prayer, and thought, their little daughter ceased to be 'the innocent troubler of their quiet'.

The last two of the Pastor's tales link the vale of Grasmere with a wider world. The memorial poem on young George Dawson (called 'Oswald' in the tale) rises almost to the height of a heroic elegy. He was a 'peasant-youth' and asked 'no higher name', but nature had given him a 'scholar's genius' and the 'spirit of a hero'. Both qualities are illustrated in his exploits in his 'unpretending valley'. Nowhere else does Wordsworth describe so vividly the local sports of peacetime or the spirit of Grasmere during the

---

[1] *The Excursion*, VII. 299–302.   [2] Ibid. 632–94.

alarm of invasion in 1803 when young 'Oswald' led forth his comrades

> From their shy solitude, to face the world,
> With a gay confidence and seemly pride . . .[1]

How much of Wordsworth's heart and hopes are in the lines which express what George Dawson stood for at that time!

> in [him] our country showed,
> As in a favourite son, most beautiful.
> In spite of vice, and misery, and disease,
> Spread with the spreading of her wealthy arts,
> England, the ancient and the free, appeared
> In him to stand before my swimming eyes,
> Unconquerably virtuous and secure.[2]

It is to George Dawson that his comrades look for enlightenment on the prospects of national independence and liberty against Napoleon as the map of Europe is unrolled before them on the grass. The young man met his death from a fatal chill caught — through a moment's rashness — in the heyday of his vigour. His funeral, at which he received 'a soldier's honours', is described with solemn beauty.

The last of the tales[3] is little more than a pretext for some reflections from the Wanderer which conclude this part of *The Excursion*. A 'monumental stone' in the wall of the Church commemorates 'Sir Alfred Irthing'[4] who built a mansion in the valley in the reign of Elizabeth I. He is said to have arrived on a charger 'gorgeously bedecked with broidered housings', a belated representative of the age of chivalry. Few signs now remain in the valley of his former glory. We, too, continues the Wanderer, live in a time of change. The Knight saw chivalry decay: he saw the ancient Church overthrown. There is something in man which exults in the power of mutability: hence thoughtful people must endeavour to nourish 'the retrospective virtues'. This epilogue brings the Pastor's 'Pictures', judged as a whole, into close relation with Wordsworth's three Essays on Epitaphs written about 1809–10. The 'Pictures' are themselves 'authentic epi-

---

[1] Ibid. 774–5.   [2] Ibid. 852–8.   [3] Ibid. 923–1050.
[4] Really a member of the Knott family (Wordsworth: Fenwick Note).

taphs',[1] and many of them exemplify Wordsworth's conception of what an epitaph should be: 'truth hallowed by love — the joint offspring of the worth of the dead and the affections of the living'.

Wordsworth always keeps his strong identity, but his artistic purpose differs with the development of his mind. Various groups of poems represent a phase of thought in which he dwelt intensely for a limited time. It is perhaps the failure to recognize this that has led to the comparative neglect of the 'Pictures'. They are adapted to the Pastor's special purpose and outlook. Some of Wordsworth's best-known qualities are therefore absent, and rightly so. Very often his men and women have something of their creator's rejoicing sympathy with the moods of Nature. But here, such joy is the exception rather than the rule — a compensation, for example, for the want of hearing or sight. Nature is more often a power to be tamed or subdued. The folk of the tales have no idea that they are living in Arcadia. If they find beauty in their surroundings, it has usually been made by their own labour. Again, the stories cannot be detached from their setting without loss. Thus, the story of Ellen needs the large Christian charity of its teller, and the imagined proximity of the two graves. Besides, its effect in the series is heightened by its sequel, the story of a seducer who woke to a realization of what he had done, and 'could not find forgiveness in himself'. The very causes which have prevented the tales from becoming anthology pieces give them cohesion as a single poem. They must be read as a whole and in the right order. When their variety, harmony and subtle contrasts are taken into account, they will be recognized as an admirable achievement in the art of poetry.

These 'pictures' too, are more than a series of narratives, for they are penetrated by profound sentiment belonging to this season of the poet's life. They have a close affinity with *The White Doe of Rylstone* (1807–8), the action of which is centred in the grave of Francis Norton and the mysterious meeting of earth and heaven in the soul-experience of his sister. The burden of Wordsworth's meditations in the Essays on Epitaphs is the illumination which the near neighbourhood of a grave casts on a departed life. 'Every man has a character of his own, to the eye that has skill to

[1] *The Excursion*, v. 651.

perceive it.'[1] At one time the poet found the 'lonely roads' to be the best school for the searcher into 'the depth of human souls'. The development of his thought, since the death of his brother, brought his idea of 'infinitude' as the home of the human soul[2] nearer to the Christian conception of 'eternity'. A man's life, he now taught, is most truly judged in the blended association of the temporal and the eternal: hence, the gift of sympathic insight into character once assigned to the stimulus of Nature is now found to be encouraged by the consecrated ground of a churchyard. The rarefied realism of the stories testifies how strongly Wordsworth's mind was possessed by this belief: in substance, they are poetic; in spirit, religious. This twofold character corresponds to their relation with his other poetry.

[1] *Essay upon Epitaphs.* (*P.W.* v, p. 451).   [2] *The Prelude*, vi. 604–5.

CHAPTER X

Peter Bell; The Ruined Cottage; The White Doe of Rylstone

IT is difficult to assign either *Peter Bell* or *The Ruined Cottage* to any particular stage in Wordsworth's poetic development. Both poems were begun and provisionally ended at Alfoxden, but *Peter Bell* was not published until 1819, while *The Ruined Cottage* became part of *The Excursion*. *Peter Bell* has often been considered as an imaginative account of a conversion by natural means, but in view of lines 938–70 (on the Methodist preaching) it cannot be regarded wholly in that light, and this passage, followed by two stanzas apparently added near the time of publication, gives the story a certain kinship — in substance, though not in style — with the Pastor's tales. The poem has therefore been reserved for the present chapter. The story of Margaret in *The Ruined Cottage* was to have been interpreted at its conclusion by the 'natural wisdom' of the Pedlar (or Wanderer), but the poet's attempt never quite succeeded. The story was never wholly absorbed into *The Excursion*. With it is associated *The White Doe of Rylstone* in which the fate of Emily Norton, fundamentally similar to Margaret's, is handled by the art of a later stage in the poet's career. Though finished in 1808 its thought, in relation to Stoicism, marks an advance beyond that of *The Excursion*.

1. PETER BELL

No poem of comparable length by Wordsworth raises more questions of criticism than *Peter Bell*, and a complete examination of it cannot be attempted here. Few works of merit in the English language have been so much misjudged, since the example was set by the early parodists. 'The ludicrous parts of the poem'[1] are

[1] See *Oxford Companion to English Literature* (Oxford, 1932; 3rd ed. 1946).

still known by repute to scores of persons who have never read the
whole work, and knowledge of Peter is apt to stop short at his
indifference to the yellow primrose. Many points about the poem's
composition and history must be set aside in order that I may deal
more fully with the claims of some excellent critics that it is one of
Wordsworth's 'great imaginative poems'.

   That it is partly a work of imagination — in the special sense of
the term adopted by the poet himself — cannot be gainsaid. For
Wordsworth the power of imagination is proved in making us
aware of certain great yet common truths vital to the soul of man.
Such truths, he teaches, lie all around us, waiting to connect
themselves with our minds. The Prologue to *Peter Bell* translates
into a light and fanciful form the substance of the famous passage
in *The Recluse* to the effect that Wordsworth's imagination needs
no supernatural world or mythical heaven, in view of the awe-
compelling nature of the human mind. He declines, after a short
trial, any further flights into space provided by his little Boat
shaped like a crescent-moon, nor is he tempted by the fabled
enchantments of the Earth. He accepts the taunt of being a
'homesick Loon':

> The common growth of mother-earth
> Suffices me — her tears, her mirth,
> Her humblest mirth and tears.

Peter Bell presents a strong contrast with its counterpart, *The
Ancient Mariner*, which makes abundant use of the supernatural.
Both poems originated in discussions between the two authors on
the fundamental nature of poetry, and *Peter Bell* is the result of
their schism after an attempt to write *The Ancient Mariner* in
collaboration. Both poems are a record of redemptive remorse
following an act of cruelty to an inoffensive living creature. The
ass in Wordsworth's poem corresponds to Coleridge's albatross.
Walter Raleigh, in his *Wordsworth*, further unfolds the parallel
and the contrast between the two poems. 'The protagonist of
Wordsworth's tale, in place of the Mariner, is a drunken itinerant
potter. He has not killed an albatross, but in the course of his
reckless life he has committed a hundred more accessible crimes.
At the opening of the poem he is discovered by the light of the

moon cruelly beating a stray ass. The ordeal for the softening of
his heart begins.' The stages of this process form the main part of
the poem. Peter sees a thing of horror — not a skeleton ship, but
the body of the ass's dead master in a river. Like the Mariner, he
is thrown into a trance. On wakening, he is subject to 'Spirits of
the Mind' and in conscience-stricken fear begins to attribute
natural incidents to supernatural causes. The sound of a withered
leaf blown over the ground suggests the nearness of a pursuer.
Falling drops of blood prove to be flowing from the wound he
inflicted on the ass's head. A subterranean noise, which at other
times he would have known to proceed from miners at work,
mysteriously intensifies his guilty recollections. The worst memory
of all links itself with a dilapidated chapel: such a ruin had once
'served his turn' as the scene of his mock marriage with a young
Highland girl in the shire of Fife. The whole crime now re-enacts
itself in his imagination, ending with the vision of the mother of an
unborn child, lying dead at his feet. 'The Spirits of the Mind'
have now finished their work on Peter, and he is absorbed in
'his heart's contrition'. It is in this mood that he hears the
'clamorous' voice of a Methodist preacher proclaiming the Gospel
of repentance and forgiveness. The words fall on his ears with
instant and convincing power. The ass finally brings his rider to
the cottage of the drowned man, and Peter's newly won humanity
is proved in his sympathy with the astonishment and grief which
his story brings to the widow and her children. The bitterness of
his ordeal is now completed. After 'ten months' melancholy' he
becomes 'a good and honest man'. Raleigh's comment after a
comparison between the two poems is that '*The Ancient Mariner*
is one of the dearest possessions of English poetry. *Peter Bell* is a
deeply interesting experiment'. Does this conclusion do justice to
Wordsworth's poem?

By its date (1798) the original *Peter Bell* belongs to the most
experimental stage of Wordsworth's poetic career. He had not
attained that sureness of touch in diction and metre which marks
the best poems of 1799–1800. In the 1800 Preface he is less hopeful
that 'the language of conversation in the middle and lower classes
of society' is a fit medium for poetry than he had believed in 1798,
and he holds that such language must be 'purified'. *Peter Bell*

bears many marks of its earlier date. It purports to be a story told
extempore to a mixed rural audience, and the parts describing
Peter at his worst — his brutality to the ass — are given in the
casual gossiping manner such a group would have relished. Of
genuine poetry there are few traces. It is only when Peter's cruelty
begins to recoil on himself that the story becomes poetically alive.
The six manuscripts bear witness to Wordsworth's efforts to purify
the offending parts and he did much by sheer literary ingenuity.
But to have removed all the ruder features would have fatally
weakened the character of the poem. The ass still *grinned*; 'girl'
still rhymes dialectally with 'squirrel'. Wordsworth might claim
that the style of the revised poem was 'not negligent', but *Peter
Bell* had been begun as an experiment, and the fact could not be
disguised.

Nevertheless Wordsworth was right in his high esteem of the
poem, once it develops from a local entertainment into a serious
and pathetic story of moral regeneration. Seldom has the transformation of a sub-human brute into a living soul been traced
with such subtle originality.

> Mit ahnungsvollem, heil'gem Grauen
> In uns die bessre Seele weckt.[1]

Conversion is sometimes instantaneous, and poetry has generally
emphasized its strong dramatic contrasts. Browning does this in
Ned Bratts, so does Masefield in *The Everlasting Mercy*. But to
represent the painful awakening of a petrified conscience, step by
step, within the bounds of common occurrences was a bolder and
not less worthy plan, performed by the poet without any model to
guide him. It is Wordsworth's first great poem on the holiness of
the heart's affections and it closes with a simple directness
befitting the theme. On hearing the words of the Methodist
Preacher, 'clamorous' though they are, Peter experiences the joy
of a repentant sinner.

Peter Bell was conceived in the most sanguine period of Wordsworth's poetic life and under the stimulus of Coleridge's society.
That he should have been able to write a poem which is in some
sense a rival of *The Ancient Mariner* is an astonishing proof of

---

[1] Goethe, *Faust*, i. 1180–1.

intellectual independence. His imagination finds congenial employment when Nature begins to act on Peter, and from that point the story takes care of itself. But in complete alienation from natural feelings Peter's mind resists imaginative description: crude realism with metre 'superadded' was not the solution, and the intermittent touches of lyrical beauty land the poet in the old mistake of the 'two voices'. At Alfoxden, Wordsworth's mastery of the art of poetry was not yet commensurate with his imaginative reach. *Peter Bell* is a poem which opens in dim faith and emerges into clear vision. It is thus the converse of *The Ruined Cottage*, a poem begun and continued with wonderful success but never perfectly ended, notwithstanding intense effort.

2. THE RUINED COTTAGE

The Ruined Cottage, in spite of its apparent simplicity, is really a synthesis of some of the poet's deepest convictions. It originated in his brooding on the human aspects of a country cottage which had slowly fallen into decay and become absorbed into the landscape. Traces of departed human life are blended with the ruined walls and half-wild overgrowth of vegetation, making the whole scene a document awaiting interpretation. The ruin has its own *religio loci*: for Nature, to the poetic eye, has preserved something of the spirit of the last inhabitant. Can an empty cottage be haunted by a good spirit? The Wanderer who tells the story secretly believes it can, though he deprecates the thought as foolish. The pathetic fallacy of the poets is false to fact, but obedient to 'the strong creative power of human passion'. The story of Margaret works so powerfully on the listening poet that he too feels with the Wanderer

> That secret spirit of humanity
> Which, 'mid the calm oblivious tendencies
> Of nature, 'mid her plants, and weeds, and flowers,
> And silent overgrowings, still survived.[1]

There was nothing outwardly striking in Margaret's story. It was 'a common tale, an ordinary sorrow of man's life, a tale of silent suffering'. Her affectionate and once thriving husband was

[1] *The Excursion*, i. 927–30.

ruined by the economic disaster following on war. Finally, in desperation, he enlisted for foreign service, leaving Margaret secretly in order to spare her the misery of following a soldier's life. For 'nine tedious years' she lingered in solitude and increasing poverty, 'a Wife and Widow'. 'She was a woman of a steady mind', and never gave up hope of her husband's return. Hence she clung to the cottage, asking news of her husband from every passing soldier or sailor. But he never came.

In the life of this good woman, closely associated with the one spot on earth that she loved, there was the perfect subject for illustrating the truth which had been borne in upon Wordsworth as he wrote *The Borderers*:

> Suffering is permanent, obscure and dark,
> And shares the nature of infinity.[1]

Many poets have known this, but how can the suffering of the innocent compare with the attractions for poetry of a great and exciting action? The doubtful success which poets have made of the patient Griselda illustrates the difficulties of the task. But in the twin existence of Margaret and her cottage Wordsworth found the way, needing, however, an observer who would naturally visit the place at intervals over a long period. He had recourse to the occupation of a pedlar, in which he had taken a lively interest in boyhood. His own Pedlar (or Wanderer) is the clear-sighted annalist of Margaret's life both before and after her misfortunes. He records, with a minute exactness no reader can forget, the progressive signs of neglect in the once trim cottage and garden. They betoken the slow blighting of hope in her life: from a fixed and happy possession rooted in religious faith (ll. 533–4), to brave cheerfulness under the first adversity (l. 550), to a courageous effort after her husband's enlistment (l. 685), to an unloved burden in his prolonged absence (ll. 812–13), and finally to a torturing instinct 'fast rooted in her heart' (ll. 913–14). No praise is too high for the art with which the homely phrases are charged with emotion, nor has Nature ever been more intimately linked with the history of a human heart. For suggestiveness of description it would be hard to surpass the lines:

[1] *The Borderers*, ll. 1543–4.

                                                From within
    Her solitary infant cried aloud;
    Then, like a blast that dies away self-stilled,
    The voice was silent.[1]

Nothing of comparable quality in English poetry is written with
less parade than this poem.

But the Wanderer is not merely the chronicler of Margaret's
story: he is its indispensable interpreter. Wordsworth in his own
person could have made it a tale of equal pathos: but what 'worthy
purpose' would it serve? Something more mature than the poet's
buoyant natural philosophy of *Tintern Abbey* was required. The
story of Margaret hardly confirms the cheerful faith that all
which we behold is full of blessings. The Wanderer, as finally
developed from the simple Pedlar of Hawkshead, is more advanced
in faith than the poet himself. With his mystical intercourse with
Nature he combined an early acquired sense of duty and an
unweakened fidelity to the Theistic teaching of the Scottish
Church. Thus fortified he could face the tragic facts of life with a
habitual stability not attained by the poet himself until some
seven years later. The declaration of Wordsworth in the *Elegiac
Stanzas on a Picture of Peele Castle* is made by the Wanderer in
the earliest version of *The Ruined Cottage* —

                        that there is often found
    In mournful thoughts, and always might be found,
    A power to virtue friendly; were't not so
    I am a dreamer among men — indeed
    An idle dreamer.[2]

Thus in the character of another, Wordsworth anticipates the
lines of his own philosophical development. The first draft of *The
Ruined Cottage* was completed by 1798.

Margaret's hopes end in her death, and the bare fact alone is all
that is recorded in the original poem. Some 'reconciling conclusion'
was needed and the poet exerted himself to find one. Finally, he
wrote a passage which includes fourteen lines almost identical
with the corresponding part in *The Excursion*. Beginning with the
line:

[1] *The Excursion*, i. 735–8.   [2] *P.W.* v, p. 393.

> She sleeps in the calm earth and peace is here,

the passage ends:

> That what we feel of sorrow and despair
> From ruin and from change, and all the grief
> The passing shews of being leave behind,
> Appeared an idle dream that could not live
> Where meditation was. I turned away
> And walked along my road in happiness.[1]

Here the Wanderer is speaking entirely in character, but Wordsworth could not rest content with the vague word 'meditation'. In
the last version (1845) he gave the whole conclusion of the poem an
unequivocally Christian character, both in ll. 934–9, which were
added, and in an expansion of the lines after 'an idle dream', which
now read:

>   that could maintain,
> Nowhere, dominion o'er the enlightened spirit
> Whose meditative sympathies repose
> Upon the breast of Faith. I turned away, &c.

These alterations leave the passage inconsistent with the
Wanderer's characteristic point of view. His thoughts have
hitherto been drawn from 'natural wisdom' and the Theism of his
upbringing. He is not the spokesman of a specific Christian faith.
We must regret that the plan of the poem did not allow an epitaph
on Margaret to have been spoken by the Pastor. But it appears
to me that the extra knowledge we gain of Wordsworth's mind
near the end of his life should atone for his inconsistent attribu-
tion of these new lines to the Wanderer. That was better than
leaving the thoughts unspoken.

The Ruined Cottage is in itself so powerful a poem, and so
central to Wordsworth's deepest thought, that it has seemed best
to consider it apart from *The Excursion*. Up to 1802 it was still
regarded by the Wordsworths as a separate poem, and it is so
printed in Matthew Arnold's Selections under the title of
'Margaret'.

[1] Ibid. v, p. 403.

3. THE WHITE DOE OF RYLSTONE

The White Doe of Rylstone was finished in 1808 but not published until 1815. It is another tale of the 'silent suffering' of a good woman in extreme adversity, and her release by death, spiritually unconquered. But the treatment is completely different. Instead of the unadorned facts of an obscure life related by a pedlar, we have, in the later poem, a setting of high national import — the Catholic rising in the North in the reign of Elizabeth I, to which is added the local tradition of a White Doe, beautifully elaborated by the poet. Emily Norton, the central figure, is enabled to mount through her sufferings to an unearthly peace; the White Doe — a creature between earth and heaven — being the means and sharer of her beatification.

In some respects, *The White Doe* is also a successor to *Brougham Castle*: both poems, besides being founded in the local traditions of Northern England, contrast the martial virtues with the higher fortitude of patience. *The White Doe* has also been compared with Coleridge's *Christabel*, and with Scott's *Lay of the Last Minstrel*, each of the three poems being 'a tale of feudal times, having as its heroine a lady of high birth surrounded by warring hates and the violence of battle, to which her innocence and beauty afford a striking contrast; each has its setting of northern landscape and medieval architecture, and each is in part bathed in the romantic atmosphere of moonlight'.[1] But romance has little place at the heart of Wordsworth's poem: the beautiful descriptions of Bolton Priory and of Rylstone Hall (the seat of the Nortons) are only incidental to the main theme — the spiritual discipline of Emily and Francis Norton.

Wordsworth was not satisfied with his treatment of the 'physical action' of *The White Doe*, and admitted that the style of the 'business parts' had a 'feebleness of character'. This was inevitable and indeed, in one sense, almost desirable. He declares in *The Recluse* that he could not read a tale of two brave vessels fighting to the death, without being more pleased than a wise man ought to be. Nor could he follow the fortunes of the elder Norton and his eight sons marching to support the headstrong rebellion and

[1] *P.W.* iii, p. 546.

finally losing their lives at York, true to their cause, without a stirring of the spirit. But his sympathies were divided: he knew that the rising was at best a heroic mistake. Rightly considered, it was something much worse, for the Nortons' Banner, figuring the Five Wounds of Christ, was — as Francis[1] and Emily both felt — a profanation. Emily had wrought it at her father's bidding, but with foreboding afterthought: it was 'an unblest work'. The bravest of the Nortons was Francis, the eldest son and a Protestant, who incurred his father's wrath by refusing to join the rising. He followed it unarmed, in order to render his family what services he could.

The conflict inherent in the poem, which deals sympathetically with two opposing sets of values, appears in Francis's tragic fate. He had shown to Emily what course was required of her in the light of his own uncompromising idealism. When left alone at Rylstone by her father and brothers, she feels an overpowering impulse to hasten to the scene of action, but she is restrained by the thought that to Francis this would seem a betrayal of her higher self:

> She meets the insuperable bar,
> The injunction by her Brother laid;
> His parting charge — but ill obeyed —
> That interdicted all debate,
> All prayer for this cause or for that;
> All efforts that would turn aside
> The headstrong current of their fate:
> *Her duty is to stand and wait*;
> In resignation to abide
> The shock, AND FINALLY SECURE
> O'ER PAIN AND GRIEF A TRIUMPH PURE.[2]

Francis himself is faced by a terrible dilemma. Admitted to York Castle before the execution of his father, with whom he is now reconciled, he receives his last request. The elder Norton cannot restore the ancient faith, but he may 'attest' it by having the Banner laid in Bolton Priory. What son could refuse? Yet Francis is not guiltless, for to him the Banner is 'unhallowed', and, as

---

[1] *White Doe*, 501.
[2] Ibid. 1062–72 (Wordsworth's italics and capitals).

Wordsworth reminds us, 'Throughout [the poem], objects (the Banner, for instance) derive their influence, not from properties inherent in themselves, not from what they *are* actually in themselves, but from such as are *bestowed* upon them by the minds of those who are conversant with or affected by those objects.' Thus, all the guilt involved in an armed insurrection is associated with the Banner, and the noble Francis is tragically involved:

> What hath he done? what promise made?
> Oh weak, weak moment! to what end
> Can such a vain oblation tend,
> And he the Bearer?[1]

He foresees his destruction, and remembers his prophecy to Emily that the Nortons 'are doomed to perish utterly'. His death at the hands of Sir George Bowes and his followers is the Nemesis: it is his body, not the Banner, that finds its way to Bolton Priory. Unlike Emily, he has not been 'held above The infirmities of mortal love'. The poem begins with the White Doe at his grave, and so it ends.

There may be some weakness in the 'business parts' of the poem, but in all that relates to Emily and the White Doe there is an enchanting beauty. The Doe is the link between the ruined home of the Nortons and Bolton Priory, which she visits 'every sabbath'. There she appears in the opening canto: she is invested with a strange awe in the minds of the rural worshippers. The beauty of the Priory is enhanced by the presence of the delicate creature as she glides among the ruins from shadow to sunshine, seeming to the fancy to possess a pilgrim's reverence for the once holy places. She passes on until she lays herself in quietness 'beside the ridge of a grassy grave'. The poem then turns back to retrace past events, and the Doe's next appearance is by moonlight in the spacious gardens of Rylstone Hall. Emily's father and brothers have left their home to join the rising. Heart-sick in her solitude, she first rejects the Doe's advances, but then softens to this friend of her childhood, finding in her a link with the mother who taught her 'to worship in simplicity the invisible God'.

In the last canto the deeper meaning of the Doe's mystical

---

[1] Ibid. 1394–7.

relation with Emily is unfolded. The mansion of the Nortons has
been laid waste, and Emily herself personifies the desolation she
has been schooled by her brother to expect. By utterly renouncing
every thought of joy she has won a terrible victory over her own
humanity:

> Her soul doth in itself stand fast,
> Sustained by memory of the past
> And strength of Reason; held above
> The infirmities of mortal love;
> Undaunted, lofty, calm, and stable,
> And awfully impenetrable.[1]

But the Doe finds her out in her solitude and awakens the memory
of the past, its delights and sorrows, which she thought she had
laid to sleep for ever. She can no longer bear the old associations
and seeks an abode among strange scenes which gradually link
themselves with her heart. Thus restored, and with her now
inseparable companion, she has the strength to return to Rylstone
and to give heed to the sabbath music of the church bells attuned
to the words, 'God us ayde'. The past thus revives in her mind,
solemn and unearthly, like a holy spring-day. The unhoping
stoicism enjoined by her brother is replaced by a sacred resigna-
tion. Dead to all earthly pleasure, she is yet free, while still on
earth, to tread

> A more divine and loftier way!
> Even such this blessèd Pilgrim trod,
> By sorrow lifted towards her God . . .
> At length thus faintly, faintly tied
> To earth, she was set free, and died.[2]

But the Doe does not only raise Emily from a barren renunciation.
She remains on earth to haunt those spots which Emily had most
loved. The poem ends like a faint impalpable music, and our
minds are left with the image of a milk-white doe, immortal and
unchanged.

Wordsworth called the poem 'a mortal song' encouraged by
'celestial power'. One of its critics maintains that 'there is a
sudden loss of clarity' at the end 'where it becomes uncertain

---

[1] *The White Doe*, ll. 1623–8.   [2] Ibid. ll. 1849–65.

whether Emily's victory is of earth or of heaven'.[1] The remark is suggestive, but the life of a poet's thought lies in its development. The point of this particular judgement will, I think, disappear in a wider view. That there is a theological incompleteness in the poetry of these middle years of Wordsworth's life must be admitted. He is approaching theology in his own way — from the standpoint of 'natural wisdom' — and he affirms no more than he knows at the time. Peter Bell is brought to repentance by a Methodist preacher, but we do not know whether he becomes a Methodist himself. The Solitary is deeply impressed and partly changed by the Wanderer and the Pastor, but again we are not told whether he was restored to 'the Christian faith in which he had been educated'.[2] Instead of deploring Wordsworth's 'indecision', is it not more noteworthy that, while still working within his own imaginative sphere, he inevitably approached the Christian view of man's moral life — its depth, its needs, its incompleteness without a higher revelation? Such surely is the impression produced by the profoundly conceived poems discussed in this chapter. Nor is the final stage of the poet's own beliefs concealed from us. We know it from the work of his last fifteen years.

[1] J. Jones, *The Egotistical Sublime, A History of Wordsworth's Imagination* (Chatto & Windus, 1954), p. 153.

[2] See Fenwick Note (24 June 1843).

CHAPTER XI

The Classical Sublime, 1814-1821

DURING a period of some seven years — from 1814 to 1821 — Wordsworth produced a group of poems marked by certain common features of spirit and form and differing in a measure from most of his earlier and later work. Some of the new poems are the successors to the *Ode to Duty*, attaining at their best the same severe ethical beauty. The 'spontaneous overflow of powerful feelings', 'the deep power of joy', had no longer the creative power or the spiritual sufficiency of earlier years. Nor was there any great task on hand to demand the concentration of his powers. In *The Excursion* he had included much of his best earlier work, which might otherwise have remained as a stimulus to continue the now shadowy *Recluse*. Except for the brief return of crisis in 1815, the fever of the Napoleonic wars was at an end. Thus there was no external call for the exertion of the poet's intellectual powers, his ethical fervour, or his passion for great poetry, all still at their height.

In 1815 Wordsworth published his collected short poems in two volumes, 'including', said the title-page, 'Lyrical Ballads, Additional Poems, a New Preface, and A Supplementary Essay'. An epoch of his life is closed, and the poet is looking before and after. Both Preface and Essay, while dealing with large critical issues, are closely concerned with Wordsworth's own powers and status as a poet. Confident in the verdict of the future, he places himself among those of our poets whose very originality was a stumbling-block to their contemporaries. His own strength lies in the Sublime and the Pathetic, the former being something of a barrier between him and the age. 'And for the sublime', he says, '— if we consider what are the cares that occupy the passing day, and how remote is the practice and the course of life from the sources of sublimity, in the soul of Man, can it be wondered that there is little existing preparation for a poet charged with a new mission to extend its kingdom, and to augment and spread its enjoyments?' Wordsworth had written sublime poetry, and he knew it. But could he in the new and uncertain period which he was entering, 'extend its kingdom' into fresh areas? Part of the answer depends on the quality of the occasional and quasi-classical poems which he wrote between 1814 and 1821.

The various causes of Wordsworth's renewed interest in the Greek and Roman classics are complex, but the fact itself need not surprise us. His 'knowledge of classical literature', says de Selincourt, 'and his affection for it dates from his schooldays, and had always been stronger than is usually recognized.' His mind needed a new orientation after long and intense creative effort in his peculiar field. 'No mortal man', says Dr. Batho,[1] 'could have kept up the pace of the years from 1797 to 1807 for another ten years', though in fact Wordsworth relaxed little until 1814. His removal in the previous year from Grasmere to Rydal Mount was itself a breach with the past, and his growing intimacy with Sir George Beaumont (in spite of Wordsworth's 'terrific democratic notions')[2] was symptomatic of developing views. The harbinger of his new poetic phase is *Laodamia*. It is founded on the description of the Underworld in *Aeneid* vi, where Aeneas sees the unhappy subject of the poem among other victims of love. Ovid and Euripides suggested minor features of the work. Having found his way back to the classics, Wordsworth remained with them for several years. Seneca was already one of his favourite authors. His love of Virgil led him to translate the first three Books of the *Aeneid* into heroic verse between 1819 and 1823.

An assimilation of Wordsworth's view of nature, even though temporary, to a Roman mode may seem more surprising than a choice of subject from Virgil or Plutarch. There was, however, an anticipation of this novelty in some of his early, though less characteristic, work. In the full vigour of his early inspiration, Wordsworth had been little troubled by a sense of mortality in the world of nature. His contemplative absorption in *one* bird or *one* tree, or on a number of units seen instantaneously, such as the forty cattle feeding like one, or the host of daffodils seen at a

---

[1] *The Later Wordsworth*, p. 315.

[2] *Autobiography of B. R. Haydon*, p. 126 (O.U.P., World's Classics).

glance, had satisfied his imagination: the single object was sublimated into something higher than its ordinary self. But on occasion his mind seized on the life of a whole species in the natural order.[1] There is an instance of this in the poem *Water Fowl*, composed in 1800, though first published in the *Guide to the Lakes* (1823). It describes the intricate evolutions of a 'company' of birds, as if the species were displaying its character to the eye of the gazer, to whom these 'feathered tenants of the flood' are like a 'genus' or 'proles' of Latin poetry. The generalized view appears again in the poem *To the Clouds*, written in 1808. Every reader remembers Wordsworth's single clouds, mostly slow-moving or motionless. But the clouds of this poem sweep across the sky, not as units, but as an 'army', 'an endless flight of birds', 'a long procession'. In merging the individual in the group or species, both these poems anticipate the *Vernal Ode* (1817) — an unusual type of poem for Wordsworth, composed, as he said, 'to place in view the immortality of succession, where immortality is denied, as far as we know, to the individual creature'.

Laodamia, the first of three short narrative poems, each of them inspired by a high principle or ideal, was finished in 1814 and later twice revised, with important changes in the conclusion. The situation is based on an episode in the Trojan War. Protesilaus, the husband of Laodamia, knew from the Delphic oracle that the first Greek to land on Trojan soil would be killed, but was willing to sacrifice himself for his country's honour, and was slain by Hector. Laodamia implores the gods to restore her dead husband to her sight, and the boon is granted, but Protesilaus is to remain among the living for no more than three hours. He adjures Laodamia to 'mourn meekly' when he departs, but her passion of love is too strong, and when he is summoned away, she falls dead on the floor of the palace. The human implications of this situation stirred Wordsworth so profoundly that his poem is one of the grandest he ever wrote. Passion and reason, human love and heroic daring, pathos and sublimity, the mortal and the immortal, contend in its glowing lines. Over the discord, stands the rock-like stability of the central passage:

[1] See also pp. 146–7.

> Be taught, O faithful Consort, to control
> Rebellious passion: for the Gods approve
> The depth, and not the tumult, of the soul;
> A fervent, not ungovernable, love.

How deeply Wordsworth's heart and judgement were engaged in
this poem is shown by his difficulty in arriving at the right
conclusion. No doubt the final version in which Laodamia is
separated from the 'happy Ghosts' of the Underworld, but only
for an 'appointed time', is the one most consonant with the tenor
of the poem. The stern conclusion in which she was sentenced 'to
wander in a grosser clime' stood only for a few years. But the
earliest ending, inconsistent though it is with Virgil, has a note of
pathos which gives the lines an unforgettable beauty:

> Ah, judge her gently who so deeply loved!
> Her, who, in reason's spite, yet without crime,
> Was in a trance of passion thus removed;
> Delivered from the galling yoke of time
> And these frail elements — to gather flowers
> Of blissful quiet 'mid unfading bowers.

Nothing reminds us more forcibly than this cancelled stanza of the
emotion which underlies the apparent calm of Wordsworth's best
poetry.

Artegal and Elidure (1815), like *Laodamia*, presents a situation
which appealed to Wordsworth's 'natural heart'. Any ancient tale
of affection between brothers would have attracted him, and
Artegal and Elidure is a tale of fraternal love tested and
triumphant. The story has not the prestige of Greek or Latin
poetry, but was chosen 'as a token of affectionate respect for
the memory of Milton', from whose *History of Britain* the
ancient British legend is taken. The poem has something of the
serene cheerfulness which Wordsworth associated with Milton's
character, and its strength lies in the reality it gives to the
implications of an extraordinary situation. Artegal (Milton's
'Archigallo'), the elder brother of Elidure, proves so bad a king
that he is deposed and exiled, Elidure being crowned in his stead.
After a season, Artegal returns secretly to his native country,
desiring only 'a place of safe retreat', but is recognized by his

brother. With high magnanimity, Elidure insists on restoring the power which, in his mind, he had 'held in trust'. Artegal deprecates the noble offer as impolitic, but Elidure carries his point, acts cautiously for a time, and by his infectious generosity finally turns the restored Artegal into 'Earth's noblest penitent'. The poem was written in the last year of the Napoleonic wars, and Wordsworth's mind, long strained in the effort of supporting his own and the nation's *morale* against military despotism, relieved itself in this Quixotic legend on the force of example in noble action.

The story of *Dion* (composed 1816) is closely parallel to the tragedy of Brutus in *Julius Caesar* and, like Shakespeare's play, was founded on Plutarch. Dion, a noble exile from Syracuse, embraces the political teaching of Plato and returns at the head of five thousand warriors to Sicily, where he is welcomed 'as if a very Deity'. But in order to give effect to the 'sacred laws' of Philosophy he employs unrighteous means, and stains

> the robes of civil power with blood,
> Unjustly shed, though for the public good.

That his crime has left indelible marks on his soul is brought home to him by a terrifying apparition; but he is spared the misery of long remorse, being slain by political rivals. The truth embodied in his tragedy and expressed in the final lines was one of the keystones in Wordsworth's later teaching:

> Him only pleasure leads, and peace attends,
> Him, only him, the shield of Jove defends,
> Whose means are fair and spotless as his ends.

Wordsworth 'came to trust in the slow and patient processes of divine action and in those gradual changes in human institutions which imitate them, rather than in the hasty measures which promise well and lead to confusion'.[1] The merit of *Dion* lies in its exalted ethical strain. Instead of developing a single situation as in the two poems just discussed, Wordsworth has here packed an entire tragedy into little more than a hundred and twenty lines. This has literally 'cramped his style'. Originally the poem began with a beautiful description of a swan designed, as the poet said,

---

[1] Batho, *The Later Wordsworth*, p. 233.

to prepare 'for the due effect of the allusion to the genius of Plato'. The poet afterwards 'displaced' this passage as distracting and too long: had he left it, the rugged conciseness of the poem would have been somewhat softened.[1]

Four poems composed in the following year (1817) give a varied picture of Wordsworth's mind in this middle part of his career. He is loyal to his past but recognizes that he has outgrown the season for 'vernal ecstasies and passion's feverish dreams'. Like all religious-minded men, he had his moments of deep depression, when he failed to keep the 'heights which the soul is competent to gain'. Part of a sonnet published two years later ('I watch, and long have watched, with calm regret Yon slowly-sinking star') expresses this darker mood:

> Angels and gods! We struggle with our fate,
> While health, power, glory, from their height decline,
> Depressed; and then extinguished: and our state,
> In this, how different, lost Star, from thine,
> That no to-morrow shall our beams restore!

Rebelling against such moods, Wordsworth strove to draw strength and refreshment from the permanence of the natural order. In this attempt, his writing loses some of the intimate personal charm which is one of its chief attractions. But his refusal to surrender to time gives the poetry of this period a spiritual elevation and austere beauty of its own. Moreover, it augurs well for the work of his third and last period.

The heart of the *Vernal Ode* is in two passages (strophes iii and iv) on the 'immortality of succession'. The first of these is uttered by a celestial 'Stranger', described in the opening lines, who first celebrates in song the emblematic eternity of the nightly sky and next the perpetual cycle of the seasons:

> 'Mortals, rejoice! the very Angels quit
> Their mansions unsusceptible of change,
> Amid your pleasant bowers to sit,
> And through your sweet vicissitudes to range!'

In the following strophe the poet passes from this exalted strain

[1] The cancelled passage was afterwards 'attached to the poem' but not fully restored to it.

and imagines himself in company with the 'mild pastoral Muse'
amid homely country sights,

> To lie and listen — till o'erdrowsèd sense
> Sinks, hardly conscious of the influence —
> To the soft murmur of the vagrant Bee.
> — A slender sound! yet hoary Time
> Doth to the *Soul* exalt it with the chime
> Of all his years; — a company
> Of ages coming, ages gone.

The transition in the quality and style of the poetry from the
first part to the second is very marked. After all, Wordsworth's
strength does not rest in the contemplation of generalized nature,
but in the power to feel the infinite significance of individual
things. It is the one bee, not 'the shadow-casting race of trees',
that gives the poem its real distinction. The poet felt this when
he chose the motto from Pliny that stands at the head of the Ode:
'Rerum Natura tota est nusquam magis quam in minimis.' The
pregnant style of the concluding lines (especially 101–24) with
their accumulation of compact phrases belongs to a new order of
Wordsworth's poetry and anticipates the manner of his ode on
The Power of Sound.

The Pass of Kirkstone is a synthesis of two phases in Wordsworth's poetic life: it unites Duty with Joy. The Pass had become
his neighbour by his removal to Rydal Mount, which lies near the
beginning of the ascent, though the climb is too stiff for a daily
walk. In the poem, his arduous struggle up the Pass corresponds
to the moral strain of his middle life during the War. At the
summit, midway between Ambleside and Patterdale, his mind is
invigorated by the sight of the inverted rocky arch, unchanged
since the Roman legions passed through it. After panting up the
hill of duty men may be thankful for the discipline of constraint,
which often releases a new power of enjoyment, as Wordsworth
now finds, perceiving 'how beautiful the world below' (ll. 53–86).
Rapid changes of one thought or image to another, often in short,
crisp phrases, are skilfully managed, and the poem is a fine
example of the subjective sublime.

In the *Ode to Lycoris*, a poem addressed to Dorothy Wordsworth,
the poet continues to extend his early discoveries in self-knowledge

to the less susceptible period of middle life. He is now 'a bard of
ebbing time'. The young, he reminds his sister, prefer autumn to
spring, as they prefer twilight to dawn:

> Sad fancies do we then affect,
> In luxury of disrespect
> To our own prodigal excess
> Of too familiar happiness.

It is also the natural impulse of the mature to welcome 'the year's
decline' with its 'milder suns' and 'harvest hope'. But is it wise at
this time of life to indulge purely passive feeling?

> Something whispers to my heart
> That, as we downward tend,
> Lycoris! life requires an *art*
> To which our souls must bend.

That the preference should now be given to the spring is therefore
required as an act of self-discipline:

> Still, as we nearer draw to
> life's dark goal,
> Be hopeful Spring the
> favourite of the Soul!

The poem marks the middle stage in the development of the
author's 'vernal hopes': the last is reached in a poem of some
fourteen years later, *The Primrose of the Rock*. *The Ode to
Lycoris* has a classical neatness and restraint: it also contains
several classical allusions; for instance, the name 'Lycoris' is
borrowed from Virgil's Tenth Eclogue. The author, says Wordsworth in a note, has retraced his steps 'in the regions of fancy
which delighted him in his boyhood, when he first became
acquainted with the Greek and Roman Poets'.

Any 'classical' features in the poem *Composed upon an Evening
of Extraordinary Splendour and Beauty* (1817) are external — the
structural identity of the elaborate stanzas, as in certain of the
odes of Gray, and the somewhat Latinized diction. But in essence,
nothing could owe less to the past than this 'effusion' on 'one
transcendent hour'. It is like a sudden illumination from another
world — a visible realization of the poet's dream of

L   G.U.W.

> An ampler ether, a diviner air,
> And fields invested with purpureal gleams.

Sky and earth meet in some of the most inspired descriptions Wordsworth ever wrote. To communicate his rapture he associates it with the Immortality *Ode*: the splendour of the sunset recalls the 'visionary gleam' of his childhood:

> the light
> Full early lost, and fruitlessly deplored;
> Which, at this moment, on my waking sight
> Appears to shine, by miracle restored.

But the restoration is imaginary, not real. The 'visionary gleam' was not an extraordinary but ephemeral lustre like this sunset: it shone continuously on 'the earth, and every common sight'. 'This is the last of Wordsworth's great visionary poems', say the Editors of a well-known anthology, 'prompted by "that blessed mood, in which . . . we see into the life of things".' But the poem is inspired by a sunset, not a mood: it is less a revival from the past than an augury of the future. This was indicated when Wordsworth later transferred it from the *Poems of the Imagination* to the group of *Evening Voluntaries*.

The *Ode to Enterprise* (1821) is separated by four years from the last four poems discussed but it is one of the most classically conceived of all. It has been undeservedly neglected, partly, no doubt, because it is superficially alien to the so-called 'philosophy of nature'. The poet is again seeking new objects of hope and admiration, without being false to the old, and he does so in one passage with considerable boldness, though in full accordance with the principles of the 1802 Preface. The Poet, he there tells us, 'will be ready to follow the steps of the Man of Science, carrying sensation into the midst of the objects of the Science itself'. Successive stages in the Progress of Enterprise, daughter of Hope and Young Ambition, are traced in the Ode, among them her contemporary triumphs in the field of invention:

> And hast Thou not with triumph seen
> How soaring Mortals glide between
> Or through the clouds, and brave the light
> With bolder than Icarian flight?

How they, in bells of crystal, dive —
Where winds and waters cease to strive —
For no unholy visitings,
Among the monsters of the Deep;
And all the sad and precious things
Which there in ghastly silence sleep?
Or, adverse tides and currents headed,
And breathless calms no longer dreaded,
In never-slackening voyage go
Straight as an arrow from the bow;
And, slighting sails and scorning oars,
Keep faith with Time on distant shores?

Having paid tribute to material progress, the poet passes to the
enterprise of Bard and Sage in the world of mind; then to enterprise of the Patriot's soul to restore a prostrate nation. He closes
with a spirited appeal to Enterprise to cherish her 'favourite Isle'
in the days of her prosperity: to 'quicken the slothful, and exalt
the vile', and to invigorate the ambitions of her worthier children.
The poem was greatly admired by Landor. 'Nothing can be
conceived more poetical than the *Ode to Enterprise*', he wrote to
the author, adding that if Porson were still alive, 'he would be
forced to acknowledge that you had beaten his own trained bands
at their own weapons.' The noble humanity of Wordsworth's
poem, its patriotism, its sense of history, and its praise of the
strenuous virtues, are all congenial to the spirit of the classical
ode. Even Macaulay, in general no lover of Wordsworth, would
surely have rejoiced in this timely and forward-looking poem.

The classical phase described in this chapter is partly a link,
partly a barrier, between Wordsworth's earlier and later poetry.
It was essentially temporary; Wordsworth could not have
continued in this path without losing contact with his main
sources of strength. How actively past emotions survived, appears
in the additions he made to the version of *Vaudracour and Julia*,
which he had written in *The Prelude* and was preparing for
publication in 1820. The later version, as Mrs. Moorman points
out, 'contains lines of intensity of feeling second to none that he
wrote, in spite of the weakness of the poem as a whole; and these
lines were most of them added about the time when the poem was
revised for publication, that is, quite late in Wordsworth's poetic

life, at a time when it is usual to suppose that he had practically ceased to write great poetry.'[1] None the less the change in Wordsworth's later writing must be recognized. It was becoming less true of his poems that 'the feeling therein developed gives importance to the action and situation'. His subjects are chosen more and more for their intrinsic value. Art and science, books and history, play a larger part in his poetic thought. Thus we may compare his early sonnet, 'Nuns fret not', based wholly on his inner meditations, with its later counterpart, 'Scorn not the sonnet', which appeals to the practice of seven other poets. Natural facts count for more in relation to fancy and feeling, as appears in a comparison of *A Wren's Nest* (1833) with the early lyric *To the Cuckoo* (1802). The long tours of Wordsworth's later life enabled him to transplant old enthusiasms to new scenes. His narrative poems carry his knowledge of the human heart into unexpected places. The 'deep power of joy' is succeeded by a new spiritual vision. These are among the features of his later work. After his classical phase he rediscovered the truth asserted in the Preface to his Poems of 1815, that Hebrew rather than classical poetry is the true source of the sublime. This is felt especially in his last great ode, *On the Power of Sound*.

[1] M. Moorman, *Wordsworth: Early Years*, p. 184.

CHAPTER XII

Three Series of Sonnets

1. POEMS DEDICATED TO NATIONAL INDEPENDENCE AND LIBERTY (1807–11)

'FROM want of resolution to take up anything of length', wrote Wordsworth in later life, 'I have filled up many a moment in writing Sonnets, which, if I had never fallen into the practice, might easily have been better employed.' The application of this remark is limited to the *Miscellaneous Sonnets*, for his sequences have themselves much of the character of long poems. The Sonnets of Shakespeare are often read as a single composition, but Wordsworth's sequences, which are more closely articulated, are seldom regarded as anything but a mine for the anthologist. This practice conceals some important features of his art and thought, and in the present chapter an attempt is made to view three groups of sonnets as single poems. The first to be considered is the second set of *Sonnets Dedicated to Liberty*,[1] which, unlike the better known first group, are stronger and more impressive in their cohesion than as units. These *Sonnets* take us back a few years from the point we have reached in this survey of Wordsworth's poetry: the other two sequences follow chronologically from the previous chapter.

The thirty-three sonnets of Part II on *National Independence and Liberty*, mostly written between 1807 and 1811, present a certain contrast with those of 1802–6. As long as Great Britain was united to repel the invader and could look to such men in high place as Nelson and Fox, the sense of danger and national unworthiness was overshadowed by a larger hope and pride. But

---

[1] This is a title used in 1807. The thirty-three sonnets referring to the years 1807–11 continue as a second sequence on a wider plan, and they later became the first portion of a larger group constituting Part II of *Poems Dedicated to National Independence and Liberty*.

the death of Nelson in 1805, and of Fox in 1806, changed the situation. There was no statesman left at home who, in the poet's view, had the heart and mind to understand the vastness of the issues involved in the struggle with Napoleon. From 1807 onwards Wordsworth surveyed events in Europe with a wide-embracing vision, like Hardy's or Tolstoy's. The sonnets of 1807–11 are the record of an inspired tenacity of hope in repeated disappointments, and of faith that tyranny supported by mere military force cannot endure for ever.

The first six sonnets of this series are a miscellaneous group giving no clear promise of what is to follow. The fifth has an undertone of deep sadness in its comparison of the peace at Grasmere with

> earth's groaning field,
> Where ruthless mortals wage incessant wars.

Then at the seventh, the tone changes abruptly, and a strain of poetry begins which culminates in the great sonnet, *1811* (xxxiii). The poet has linked himself in sympathy with the Spanish rising against Napoleon, and his solitude is peopled with living hopes:

> Here, mighty Nature! in this school sublime
> I weigh the hopes and fears of suffering Spain;
> For her consult the auguries of time,
> And through the human heart explore my way;
> And look and listen — gathering, whence I may,
> Triumph, and thoughts no bondage can restrain.[1]

For Wordsworth, the rising in Madrid of 2 May 1808 against the French occupation was an event comparable to the outbreak of the French Revolution — as popular, spontaneous, and passionate. Like many of his countrymen he was bitterly disappointed when, after a victory over the French, the generals of a British force sent to aid the Spaniards signed a Convention to repatriate the defeated forces in British ships. As long as the Spanish war was considered as a mere military action, it could not fail to be of limited effect. If, however, it could be incorporated into a movement of national resistance over the whole of Europe, it would be the centre of a new hope for millions under Napoleon's despotism.

---

[1] *Poems Dedicated to National Independence and Liberty*, Part II. vii.

'His first and last thoughts', wrote Dorothy of her brother at this time, 'are of Spain and Portugal.' He was then writing his Tract on the Convention of Cintra, which he compares to a prose poem: 'an impassioned strain, without aid of numbers'.[1] It labours to convert an immense load of facts and arguments into a prophetic vision, and though the style is tortuous the faith is clear. He writes as if with a mission to express the inarticulate hopes of freedom-loving people throughout Europe, bidding them look to heaven and their own hearts for the only strength mightier than Napoleon's battalions. Events proved him right. Napoleon was overthrown as he prophesied. The force to which he appealed, later called Nationalism, was to play a glorious part in effecting the liberation of oppressed peoples.

Of these thirty-three sonnets only fourteen deal directly with Spain, but if the poet's thoughts fly to other lands they soon return to their starting-point. The impalpable spirit of Liberty spreads far and wide:

> No foot may chase,
> No eye can follow, to a fatal place
> That power, that spirit, whether on the wing
> Like the strong wind, or sleeping like the wind
> Within its awful caves.[2]

During this soul-testing time the poet cannot spare a word of praise for organized military resistance to the tyrant, for he is bent on exposing the great heresy of the age:

> O'erweening Statesmen have full long relied
> On fleets and armies, and external wealth:
> But from *within* proceeds a Nation's health.[3]

Seldom in Wordsworth's life was his mind sustained at a higher pitch of enthusiasm than in the composition of these sonnets and the Tract. On the outcome of the struggle he has staked his earthly hopes for man.

Sonnets ix–xi are on the rising under the Tyrolese patriot, Andreas Hofer, no strange portent to the poet who knew that the 'stern Nymph', Liberty, was an inhabitant of the mountains. And thus,

[1] Ibid. viii. [2] Ibid. xxxii. [3] Ibid. xxix.

> If sapient Germany must lie deprest,
> Beneath the brutal sword,[1]

something has been done for the cause by 'a few strong instincts
and a few plain rules'.[2] But in Spain Liberty was not dependent
upon the barriers of Nature: 'There is a bulwark in the soul'. This
was proved by the citizens of Saragossa — men and women, 'naked
to the gales of fiercely-breathing war',[3] who defended their city
in what J. Holland Rose (writing in 1894) calls 'the most desperate
defence of modern times'. Sonnets xv and xvi, written when the
resistance of the Tyrol and Saragossa was at last at an end are
conceived in the spirit of the great sonnet to Toussaint l'Ouverture.
In three sonnets (xix–xxi) the poet meditates on the folly of
wooing Fortune for her fickle favours, like the Adventurer who is
now at an elevation,

> Round which the elements of worldly might
> Beneath his haughty feet, like clouds, are laid.
> O joyless power that stands by lawless force![4]

Sonnets xxiii–xxxi return to Spain where the people in 'the might
Of martyrdom, and fortitude, and right' still 'baffle that imperial
Slave'.[5] Wordsworth had acquired a true insight into the Spanish
national character which in its severer and more idealistic aspects
had a striking resemblance to his own. There are three sonnets
appealing to the local patriotism of the stubborn Biscayans
(xxiv–xxvi), and in Sonnet xxviii the poet praises a national
stiffness of bearing, more to be trusted than 'pliancy of mind':

> and be there joined
> Patience and temperance with this high reserve,
> Honour that knows the path and will not swerve;
> Affections which, if put to proof, are kind;
> And piety towards God. Such men of old
> Were England's native growth; and throughout Spain,
> (Thanks to high God) forests of such remain.

The Spanish group is closed by two exultant sonnets (xxx, xxxi)
on the elusive but indomitable 'Guerrillas' in their opposition to
the French forces.

[1] Ibid. xii.   [2] Ibid.
[3] Ibid. xiii.   [4] Ibid. xxi.   [5] Ibid. xxiii.

The series comes to an end in two sonnets of a more general character. The last 'Here pause: the poet claims at least this praise . . .' is included in many anthologies, and its predecessor is hardly less known. No doubt, the poet has put the quintessence of his thought into these two final pieces, and of the whole series they are the ones which could least be spared. But many of the preceding sonnets are inferior only in being more closely bound up with the history of the time. The whole 1807–11 group, together with the Cintra Tract, are a record of Wordsworth's inspired vision, courage, and hope during a great European crisis.

2. THE RIVER DUDDON

The River Duddon, a Series of Sonnets — 'one poem', as Mary Wordsworth said — was published along with other poems in 1820. 'To which is annexed', continued the title-page, 'A Topographical Description of the Country of the Lakes, in the North of England'. This volume was more immediately successful than any other published by the poet. Two years later the *Guide to the Lakes* was produced separately and it has since been many times reprinted. The Duddon Sonnets shared the popularity of the Guide. 'My sonnets to the river Duddon', said Wordsworth in 1849, 'have been wonderfully popular. Properly speaking, nothing that I ever wrote has been popular, but they have been more warmly received'.[1] The date of publication is significant. 1820 is the year chosen by De Quincey to mark the turning-point in Wordsworth's reputation: 'up to 1820', he wrote, 'the name of Wordsworth was trampled under foot; from 1820 to 1830 it was militant; from 1830 to 1835 it has been triumphant.'[2]

To some extent, the early popularity of the Duddon Sonnets may have been due to the very limitation of their value as poetry. De Selincourt asserts that with the exception of 'After-thought'[3] they are not 'generally regarded today as ranking high among Wordsworth's poetry'. 'After-thought' has indeed the note of

[1] *P.W.* iii, p. 505.   [2] T. Hutchinson, Oxford *Wordsworth* (p. xxx).

[3] Matthew Arnold includes this and two more of the Duddon series among the sixty sonnets in his selection, *Poems of Wordsworth*.

great poetry in its powerful appeal to something in us beyond time and place: the sonnets of the series itself, on the other hand, are, in Wordsworth's own term, 'loco-descriptive'. But the subject had special attractions. 'The power of waters over the minds of Poets', he wrote, 'has been acknowledged from the earliest ages', and the history of the Church in England is for him a 'holy river'. The Duddon sonnets are more poetic than pure description and more descriptive than the higher poetry.

Wordsworth does not associate the Duddon with any events at the centre of his own or his country's life, in the manner, for instance, of Dante describing the course of the Arno through the Tuscan cities. He does not make it vocal with the music of words, like Tennyson's *Brook*. A sonnet sequence might seem ill adapted for describing a river, compared with the flowing measures of Dante and Tennyson. But what Wordsworth offers in his sonnets is something unusual, perhaps unique. He gives himself up completely to the river, body and mind, for one imaginary day. The Duddon is a small stream — by the evening the poet has traversed its entire course. Inevitably, the poetry is circumscribed by the modest nature of the theme. The use of the sonnet-form justifies itself in the end: it proves well adapted to meditation alternating with description. The sonnets occupied the poet at intervals from 1806 to 1820. He had known the river from his childhood: 'long-loved Duddon is my theme'.

The starting-point of the poet is the top of the Wrynose Pass near the Three-Shire stone where Cumberland, Westmorland, and Lancashire meet. The rough track over the Pass of Wordsworth's time is now a motor-road. The poet must have often made a path of his own, forcing his way through whatever rugged or boggy ground the Duddon chose to take. The river begins amid mist and rain, a 'child of the clouds', cradled on ground high enough to be spangled with frost when only a few miles away the valleys are faint with heat.[1] The tiny stream has scarcely come to life before its power is felt among the rocks and earth in shedding round itself 'a gleam of brilliant moss'.[2] Soon the 'nursling of the mountain' begins to assume a half definite form like a loosely-

---

[1] *The River Duddon, a Series of Sonnets*, ii.
[2] Ibid. iii.

scattered chain, as the poet looks down into the long valley or 'bottom' stretching before him,

> Or rather thou appear'st a glistering snake,
> Silent, and to the gazer's eye untrue,
> Thridding with sinuous lapse the rushes, through
> Dwarf willows gliding, and by ferny brake.[1]

So far we have had faithful description in half-lyrical verse, but a higher strain is sounded in sonnet v. The four opening lines look back to the 'sullen' and 'craggy' solitude now left behind; then the eye is carried on to the first cluster of trees in the river's course — green alders, ashes,

> And birch-trees risen in silver colonnade,[2]

among which a cottage too stands in the Wrynose waste, where 'ruddy children' sport in a wildness which has no power to oppress their gaiety:

> light as endless May
> On infant bosoms lonely Nature lies.[3]

The river is still a mountain stream, but more tokens of settled life begin to appear. The 'slender voice' of the wren is heard: stepping-stones offer a passage over the stream,

> with interspace
> For the clear waters to pursue their race
> Without restraint;[4]

but not without danger in winter, when to cross the 'dizzy flood' requires some boldness even in the young and active.[5] As the poet gazes into the deepening stream and its rocky bed, objects are seen to stir the fancy: a 'faery chasm',[6]

> Wild shapes for many a strange comparison!
> Niagaras, Alpine passes, and anon
> Abodes of Naiads, calm abysses pure.[7]

The transformation of the little mountain beck into a river of classical proportions is reflected in the language and allusions of

[1] Ibid. iv.   [2] Ibid. v.   [3] Ibid. v.
[4] Ibid. ix.   [5] Ibid. x.   [6] Ibid. xi.   [7] Ibid. xii.

sonnet xx: the river, flowing smoothly with 'liquid lapse serene' would have 'beautified Elysium', and when it dashes over the next precipice, it will

> Dance, like a Bacchanal, from rock to rock,
> Tossing her frantic thyrsus wide and high![1]

The Duddon now broadens out in the lower land near the sea, and the more open valley enters the great system of the Lakeland landscape.[2] But the poet, after his exertions, is glad to find a nook which 'proffers to enclose body and mind'. Three sonnets (xxiv–xxvi) record his meditations as he rests in the heat of the afternoon, and there is a touching reflection that Dorothy is no longer fit for the present expedition:

> Rough ways my steps have trod; — too rough and long
> For her companionship; here dwells soft ease:
> With sweets that she partakes not some distaste
> Mingles, and lurking consciousness of wrong.[3]

A vigorous sonnet follows (xxvi) which dispels the languor of the sultry hour and reviews the debt of the poet's whole life — childhood, youth, and manhood — to the 'bold brood' of impetuous waters:

> Pure as the morning, fretful, boisterous, keen.[4]

As he nears the 'Kirk of Ulpha' (xxx, xxxi) with its 'wave-washed'[5] churchyard, there is a hint of natural fatigue; and the poet is not sorry that the easy terms of his companionship with the river allow him to take a short cut through the grass to avoid forcing his way through a 'rough copse'. The concluding sonnets (xxxii and xxxiii) were originally one, consisting of the octave of the former and the sestet of the latter. It is a pity that the poet made the change, adding alien references to the Thames, which distract the reader's mind from the wide stretch of sands where the river enters the sea:

[1] Ibid. xx (written in 1817).　　[2] Ibid. xxiii.

[3] Ibid. xxv.　　[4] Ibid. xxvi.

[5] Ulpha Church 'is situated on a little knoll of rock below the curve of which the Duddon flows'. I owe this information to Mr. Norman Nicholson.

Gliding in silence with unfettered sweep.[1]

No one who knows the Duddon can forget its final course over the Duddon Sands, and the original end to the series is not only better in itself but more in harmony with the glorious 'After-thought' (xxxiv).

A careful reading of the Duddon Sonnets tends to disabuse one's mind of the common belief that all but Wordsworth's greatest poetry is negligible. It is true that the finest sonnets of the series (v, xxvi and xxxiv) stand out from the rest, but to some the series as a whole will be as delightful as the Duddon itself, for Wordsworth has made the river peculiarly his own. Such writing must owe part of its attraction to an interest in the region described. No doubt those who know the Duddon already will enjoy the sonnets most, but the popularity of the series in Wordsworth's own time suggests that it was able to kindle an interest in many readers to whom the river was unknown. It will surely do this for others among Wordsworth's readers, scattered over a large part of the world, who are drawn for one reason or another to this most purely 'loco-descriptive' of all his mature poems.

3. ECCLESIASTICAL SONNETS

The *Ecclesiastical Sonnets* (originally 'Sketches')[2] have suffered in reputation from their title and perhaps also from their supposed subject. Of the 132 sonnets in the series not more than half a dozen at the most have found their way into anthologies. Wordsworth did not intend to write a succession of short poems. 'The Reader', he hoped, 'will find that the pictures are often so closely connected as to have jointly the effect of passages of a poem in a form of stanza to which there is no objection but one that bears on the Poet only — its difficulty.' The sonnets do, in fact, form a continuous poem, not indeed unified by the same treatment throughout, for there is some change of standpoint in Part III, but connected sufficiently to justify the poet's comparison with a

[1] Ibid. xxxii.
[2] *Ecclesiastical Sonnets*, ed. A. F. Potts (Yale University Press, 1922).

river, like the Duddon series itself, or those which trace 'the nobler Stream of Liberty'.[1] To readers who know only a few specimen sonnets, the poem must remain virtually a closed book.

The origin of the *Sonnets* lies in Wordsworth's lifelong sense of what the 'spires', the 'steeple-towers', and the 'chapels lurking among trees', meant to the rural life of England, and thence to the whole body politic. At the height of his Gallic fervour he had been conscious of his love for 'the sight of a village steeple'. *The Excursion* links the 'holy structures' with all that is noblest in patriotic feeling, in 'human charity and social love'. Two passages in that poem (VI. 1–41 and IX. 679–754), spoken respectively by the Poet and the Pastor, are the 'Ecclesiastical poem' in miniature. Much reading was of course needed for the work itself. In spite of the handicap of bad eyesight — only intermittently relieved from 1820 onwards — Wordsworth read many standard authorities on English Church History, from Bede's *Historia Ecclesiastica* to Sharon Turner's *History of the Anglo-Saxons from the earliest period to the Norman Conquest* (1799–1805). Fuller's *Church History of Britain* was another of his main sources; and his notes refer to ten other authorities. Wordsworth's position as an Anglican involves no hostility to the Church of Rome, though he deplores her interference in politics. He added two sonnets[2] to the original number 'to do more justice to the Papal Church' for the services which she rendered 'to Christianity and humanity in the middle ages'.

It was noted by the author himself that the *Sonnets* were written 'long before the Oxford Tract movement' and therefore 'long before Ecclesiastical History and points of doctrine had excited the interest with which they have been recently enquired into and discussed'. In bringing church history into the sphere of general literature he was a pioneer, especially in respect of the earlier stages of the subject. Of the three parts of the poem, the last — on the Church of England since the Restoration — has least novelty. Certain events in the record, such as the martyrdom of Latimer and Ridley, were known in thousands of English homes from Foxe's 'Book of Martyrs'. 'The Church in England' was a subject which appealed to Wordsworth in its entirety. In

---

[1] Ibid. I. i.   [2] Probably Ibid. II. ii and ix.

the continuity of so ancient an institution, and its survival through violent storms from without and bitter persecution within, was a sublimity to capture the imagination:

> Truth fails not; but her outward forms that bear
> The longest date do melt like frosty rime.

Much of the poem is an expansion of these lines. Religious history is for Wordsworth a succession of wave-like movements of progress and decline: the rise of spiritual worship sustained by single-minded zealots and accompanied by humanizing influence, followed by the corruptions of worldliness and political ambition. Complicating the rise and fall of 'outward forms' is the pressure o great secular events, the whole process being a field for the emergence of outstanding personalities. Such in outline is the pageant unrolled in the poem.

The historical content of the *Sonnets*, however, is only of secondary interest in the present study. What chiefly concerns us is Wordsworth's general philosophy of religion as developed from his early intuitions as a poet. For him the fulfilment of man's religious instincts was 'to adore the Invisible and Him alone',[1] but any incitement which raises men from their ignorance or apathy serves a religious purpose. Imagination is 'the mightiest lever known to the moral world'.[2] 'Our slack devotion' needs all the stimulus it can get. There is often a poetry in religious 'forms' and Wordsworth defends it throughout the series:

> Nor scorn the aid which Fancy oft doth lend
> The Soul's eternal interests to promote.[3]

He deplores the iconoclasm of the Reformation, and one of the most poetic parts of the series is the group of sonnets[4] on the loss to human values — 'the pillage of man's ancient heart' — in the dissolution of the monasteries. The climax of this group is the sonnet, 'The Virgin', which Dr. Batho calls 'a reverent invocation'. It is also an exquisite expression of the poetry latent in this cult. The poet's attitude is the same in the sonnets on the religious controversies of the early seventeenth century in England. Not

---

[1] Ibid. xi.   [2] Ibid. i. xxxiv.
[3] Ibid. xviii.   [4] Ibid. ii. xxi–xxv.

only does he regret the abolition of 'graceful rites' by 'our scrupulous Sires',[1] but he recalls with approval, in a note on Sonnet II xlv, the words of Laud 'upon the true and inward worship of God, which while we live in the body, needs external helps, and all little enough to keep it in any vigour'.[2] Wordsworth continued to urge this view in later poems such as *Devotional Incitements*, which extend the activity of eye and ear, of fancy and the affections, to the sphere of religious worship. Such was his consistent attitude in the long middle stage of his poetic career before his final entry into a more purely spiritual phase.

Through much of its course the poem is subject to the facts of history, but in the second portion of Part III invention finds freer scope. Sonnet xvii, 'Places of Worship', introduces a group of sonnets on the human aspects of religious rites — the consecration by the Church of the several ages of man from birth to death. Here the intimacies of rural life are touchingly blended with the solemnity of immemorial custom. In 'Baptism', for instance, the poet imagines thoughts of the coming festivity and the sound of the infant's crying at the font as intruding on the ceremony, until the associations of the churchyard

> Recall the wandering Soul to sympathy
> With what man hopes from Heaven, yet fears from Earth.

Hale White thought that there is 'nothing stronger in the whole series' than this sonnet and 'Thanksgiving after Childbirth' (xxvii). Both are later additions to the original series, as are also the two beautiful sonnets on Confirmation. Finally, our thoughts are brought back to the links which bind the humblest churches of recent date to the sacred history which has been traced to its origins, and the series concludes in the contemplation of some of the greatest temples in the land:

> They dreamt not of a perishable home
> Who thus could build.[3]

In his earlier poetry Wordsworth had shown how

> The external World is fitted to the Mind;

---

[1] Ibid. III. xxxiii.   [2] *P.W.* iii, p. 568.
[3] *Ecclesiastical Sonnets*, III. xlv.

so, on another level, the liturgy and rites of the Christian Church, long acclimatized to English soil, satisfy the needs of man in the supreme hours of life —

> if the intensities of hope and fear
> Attract us still, and passionate exercise
> Of lofty thoughts.[1]

[1] Ibid. xix.

CHAPTER XIII

The Lighter Muse

R EADERS of Wordsworth used to be told that he was deficient in humour, and that if his poetry provokes a smile, it is probably against his intention. Hazlitt, however, observing the poet for the first time, detected 'a convulsive inclination to laughter about the mouth, a good deal at variance with the solemn, stately expression of the rest of his face'. The notion of a humourless poet has been rightly contested.[1] Humour was an element of his genius though, as Hazlitt suggests, it was kept under control. Wordsworth had the characteristic English delight in 'originals', expressed in the novels and art of the age. One of his most amusing poems invokes the genius of Bewick, 'and the skill which he learned on the banks of the Tyne'. There is, as we have seen, an element of humour in *The Idiot Boy*. There is humour in the comparison of Rob Roy with Napoleon. In particular, humour is present in many of the poems founded on London memories, though seldom as their main characteristic. Indeed, a highly poetic incongruity is often the secret of their peculiar success. Thus, in *The Reverie of Poor Susan*, it is but a step from the semi-humour of the lines,

> Bright volumes of vapour through Lothbury glide,
> And a river flows on through the vale of Cheapside,

to the simple sublimity of

> She looks, and her heart is in heaven.

The Farmer of Tilsbury Vale, on the other hand, is a purely humorous sketch of an 'original' — an earthbound counterpart to Poor Susan. Like her, he is out of his element in London, and

> His heart all the while is in Tilsbury Vale.

[1] e.g. by John E. Jordan, 'Wordsworth's Humor', in *P.M.L.A.* (March 1958).

Another humorous poem is the village comedy of *The Two Thieves* in which a couple of culprits, at the extremes of age, a grandfather and a grandson, separated by ninety years, practise their harmless pilferings, like caricatures of Michael and Luke:

> in us the old and young
> Have played together.

But here the poet is not quite content with the charm of innocent roguery. The poem is related to the other *Lyrical Ballads* by its 'worthy purpose': it 'lifts up the veil of our nature'.

The radical distinction in Wordsworth's poetry is not between the serious and the humorous, but between Imagination and Fancy. The Muse to whom he dedicated himself in early manhood was Imagination, the 'image of right reason': but the Muse of his boyhood was Fancy, who pleases herself and has only a childlike concern with Truth. She may luxuriate in the Pathetic, but is a stranger to the Sublime. She was a favourite of Wordsworth's adolescence: she remained so in his first year at Cambridge and until the decisive experience of his first summer vacation. Fancy is a moralist in her way and delights in fables, but does not contemplate the tragic cleavage between Good and Evil. She is the lighter Muse: her devotees are young poets,[1] and she may revisit them when they have children of their own, and sometimes, though rarely, in the repose of their old age.

Let us hear the poet's own words on this matter. 'The law under which the processes of Fancy are carried on is as capricious as the accidents of things, and the effects are surprising, playful, ludicrous, amusing, tender, or pathetic, as the objects happen to be appositely produced or fortunately combined. Fancy depends upon the rapidity and profusion with which she scatters her thoughts and images; trusting that their number, and the felicity with which they are linked together, will make amends for the want of individual value: or she prides herself upon the curious subtilty and the successful elaboration with which she can detect their lurking affinities. . . . Fancy is given to quicken and beguile the temporal part of our nature, Imagination to incite and to support the eternal.' He adds that at times 'Fancy ambitiously

---

[1] Cf. *The Prelude*, VIII. 365–458.

aims at a rivalship with Imagination, and Imagination stoops to work with the materials of Fancy.'[1] That which gives unity to Wordsworth's poetry is the prevalence of Imagination. Fancy collects but does not unite.

Of all the poems inspired by Fancy none are truer to type than two of his pieces *To the Daisy*. In one ('With little here . . .') he sits and 'plays with similes' until Fancy's kaleidoscopic activity comes to rest in the white light of truth:

> Bright *Flower*! for by that name at last,
> When all my reveries are past,
> I call thee, and to that cleave fast.

In the other ('In youth from rock to rock I went') Fancy revels in a succession of moods and thoughts, 'coming one knows not how, nor whence, Nor whither going'. *The Oak and the Broom* is a typical fable of the Fancy: the picturesque incidents of the little story illustrate the good luck — not the wise choice — of humble obscurity. A familiar of Wordsworth's fancy was his daughter Dora who, when a baby, inspired the beautiful *Address* to her, as a 'frail, feeble Monthling', and also what is best in *The Kitten and Falling Leaves*. Seldom was Wordsworth's lighter Muse in happier mood than in the lines that follow the picture of withered leaves falling from an elder-tree:

> But the Kitten, how she starts,
> Crouches, stretches, paws, and darts!
> First at one, and then its fellow,
> Just as light and just as yellow;
> There are many now — now one —
> Now they stop and there are none:
> What intenseness of desire
> In her upward eye of fire!
> With a tiger-leap half-way
> Now she meets the coming prey,
> Lets it go as fast, and then
> Has it in her power again:
> Now she works with three or four,
> Like an Indian conjuror;
> Quick as he in feats of art,
> Far beyond in joy of heart . . .

[1] *Preface to the Edition of 1815.*

But it is hard to conclude this strain, and the final lines on 'Life's falling Leaf' do not keep the careless charm of the beginning.

The Waggoner is the best of the longer poems of the Fancy. The opening passage is exceptional in Wordsworth and is meant to create the right kind of expectation for the story which is to follow. The first lines describe the oppression of a hot summer night before a thunderstorm:

> The air, as in a lion's den,
> Is close and hot; —

so introducing 'a play of the fancy on a domestic incident and lowly character'.[1] It is a night when emotions are keyed up to a higher pitch than usual. *The Waggoner* has of course been compared with *Tam o' Shanter*, but the two works have only a superficial resemblance. Burns's poem is on the craving in the blood for an illusory triumph over the ills of life. Benjamin, the Waggoner, though a 'frail Child of thirsty clay' has no need to drown his sorrows: he loves his work and his horses, and but for a combination of circumstances would never have been betrayed into the good-natured weakness which cost him his place. His tale, as Lamb said, is told in 'a spirit of beautiful tolerance'. Benjamin is locally famous for the skill with which he drives his eight-horse team up the mountain-roads without using his whip. But his over-fondness for wayside inns has nearly cost him the favour of his employer. On this hot June night, having resisted the lure of one inn, he is overtaken by a terrific thunderstorm at the head of a Lakeland pass. There he falls in with a retired sailor who is travelling with a model on wheels of Nelson's 'Flag-ship at the Nile'. At the foot of the pass the two men are driven to take refuge in a small inn where a 'Merry-night' is in progress. Amid the excitement of the dancing and the enthusiasm over the sailor's exhibit and stories — Nelson is the national idol — all scruples vanish, and Benjamin ends the night with 'a deep, determined, desperate draught'. The next morning, when the men continue their journey, still in wild spirits, a trifling accident has grave results: a mastiff which accompanies the wagon — a favourite animal of Benjamin's master — is hurt by a kick (given

[1] Wordsworth to the Hon. Justice Coleridge. (*P.W.* ii, p. 501).

in self-defence) from the sailor's donkey. The injury is detected by the owner: Benjamin is dismissed, and as no driver of his skill can be found, both 'Waggoner and Wain' disappear from the road, where they have long been familiar and beloved.

The poetic character of *The Waggoner* owes much to the frequent gleams of Fancy cast over the narrative. There is Fancy in the similes of the opening lines on the ominous breathlessness of the evening. There is Fancy in the description of the grotesque form of a crag above Grasmere, seen in lurid light. There is some truly Dickensian heartiness and Fancy in the lines on the merriment and good cheer in the wayside inn:

> What bustling — jostling — high and low!
> A universal overflow!
> What tankards foaming from the tap!
> What store of cakes in every lap!
> What thumping — stumping — overhead! . . .
> As if it heard the fiddle's call,
> The pewter clatters on the wall;
> The very bacon shows its feeling,
> Swinging from the smoky ceiling!

There is Fancy of another kind as the Muse declines to follow the jaded revellers in the sweetness of the morning air and prefers to wander in the enchanted beauty of the River Greta below Skiddaw. The poem, though light in spirit, is an image of 'this great world of joy and pain'. The poet accepts the facts as they were:

> For what I have and what I miss
> I sing of these; — it makes my bliss!
> Nor is it I who play the part,
> But a shy spirit in my heart,
> That comes and goes — will sometimes leap
> From hiding-places ten years deep; . . .

'Nature might not be gainsaid.' Memory and Fancy preside over the poem to the last line, and the author does not contrive a happy ending.

The lighter Muse also prevails in the third book of *The Prelude*. However much the memories of Wordsworth's first year at Cambridge were enriched by 'after-meditation', only a few of them are relevant to the development of his imagination. Between his first departure from Lakeland and his return in the following summer, life was for him a season of 'deep vacation' — so he calls the term-time of the academic year. The record is miscellaneous, deriving such unity as it has chiefly from the light play of fancy over the surface. In no other book of *The Prelude* do such details as the poet's dressing-gown, silk stockings, and hair-powder come into notice, and it is the fanciful touches that save the descriptions from banality. Thus, his 'transformation' left him with hair

> Glittering like rimy trees when frost is keen.[1]

Hurrying to College chapel in his gown, after drinking 'libations' to the memory of Milton, his appearance in the streets was 'ostrich-like'. He compares the eager scholars of the past bent over their books to

> Caterpillars eating out their way
> In silence,

and he recalls the 'playful zest of fancy' with which he regarded the less dedicated seniors of his own time,

> men unscour'd, grotesque
> In character, trick'd out like aged trees . . .

The poet defends this season of his life as belonging to Nature's

> tender scheme
> Of teaching comprehension with delight,
> And mingling playful with pathetic thoughts.[2]

One or two passages of high Imagination stand out in the narrative, but it is Fancy, and the moods associated with it, that prevails.

The character of Wordsworth's Fancy changed for a time after about 1820, and he cultivated the lighter Muse as a social grace. Linking Nature with the domestic arts, Fancy also allied itself with a new metrical precision, producing a kind of rural *vers de société*. A favourable example of such writing is *A Flower Garden* (1824) in which the merits of art and Nature are reconciled in a witty manner, playful and serious at the same time. In a few of

---

[1] *The Prelude*, III. 37 (1805).   [2] Ibid., p. 559–61.

these lighter pieces — of which the lines 'Yes! thou art fair' are among the best — he restates some of his favourite beliefs as epigrams. But such formalized fancy is far enough from the vital centre of his poetry. After 1830 he occasionally returned, for lighter verse, to 'fancies' drawn from nature in his characteristic manner,[1] and he was also visited by fleeting moments of imagination like that captured in *Airey-Force Valley* (1835), where he describes the 'gentle touch' of a little breeze on a 'light ash',

> that, pendent from the brow
> Of yon dim cave, in seeming silence makes
> A soft eye-music of slow-waving boughs,
> Powerful almost as vocal harmony
> To stay the wanderer's steps and soothe his thoughts.

Wordsworthian Fancy is centrifugal, and it needed this touch of Imagination to bring us back to our main subject.

[1] e.g. in the lines, 'So fair, so sweet, withal so sensitive' (1844).

CHAPTER XIV

The Poetry of Travel

So large a body of Wordsworth's poetry consists of 'Memorials' of various tours that a chapter must in any case be devoted to the subject. But the travel-poetry is also an illuminating commentary on the development of Wordsworth's mind, especially in the years 1820 and after. Only one of the travel sequences belongs to what is commonly called the poet's 'great' period — the *Memorials of a Tour in Scotland* in 1803 — and it is instructive to compare this collection with those which followed it. If too we bear in mind the relation of this travel-poetry to *The Excursion* and the *Ecclesiastical Sonnets*, the subject will be found to occupy a key position in a general study of Wordsworth's poetry.

The groups of poems to be considered are the following:

1. *Memorials of a Tour in Scotland*, 1803.
2. *Memorials of a Tour in Scotland*, 1814.
3. *Memorials of a Tour on the Continent*, 1820.
4. *Yarrow Revisited*, 1831.
5. *Itinerary Poems of 1833.*
6. *Memorials of a Tour in Italy*, 1837.

We have already seen how the novelty of unfamiliar life and scenes affected the character of the poems of the first tour of Scotland (1803). But this is only one aspect of them, and not the most important. They were written when Wordsworth's poetic inventiveness was at the peak of its activity, and the real point about these poems is the power and wealth of their organic life. Their relation is not based on their geographical sequence in a tour, but upon their common origin in the same creative mind. Many of Wordsworth's poems were themselves procreative: one Lucy poem begot another, one Matthew poem another; it was the same with the poem on the Daisy and with many more. In others there is an imaginative comprehensiveness which brings together diverse elements into a poetic harmony. It is the marked presence of these two features that distinguishes the first group of travel poems from some of its successors. After the 'great' period, both the poetic synthesis of diverse elements within a poem and the vital connexion of one poem with another are apt for a time to appear more faintly. The organic sequel is replaced by the meditative afterthought. Some of the travel-poems record mere isolated impressions terminating in themselves; some are echoes from more creative days. But the signs of falling-off, which are most conspicuous in the group of 1820, do not persist. The later poems tend to form themselves into harmonious sequences, and in the last three series there is a new spiritual vision. Wordsworth never ceased to feel the stimulus of the physical world, but there was a constant and fruitful effort in his late writing to adjust sense impressions to a growing soul-illumination.

1. MEMORIALS OF A TOUR IN SCOTLAND, 1803

Comments are made on some outstanding poems of the series:

Rob Roy's Grave is a late lyrical ballad and an extension of local memories of the poor man's hero to the great international topic of the day. In 1805–6,[1] Wordsworth could still imagine with unregenerate glee the freedom of 'natural society': his stirring song on the outlaw boldly claims for Rob Roy that

> in the principles of things
> *He* sought his moral creed.

How happy then would Robin have been in the day which acclaims a Bonaparte!

> 'I, too, will have my kings that take
> From me the sign of life and death.'

But no! the difference between the two ages and the two men was too great, for Rob Roy loved the *liberty* of Man. It is astonishing how much of himself Wordsworth has put into this brilliant exposure of Napoleon, as seen by other than French eyes.

The Solitary Reaper brings to a focus the following motifs which elsewhere stirred Wordsworth's imagination or deeper feelings:

[1] So dated in *P.W.* (iii, p. 445).

(*a*) The sight of a human being solitary in a wide landscape, and self-absorbed; (*b*) the desert lands of Arabia (cf. *Prelude*, V 50–140); (*c*) the return of the cuckoo in spring; (*d*) the border-ballads of ancient tragedy or warfare; (*e*) the 'ordinary sorrow of man's life'. *Glen Almain* and *To a Highland Girl* are both poems on a characteristic Wordsworthian theme — that in which a solitary scene has 'an appropriate human centre'. The lines in which the poet concludes his address to the Highland Girl are a classic example of a *religio loci* embodied in a person:

> For I, methinks, till I grow old,
> As fair before me shall behold,
> As I do now, the Cabin small,
> The Lake, the Bay, the Waterfall:
> And Thee, the Spirit of them all!

The Highland Girl reappears as one of the 'Three Cottage Girls' to whom a poem was dedicated on the Continental tour of 1820. She is only a memory, but, as a memory, is more vividly alive than either of the two maids, Italian or Helvetian, with whom she is now in company.

The Matron of Jedborough would have rejoiced the heart of the Pastor in *The Excursion*, for her cheerfulness in the presence of her stricken husband was a fine spiritual victory. She is more than cheerful — she dances gaily at the age of over seventy years. She is as noble in essence as one of Wordsworth's sublime Solitaries, and he names the source of her strength:

> let praise ascend
> To Him who is our lord and friend!
> Who from disease and suffering
> Hath called for thee a second spring;
> Repaid thee for that sore distress
> By no untimely joyousness;
> Which makes of thine a blissful state;
> And cheers thy melancholy Mate!

It is impossible to say whether Wordsworth at the time intended *Yarrow Unvisited* to be his final word on Yarrow. He continued to prefer the first of the Yarrow poems, remarking that 'imagination almost always transcends reality'. But he was to learn, as he

records in the *Elegiac Stanzas on Peele Castle*, that 'truth' also
has claims as against imagination, and he owed it to himself to
attempt a sequel to the first Yarrow poem. In course of time, the
first two poems became incomplete without a third. The three
Yarrow poems together form a thread which unites a whole
imaginative life.

2. MEMORIALS OF A TOUR IN SCOTLAND, 1814

Wordsworth's companions on this tour were his wife and Sara
Hutchinson. Had Dorothy been present her suggestions would
probably have prompted more poems and almost certainly have
added cheerfulness to the tour, but the 'Memorials' would perhaps
have lost some of their independence. *The Brownie's Cell* is a poem
on a member of the Macfarlane clan who retired to a small island
near the head of Loch Lomond in order to commemorate 'the
faded glories' of his race. His hermit-like life earned him the title
of 'the Brownie', but Wordsworth ascribes to him something of the
exalted self-dedication of a 'Patmos Saint'. The poem has a
certain harshness of tone, and the beauty of the small island
seems overcast by the sombreness of the hermit's reflections.
Wordsworth, however, had a partiality for *The Brownie's Cell*
and wrote a sequel to it in his tour of 1831. It is easy to understand Landor's admiration for the next poem — *Composed at
Cora Linn in Sight of Wallace's Tower*. 'Nothing in Pindar', he
wrote, 'is more like anything else in Pindar than the ode composed
at Cora Linn. Of all compositions in modern languages the higher
Ode is the most difficult.' Wordsworth's style has here the lofty
terseness befitting patriotic poetry and there is a rousing appeal
to historic memories. The final stanzas are worthy of the poet
at his best in the manner of the 'classical sublime'. *Yarrow Visited*
was a link with the imaginative life of the past, and its composition
was an act of justice to the present.

3. MEMORIALS OF A TOUR ON THE CONTINENT, 1820

This collection of poems had a modest origin. The poet's wife and
sister were his travelling companions, along with one or two other
intimate friends for part of the time. Most of the poems were

written soon after the return to England, being intended, according to the poet, 'to intersperse the Journals' of Mary and Dorothy. But they later assumed more independence. 'His work has grown to such importance', wrote Dorothy in 1822, 'that I have long ceased to consider it in connection with my own narrative.'

Dorothy's words may, I think, cause some disappointment to the reader who turns to these poetic *Memorials*, especially if he fails to read them to the end. The first poems, in particular, seldom rise much above the level of a journal in verse, and Dorothy's prose is on the whole a preferable medium. Many of the poems seem little more than a factual record of the stages of the journey and of incidents, some of them trivial enough, which arose on the way. Only once or twice on the tour was Wordsworth's poetic feeling deeply stirred, and there was more than one reason why he should be subject to a certain listlessness. The reception of his poems had given him little inducement to make a new comprehensive effort on a large scale. With the battle of Waterloo the excitement of great public events came to an end, and when he left England five years later he had none of the high expectations of the earlier Continental tours. Still, he had an inveterate love of travelling and the tour of 1820 was, after all, not devoid of some poetic surprises.

In the opening pieces, the sight of Bruges, of the field of Waterloo, of 'War's favourite playground' between Namur and Liège, and a few other scenes, are recorded in verse which adds a musing accompaniment to Dorothy's prose, and does hardly more than that. But after a time Wordsworth's fancy begins to work more independently. He discovers the poetic suggestiveness of certain names — 'Engelberg, the Hill of Angels' and 'Our Lady of the Snow', and is moved, as often, by the human aspect of a picture — in this instance, an indifferent painting of the son of William Tell. Later in the tour he writes a well-conceived but ill-executed sonnet on Leonardo's damaged *Last Supper* at Milan. True poetic energy appears for the first time in the poem called *The Church of San Salvador*. He had been astonished by the splendour of the view from some high ground near by, and his emotion animates some vigorous lines on the general power of a local *religio*:

> Cliffs, fountains, rivers, seasons, times —
> Let all remind the soul of heaven;
> Our slack devotion needs them all;
> And Faith — so oft of sense the thrall,
> While she, by aid of Nature, climbs —
> May hope to be forgiven.

The two closing stanzas, on the Swiss patriots Tell and Winkelried, have the heroic quality of the poem *Cora Linn*, admired by Landor,[1] but Wordsworth does not reach this height again in the series. Two of the subsequent poems are linked with the past: *The Italian Itinerant, and the Swiss Goatherd* recalls an old memory of London street-scenes recorded in *The Prelude*,[2] and, as already mentioned, *The Three Cottage Girls* is a sequel to *The Highland Girl, at Inversneyd*. Like many another English poet, he succumbs to the music of Italian place-names. He makes a pleasing tune out of some of them in *The Eclipse of the Sun, 1820*:

> The solemnising veil was drawn
> O'er villas, terraces, and towers;
> To Albogasio's olive bowers,
> Porlezza's verdant lawn,

and the *Stanzas, Composed in the Simplon Pass* opening with an apostrophe to 'Vallombrosa' are in the same romantic vein. In this poem, Italy is for him, as for Goethe, 'the climate of myrtles' and the land of the 'cool orange-bower'. Some later lines, however, *At Vallombrosa* (1837), is a better poem. *Processions* has a compact allusiveness, though on a smaller scale, like that of *The Power of Sound* (1828), but the later poem is a greater achievement in this difficult kind of writing.

The enjoyment of the tour was darkened by a fatal accident. A young American student, whom Wordsworth met by chance and soon came to esteem highly, was drowned while crossing the Lake of Zürich. His name was Frederick William Goddard. 'Seldom', wrote the poet, 'have I seen so promising a youth.' He lamented the loss in some *Elegiac Stanzas* and was gratified to learn that the poem did something to console the young man's mother.[3] But it is impossible for the critic not to feel how much the

---

[1] See p. 174.   [2] Book VII. 214–16.   [3] Harper, ii. 318–19.

whole treatment of the subject in these stanzas — in style and sentiment alike — is an echo of the elegy on the poet's brother, John. It is regrettable that Wordsworth did not fashion some new idiom in which to express his sorrow for an event, which, though sad indeed, could not cause the overwhelming grief of the earlier loss. This elegy is typical of the 1820 *Memorials* as a whole. Critically speaking, most of the good things in the collection had already been done better before, or were to be better done in the future. The chief exception is *The Church of San Salvador*.

4. YARROW REVISITED, 1831

'Poems composed during a Tour in Scotland, and on the English Border, in the Autumn of 1831' were published in 1835, along with a considerable number of other pieces, to form a volume entitled *Yarrow Revisited, and Other Poems*. Wordsworth's only companion on the tour was his daughter, Dora. With the great question of Parliamentary Reform in the air, the year was one of anxiety for the nation at large, and in particular for the poet, who says, in the *Apology* at the end of the collection:

> every day brought with it tidings new
> Of rash change, ominous for the public weal.

But the poet's mind was now largely attuned to the notion of change, and he was prepared to meet the inevitable with all the imaginative hope he could summon. His mood gives a certain harmony to the poems, and he is able to say, with justice:

> the several Lays
> Have moved in order, to each other bound
> By a continuous and acknowledged tie
> Though unapparent.[1]

The items of the group form something of a genuine poetic sequence, far superior to the haphazard effect of the 1820 *Memorials*.

The beautiful poem, *Yarrow Revisited*, sets the tone of the whole series. The river is viewed in its relation to a great writer; recalling a man grievously sick in 1831; but the reader's thoughts

[1] *Apology.*

are thrown back to an earlier visit, when Scott's life was still in its spring. Yarrow, both unseen and seen, had been a source of power to Wordsworth, and by a fine play of fancy, he suggests that Scott has extended the virtue of the stream far beyond itself:

> For Thou, upon a hundred streams,
>   By tales of love and sorrow,
> Of faithful love, undaunted truth,
>   Hast shed the power of Yarrow.

Now that Scott's career seems drawing to a close, Wordsworth indicates the benefit of pure Romance to the moral life of its readers: it sustains them against the sense of change by enlarging their view of the common lot of man:

> Nor deem that localised Romance
>   Plays false with our affections;
> Unsanctifies our tears — made sport
>   For fanciful dejections:
> Ah, no! the visions of the past
>   Sustain the heart in feeling
> Life as she is — our changeful Life,
>   With friends and kindred dealing.

Both writers had drawn riches and strength from their country's history, and it is small wonder that they felt a common dismay at the prospect of revolutionary change. They could not escape the logic of events, however deeply they deplored it. But though Scott's career was nearly finished, Wordsworth's was not, and he was prepared to continue the imaginative work of his life, surmounting his fears by such fortifying hopes as he could find or make.

Yarrow Revisited is followed by the sonnet *On the Departure of Scott for Naples*. The opening is as notable an example as can be found of the justified 'pathetic fallacy', for hardly the most literal mind would reject the fancy that Scott was, in very truth, a kindred 'Spirit of Power' for whose departure Eildon and Tweed were mourning. And the 'Sursum Corda' of the conclusion is as true to fact as it is comfortable to the heart. The sonnet is a perfect utterance for the occasion.

Four sonnets follow in which the unrepining acceptance of man's lot is found to beget a spiritual blessing of its own. In *A Place of Burial in the South of Scotland* all is redolent of 'plain old times'. No ostentation appears among the tombs 'level with earth', and therefore feeling is not offended: the union of death and life is 'not sad' when the birds renew near the graves their *jubilate* to spring. The next sonnet is on a sight to fill 'pure minds with sinless envy', for it is that of a manse where the trees and flowers have been loved and tended by a Minister who does not own or covet the heritable possession of the land. The lesson of the sonnet which follows, *Composed in Roslin Chapel, during a Storm*, is more difficult to convey in other words than its own, but it seems to teach a kind of contemplative humility. Nature is supplying the ruins with the winds for music, while herbs, natural and sculptured, approximating to the same appearance, preach 'of all things blending into one'. The group is closed by the splendid sonnet, *The Trossachs*, where every nook is a 'confessional' in which the dying year has its own sights and music to lull to rest the mortal cares of man. In all these sonnets the external world is 'exquisitely fitted' to the mind of the contemplative man who can renounce worldly passions.

The next sonnet, on the decay of Highland manners, sounds a note of urgent warning. Can imagination survive the conquests of civilization? Nearly the whole of Wordsworth's poetry is dedicated to the nourishment of man's higher life by imagination, and he can see no future for the race if imagination perishes from want of all stimulus to self-exertion:

> Then may we ask, though pleased that thought should range
> Among the conquests of civility,
> Survives imagination — to the change
> Superior? Help to virtue does she give?
> If not, O Mortals, better cease to live!

The poems now continue, balanced between despondency and hope. It is not Death that is man's enemy so much as the changes due to his own self-betrayal. The sonnet, *Eagles*, intimates that the 'Bird of Jove' must, like man, enjoy his natural freedom, or he is no better than 'a lone criminal whose life is spared'. Among the Highlanders in the Glen of Loch Etive the poet was 'mortified to observe the bitter hatred of the lower orders to their superiors; love of country seemed to have passed into its opposite',[1] and he wrote a gloomy sonnet on the changes

> That make the Patriot-spirit bow her head
> Where the all-conquering Roman feared to tread . . .[2]

yet he could still reflect with hope on the ancient spirit of reverence for 'patriarchal occupations' which made a 'wild vindictive Race' call a group of towering peaks by so grand a name as 'Shepherds of Etive Glen'.[3] Always it is the signs of earthly pride in 'heaven-offending' glories that feed his melancholy and the tokens of humility that encourage his hope:

> If rightly trained and bred,
> Humanity is humble, finds no spot
> Which her Heaven-guided feet refuse to tread.[4]

Within the sphere of natural experience, he still has a buoyant faith in the power of memory:

> Better to thank a dear and long-past day
> For joy its sunny hours were free to give
> Than blame the present, that our wish hath crost.
> Memory, like sleep, hath powers which dreams obey,
> Dreams, vivid dreams, that are not fugitive;
> How little that she cherishes is lost![5]

The progress of thought and feeling leads naturally to the more religious note which is struck in the last two sonnets of the series: *Countess's Pillar* and *Roman Antiquities*. In the second of these the poet asks:

> Heaven out of view, our wishes what are they?
> Our fond regrets tenacious in their grasp?
> The Sage's theory? the Poet's lay?

And this reflection reappears in the poems on the second tour to Scotland made two years later.

---

[1] Fenwick Note.   [2] *Composed in the Glen of Loch Etive.*
[3] *In the Sound of Mull.*
[4] *Highland Hut.* See also *The Earl of Breadalbane's Ruined Mansion* and *The Avon.*
[5] *Bothwell Castle.*

5. ITINERARY POEMS OF 1833

In 1833, Wordsworth made another tour to Scotland, partly by sea, in order to visit Staffa and Iona which had been omitted from the places seen in 1831. His companions in 1833 were his friend H. Crabb Robinson and his son John, who had recently been presented to the small living of Moresby, near Cockermouth. Though the poet was less disturbed about the state of the country than he had been on the eve of the Reform Bill, he still had many apprehensions, and there were even fears that his son's Parsonage 'might be taken from him any day by the reformed Parliament'.[1] But the country's religious future was, on the whole, a source of more hopeful thought, and the tour itself, with Iona as its destination, was partly a religious pilgrimage. On his travels Wordsworth's senses were always intensely active, but inward meditation had grown with the years to be a stronger independent force. His mind was disposed to dwell with affectionate pride on his sons John and William; he felt an ever-growing interest in the ancient memorials of Christianity scattered over the land; he was even learning to meet signs of insensibility to the beauty of nature with a courageous tolerance. The finer essence of this new self-discipline, with its increase of spiritual vision, is conveyed in the quiet but exquisite sonnet which closes this series of poems.

By this time, Wordsworth had exploited the possibilities of the sonnet-form to the full — at least, for his own purposes. He was becoming impatient of its restraints, and he shows this by a relaxed attention to formal standards. One sonnet (*Cave of Staffa* xxx) is marred by an unusually careless line; another (xix) called by Wordsworth an 'unpretending sonnet' is by his brother-in-law, Henry Hutchinson; a third (xxxiii) ends with four lines from a sonnet by the Rev. Thomas Russell. His friend, Barron Field, pointed out the 'superfluous syllables' in a line of the original version of Sonnet xiv. On the other hand, he was extending his range of verse-forms. Among his experiments, the most interesting

[1] Dora Wordsworth to Edward Quillinan, Feb. 1834. See Sonnet ix, *To a Friend*. Note: Sonnets in this section are numbered as in *Itinerary Poems of 1833* (*P.W.* iv, pp. 20–55).

is his poem suggested by 'the Headlands of St. Bees'.[1] In this work, he has adopted the stanza-form 'and something in the style of versification'[2] from a poem, *St. Monica*, by Charlotte Smith (1749–1806). The scheme requires the use of two different rhymes to the name 'St. Bees' in every stanza, and there are eighteen stanzas in all. Wordsworth hardly meets this challenge with the gay virtuosity of a youthful Swinburne — some of his rhymes are repeated — but he acquits himself very creditably. Other examples of metrical experiment will be mentioned in the next chapter. Though Wordsworth was never among the acrobats in verse, the new nimbleness which he was showing in his sixties is certainly remarkable.

Wordsworth's critics have generally emphasized his dread of change at this period of his life, and have failed to do justice to his openness of mind, in several new directions. No one has ever longed more passionately that the beauty of the land, as he had known it in childhood, should be preserved for future generations; but he always taught that, for a right-thinking man, the health of the social order is involved in the true enjoyment of landscape. He also came to realize that appreciation of natural beauty — especially in its highest form — is not easily learned by city-dwellers, and that the new arts of a more mechanical age may possess a beauty, and even a grandeur, of their own. The issue between spiritual freedom and slavery was always, to his mind, more profound than the issue between beauty and ugliness. Such thoughts were sometimes suggested to Wordsworth as he made his tour of 1833 through Keswick to Cockermouth; to Workington, with its memories of Mary, Queen of Scots; and so by sea to the Isle of Man, to the Clyde, to Staffa and Iona.

In the early stages of the tour, personal memories and family affections are in the ascendant. Thoughts at Cockermouth of his 'buried Little-ones' (Catharine and Thomas) move him to an expression of great tenderness in Sonnet vi, and this is followed by an *Address from the Spirit of Cockermouth Castle* recalling the stern lesson he received in childhood from the 'soul-appalling

---

[1] *Stanzas suggested in a steamboat off Saint Bees' Heads, on the Coast of Cumberland.*

[2] Wordsworth's note (*P.W.* iv, p. 403).

darkness' of the ruins. In an affectionate sonnet *To a Friend* (ix) he exhorts his son John, 'Pastor and Patriot', to be firm in his sacred calling at a time when only the unthinking can ignore the threats to the Church, and a little later, in Sonnet xvii, another son, William, is praised for the 'timely aid' by which he saved a boy from drowning off the Isle of Man.

Broad reflections on Past and Present begin to emerge, and he is tempted to regret the 'pious ignorance' of the ages of Faith, which were more friendly to poetry (xii, xiii),

> O Fancy, what an age was *that* for song!

He admits that the 'past illusions' of a pre-scientific age should not be longed for but, like the Tractarians, he rates spiritual values above intellectual progress. His mind, however, is not closed to the entry of new truths: he has flashes of fresh insight into the human heart and he can also admit that beauty may reveal itself in forms which he had supposed hostile to nature. As his steam-boat passes Ailsa Craig in the Firth of Clyde during an eclipse of the sun, he observes how these rare and splendid sights fail to attract several persons on deck 'of the poor and labouring class',[1] but he is equally 'struck by their cheerful talk with each other',[2] and he reflects that they are

> Though poor, yet rich, without the wealth of books,
> Or aught that watchful Love to Nature owes
> For her mute Powers, fix'd Forms, or transient Shows.[3]

He explained to Miss Fenwick that he regarded the happiness and even lives[4] of such persons as a compensation for their want of 'refined taste', the possessors of which are often 'self-tormentors'. In a remarkable sonnet (xlii), inspired by what he calls the 'magnificent viaduct' over the River Eden at Corby, he allays his fears about the changes which the new industrial age may bring to the peace of the northern fells:

> *Steamboats, Viaducts, and Railways*
> Motions and Means, on land and sea at war
> With old poetic feeling, not for this,

---

[1] Fenwick Note.   [2] Ibid.

[3] *In the Frith of Clyde, Ailsa Crag* (xxiii).

[4] Consistency 'in the management of their lives' (Fenwick Note).

> Shall ye, by Poets even, be judged amiss!
> Nor shall your presence, howsoe'er it mar
> The loveliness of Nature, prove a bar
> To the Mind's gaining that prophetic sense
> Of future change, that point of vision, whence
> May be discovered what in soul ye are.
> In spite of all that beauty may disown
> In your harsh features, Nature doth embrace
> Her lawful offspring in Man's art; and Time,
> Pleased with your triumphs o'er his brother Space,
> Accepts from your bold hands the proffered crown
> Of hope, and smiles on you with cheer sublime.

Wordsworth was then nearing Rydal, having visited the Cave of Staffa and Iona, afterwards passing near to Mossgiel Farm, the home of Burns. The sonnet (xxxviii) he wrote on this last occasion is a delightful example of his poetry in its luminous autumnal phase.

The poem, *Stanzas suggested in a Steamboat off St. Bees' Heads*, has links with *The Excursion* and the *Ecclesiastical Sonnets*, but it shows Wordsworth's thought at a further development than in either of these poems. No other composition of the poet illustrates so clearly the religious extension of impressions produced by an aspect of nature. The poem originates in the imaginative impact of the 'towering Headlands' of St. Bees — their threat of danger, their challenge to courage. The place was first humanized by the arrival of Bega on the Cumbrian coast, and her foundation there of a Chantry. This first 'religious Mansion' was destroyed by the Danes; revived as an Abbey, it became the guardian of man's whole welfare, temporal and spiritual. The use of 'intercessions for the soul's rest' is viewed in the most favourable light:

> Are not, in sooth, their Requiems sacred ties
> Woven out of passion's sharpest agonies,
> Subdued, composed, and formalized by art,
> To fix a wiser sorrow in the heart?
> The prayer for them whose hour is past away,
> Says to the Living, profit while ye may![1]

[1] ll. 73–78.

The 'benign influences' which Wordsworth had once sought and found in the intercourse between Man and Nature are here transferred, in his mind, to this religious house. After the 'sweeping overthrow' suffered in the Reformation, it is restored as a 'new-born College' 'for the education of ministers for the English Church', where — the poet hopes — the spirit of faith, represented in the past by 'bold credulities', may prevail against the Genius of the Age in which 'Matter and Spirit are as one Machine'. The importance of the poem in the history of religion is indicated in F. W. Faber's preface to his 'Life of St. Bega', printed in *Lives of the English Saints*, 1844, edited by J. H. Newman. Referring to Wordsworth's 'beautiful stanzas', Faber notes that they were written as long before as 1833. 'The date', he continues, 'is noticed as giving a fresh instance of the remarkable way in which his poems did in divers places anticipate the revival of catholic doctrines among us.' In execution, the St. Bees poem, as already suggested, is something of a *tour de force*, but the feeling that Wordsworth is using a difficult medium is soon lost in admiration for the eloquent progress of the argument.

With his talent for good endings, Wordsworth gave the series a beautiful conclusion in the sonnet, 'Most sweet it is with unuplifted eyes'. The lines flow easily, from the peace of a self-imposed discipline. Delight in the senses is not abolished, but controlled in the interests of 'soul-illumination', or as Wordsworth here puts it, the inspiration shed by the 'Mind's internal heaven'.

6. MEMORIALS OF A TOUR IN ITALY, 1837

These *Memorials* did not appear for five years, when they were published in *Poems, chiefly of early and late years* (1842). The tour, taken in company with Crabb Robinson, had been stimulating, but it had come late in Wordsworth's life. 'I have matter for volumes', he said, 'had I but youth to work it up.' Some of the poems reflect an elderly man's dependence on home memories when abroad, but many show a lively sense of the great historic panorama displayed in Italy and its bearing upon the most vital human concerns. The conflict between old affections and new impressions is not the keynote of the whole collection, but it is

strongly presented in the two opening poems. The blank verse
poem, *Musings near Aquapendente, April, 1837*, was written some
four years after the time to which it refers. Among the Apennines
with their waterfalls, fresh verdure, and flowering broom, his
thoughts fly to an inward vision of Helvellyn, with the 'crisp
moss' of its long summit, and its eastward prospect of Striding
Edge where he had once climbed with Scott. Not until he has
reviewed the sad thoughts of Scott's own tour in Italy is his mind
free to range over more recent memories and hopes. He recalls the
Campo Santo of Pisa and Savona, the town of Chiabrera, whose
poems he loved. He will see the 'Sabine vales', Naples, the Rome of
'bold fictions', and above all of the Christian traditions founded
by the Apostles. Then comes a dominant thought of his later
years — the natural development of his lifelong effort to trans-
mute his poetic and intellectual joys into a power friendly to
virtue:

> By gross Utilities enslaved we need
> More of ennobling impulse from the past,
> If to the future aught of good must come
> Sounder and therefore holier than the ends
> Which, in the giddiness of self-applause,
> We covet as supreme.

A sonnet follows, *The Pine of Monte Mario at Rome*, which brings
before us the kind of tree Turner delighted to paint, and in the
distance, St. Peter's. But dominant in the poet's thoughts is the
memory that it was by his friend, Sir George Beaumont, that this
very tree was saved from destruction:

> The rescued Pine-tree, with its sky so bright
> And cloud-like beauty, rich in thoughts of home,
> Death-parted friends, and days too swift in flight,
> Supplanted the whole majesty of Rome
> (Then first apparent from the Pincian Height)
> Crowned with St. Peter's everlasting Dome.

Many of Wordsworth's thoughts, during the tour, dwell on the
power of the past, whether embodied in legend or history, to
arouse virtue in the young. There is a group of three sonnets on
the responsibilities of the historian. Once more, he would not
recall past illusions and does not breathe a word against the rising

school of scientific history. Still, he cannot fail to ask what is to take the place of the traditional teaching in which his own generation was brought up:

> for exciting youth's heroic flame,
> Assent is power, belief the soul of fact.[1]

He concludes with the hope that historians will meet the challenge and remember that in the greatest days of the art, Clio taught her servants how 'the lyre should animate, but not mislead the pen'.[2] Passing from one poem to another, we are aware how strongly Wordsworth felt the poetry of the life around him. He had learned Italian in his youth and could evidently converse on simple topics with the people of Rome (Sonnet ix). It was no doubt from such intercourse that he drew his confidence in the still distant *Risorgimento* expressed in the sonnets *At Rome* (vii) and *From the Alban Hills, looking towards Rome* (xi). In these and some other utterances the aspirations of the French Revolution seem to mingle with the faith of Mazzini. In another sphere of thought, Wordsworth shows a sympathetic insight into those efforts of others who by a route of their own were striving like him to 'spiritualize the senses'. The most interesting poem on this theme, *The Cuckoo at Laverna*, is the result of a visit to the Franciscan Convent on 25 May 1837, the poem itself being begun almost at once, but not finished until some three years later. Again the poet greets with delight the cuckoo's cry which, acting with its old power of enchantment, stirs his imagination to penetrate to the spiritual heart of the monastic life. The poem, far removed from some sentimental successors, is an original interpretation of a life long misunderstood by Protestants and now for the first time for centuries presented to English readers in its historic spirituality.[3] In this house of 'heart-freezing discipline' there is no room for 'nature and the language of the sense', but, Wordsworth recalls,

---

[1] Sonnet iv, *In Allusion to Niebuhr, and other Modern Historians.*

[2] Sonnet vi, *Plea for the Historian.*

[3] This high claim for the originality of *The Cuckoo at Laverna* was first made by Dr. Edith Batho in *The Later Wordsworth*, pp. 296–7, and is accepted by de Selincourt. As far as I know, the claim has not been seriously contested.

St. Francis had a 'milder Genius' which sometimes predominated, and then

> out of the cleansed heart
> Of that once sinful Being overflowed
> On sun, moon, stars, the nether elements,
> And every shape of creature they sustain,
> Divine affections.[1]

Hence the love and power which made his followers compare him to 'our first Parents, ere the fall'.[2] Wordsworth's mind fixes itself on two of the Convent's inmates, who are vividly pictured: an old monk in a 'sunny glade' and a young ascetic in an 'aerial cell'. Perhaps the cuckoo's cry brings to their minds, not indeed a tale of visionary hours, but *the Voice of One crying amid the Wilderness*. Some further points in this important poem will be noticed in the last chapter.

The last poem of the series, *The Pillar of Trajan*, was published ten years before the date of the tour, and was afterwards classed with the 'Italian poems'. The subject was one set for a Newdigate Prize-poem, and Wordsworth advised his son, who was then an undergraduate at Oxford, to compete. He declined; but his father wrote a poem of his own to show how the thing could be done. As was then required, the 'Prize Poem' is in heroic couplets and is a striking instance of Wordsworth's versatility. His model was evidently Dryden in one of his 'Epistles and Complimentary Addresses', and he follows the style of an earlier century to a nicety — even to the extent of rhyming 'Rome' with 'doom'. *The Pillar of Trajan* is a fine descriptive and reflective poem, containing much of Wordsworth's character, in spite of the adopted manner.

These late 'Memorials', published when Wordsworth was seventy-two, testify to the alertness of his powers at an advanced age. Independence of mind and a frequent orientation to the future are among the features of the poems. The originality of the lines on St. Francis has been noticed: was not Wordsworth also the first writer to introduce the Higher Criticism into our general literature? From the sonnet *In allusion to Niebuhr, and other Modern Historians*, this seems a fair conjecture. Browning's

---

[1] ll. 50–54.   [2] l. 63.

portrait of the German professor in *Christmas Eve* came eight years later than Wordsworth's volume, and Mr. Casaubon's tragic ignorance of the Higher Criticism in *Middlemarch*, over twenty years later still. Equally remarkable are Wordsworth's sketches of the Italian character, his enthusiasm for the Italian landscape and certain poets, and above all his anticipation of the Italian *Risorgimento*. Had he been young enough to write all he had to say,[1] he would certainly rank with Ruskin, the Brownings, and George Meredith among the chief interpreters of Italy to the Victorian world.

[1] See p. 185.

CHAPTER XV

Fantasy and Late Imagination

IN 1835 Wordsworth published *Yarrow Revisited, and Other Poems*, composed chiefly between 1826 and 1834. The contents of the volume are miscellaneous, but fall into four main groups. There are the reminiscent and topical pieces, such as the title-poem and the sonnet on Scott's departure for Naples, which cherish 'Visions of the past' in a changing present. Secondly, there are 'memorials of tours', mostly sonnets, which have already been discussed as 'poetry of travel'. The third and fourth groups are the result of new developments in the poet's mind and art. They were written under the shadow of prolonged political anxiety which lasted until a year or two after the passage of the Reform Bill, but they avoid direct reference to public affairs. I have given these two groups the titles of 'Fantasy' and 'Late Imagination'. They represent a poetic revival after several unfertile years, but are among the more neglected of the author's works.

About 1826, Wordsworth's mind was deeply exercised over the two great political questions of the day. One was the movement for the 'emancipation' of Roman Catholics, then debarred from sitting in the United Parliament of Great Britain and Ireland. Many feared that the removal of this disability would weaken the authority of the Church of England in the national life, and it is evident from the *Ecclesiastical Sonnets* how strongly Wordsworth's feelings would be opposed to the change.[1] The other anxiety was about Parliamentary Reform. In the poet's mind the danger was a violent revolution introducing measures of popular rule which could only be tolerable as the result of time and education. The activities of the 'physical force Radicals' lent colour to his apprehensions, and his darkest fears are expressed in the sombre lines

[1] See Todd, *Politics and the Poet*, pp. 159–60, 183–7.

called *The Warning*. The current of his life had drawn him irresistibly towards the defence of the fundamental order in Church and State, and the remoteness of his residence concealed from his daily sight the need for change in the electoral system. The prolonged anxiety helped to divert his creative power into new channels. He found relief and satisfaction in writing several poems on themes remote from the contemporary world, yet possessing a serious ethical content. The first, and perhaps the best, of these 'fantasies' was composed in 1828. To the same year belongs a work of a widely different kind — the last of Wordsworth's great 'comprehensive' poems, completing the series to which *Tintern Abbey* and the Immortality *Ode* belong. This was the ode-like work called *Stanzas on the Power of Sound* — a universal and prophetic poem, untroubled by political passions. It has not the qualities which make for popularity, but its place in the total fabric of the poet's work gives it the highest intellectual importance.

Two poems, harbingers of Wordsworth's latter spring, are the *Ode, Composed on May Morning* (1826), and *To May* (begun in 1826). Both are cheerful in tone, nimble in step, with light felicities of phrase and fancy, and marked by freshness of metrical effect. The *Ode* rejoices in the permanence of the Seasons underlying the decay of ancient customs, which often oppressed the poet:

> Time was, blest Power! when youths and maids
> At peep of dawn would rise,
> And wander forth, in forest glades
> Thy birth to solemnize.
> Though mute the song — to grace the rite
> Untouched the hawthorn bough,
> Thy Spirit triumphs o'er the slight;
> Man changes, but not Thou!

Another poem, *The Somnambulist*, is written in the same stanza-form as the *Ode*, elaborated with an extra line and the use of internal rhyme in the third line. An experimental interest in poetic technique characterizes Wordsworth's later years. The stanza-forms of *The Armenian Lady's Love*, *The Egyptian Maid*, *St. Bees*, and *The Power of Sound* are all unique in his poetry, being carefully chosen from other authors or designed for the purpose. Equally remarkable is the rhythmical originality with which some familiar metres are handled, especially in the *Evening Voluntaries*, where the heroic couplets have an unusual music, an echo of the serene harmony of still evenings.

Wordsworth read his 'fantasy' *The Egyptian Maid*; *or, The Romance of the Water Lily* (1828) to the friend of Tennyson, James Spedding, who described it as 'a long, romantic, wizard and fairy poem, of the time of Merlin and King Arthur, very pretty but not of the first order; but' (he added) 'I should not have expected anything so good from him which was so much out of his beat'. The poem has these qualities, but something else too. The story begins with the arrival at the Scilly Isles of a ship ('The Water Lily') from Egypt, bearing a 'peerless damsel' destined to be the bride of one of Arthur's Knights. The enchanter Merlin wantonly wrecks the ship, but the intervention of the Lady of the Lake saves the life of the maiden, though she is apparently dead when she is brought to Arthur's Court. The use of a pagan figure-head on a ship dedicated to Christian service, though a sacrilege, was expiated by the sacrifice of the ship; and the Egyptian Maid is restored to life by the touch of the saintly Galahad, to whom she is united in marriage. A short epilogue suggests the allegorical meaning of this 'wizard' story. The poem is a reverie on the mercy of Providence in redeeming the use of wrongful means, and assisting the fulfilment of a good purpose in its own manner.[1] In the recesses of his mind the poet, we may suppose, cherished the hope that the use of 'physical force' by agitators might likewise be expiated, for the nation's good; for with the aims of the Chartists, though not with their violent methods, he had considerable sympathy.[2] *The Egyptian Maid* is an exotic plant which has taken root in the ethical soil of Wordsworth's garden.

Another 'fantasy', *The Russian Fugitive*, is too slight a thing to receive more than a passing notice. 'Early in life', says the

---

[1] F. M. Todd (in *Politics and the Poet*, p. 185) quotes from a letter of Wordsworth written in 1825 on Catholic Emancipation: 'Providence will prevent evil and deduce good by agency hidden from our limited faculties.'

[2] See Batho, *The Later Wordsworth*, pp. 197, 231-3.

poet, 'the story had interested me, and I often thought it would make a pleasing subject for an Opera or Musical drama.' It certainly seems to have this character in Wordsworth's version, but he has also left the impress of his own mind upon it by making it a 'poem of the affections'. A stronger effect is produced by *The Armenian Lady's Love* (composed in 1830), a highly romantic narrative on the final attainment of a family union of three persons, much like the Wordsworth household of husband, wife, and sister. A Venetian nobleman, made captive in one of the Crusades and condemned to work as a slave in some palace gardens, wins the love of the Sultan's daughter, who declares her devotion in the spirit of Miranda to Ferdinand:

> I am your wife, if you will marry me;
> If not, I'll die your maid; to be your fellow
> You may deny me; but I'll be your servant
> Whether you will or no.

The Sultan's daughter is not daunted to learn that the Crusader has a wife at home, and to Venice they contrive to escape. The 'beautiful Deliverer' is welcomed by the rejoicing wife, and thanks to the virtue and wisdom of the three persons, they live together in perfect amity:

> Constant to the fair Armenian,
>   Gentle pleasures round her moved,
> Like a tutelary spirit
>   Reverenced, like a sister, loved.
> Christian meekness smoothed for all the path of life,
> Who, loving most, should wiseliest love, their only strife.

Wordsworth obtained this story from a work by his friend Kenelm Henry Digby, and his sympathy with the situations, together with his skilful versification in an untried stanza, make a pleasing and piquant poem, which it is interesting to compare with *The Spanish Lady's Love* in Percy's *Reliques*.

Utterly unlike the 'fantasies' is the ode entitled *Stanzas on the Power of Sound* (1828), a work of 'reason in her most exalted mood'. It is of crucial importance in the present study, though few critics have considered it seriously. The anthologists, including Arnold, generally omit it. Dr. Batho in *The Later Wordsworth* does not mention it, and Professor Harper dismisses it in a few words: 'The ambitious ode *On the Power of Sound*, a marvellous example of technical daring, is too difficult to impart that degree of pleasure without which no poem really achieves its purpose.' It is certainly one of the most compressed of Wordsworth's poems and one of the most impersonal. De Selincourt mentions two early critics who rated it highly, but the most remarkable testimony to its importance is from the poet himself. He points out that he printed it at the end of the volume, *Yarrow Revisited*, 'and in the last edition of my Poems, at the close of the Poems of the Imagination, indicating thereby my own opinion of it'.[1] To anyone who has studied Wordsworth's system of arranging his works, it will be clear that he gave *The Power of Sound* the highest position possible.

The poem is Wordsworth's last great comprehensive work on the relation of sense to the soul. Its chief predecessors, *Tintern Abbey* and the Immortality *Ode*, give priority to the eye, but in this last work, the 'organ of vision' is dismissed at the third line, and thenceforward the poem is entirely consistent with its title. *The Power of Sound* is the discharge of a debt accumulated through the whole of the poet's life to the sense of hearing. A fragment of blank verse, probably written 1798–9, is aptly quoted by Mrs. Moorman in support of her view that 'of all his senses, that of hearing seems to have brought to Wordsworth the subtlest and most spiritual delight, whether it was sound or silence that he "heard":'[2]

> The clouds are standing still in the mid heavens;
> A perfect quietness is in the air;
> The ear hears not; and yet, I know not how,
> More than the other senses does it hold
> A manifest communion with the heart.[3]

Wordsworth, who knew that there is a 'lust of the eye' impairing imaginative freedom, had no such mistrust of the ear. *Tintern Abbey* is the first great poem on the relation of the senses to his higher nature. The Immortality *Ode* recognizes that the senses do not suffice for the spiritual needs of a whole life. *The Power of*

[1] *P.W.* ii, p. 526.

[2] *Wordsworth: Early Years*, p. 80.   [3] *P.W.* v, p. 343.

Sound resumes the theme in the light of a maturer wisdom. First, the sense of hearing is taken beyond the sphere of the poet's personal experience and related objectively to animal and human life in a number of different aspects. Secondly, an impressive passage of the Immortality *Ode* — on the eternal Silence — is directly countered in the concluding stanza on the eternal Word. It is perhaps suggestive that *The Power of Sound* was composed in the year following a publication of the poet's collected works: his later life had provided vital new thought and experience which demanded expression.

Two opposite views are held by critics on Wordsworth's power of spiritual divination after the acuteness of his senses had passed its meridian. 'Age has come upon him', says Mr. J. Jones, 'as a "removal" or a "severing", and he has no other world to tell of.'[1] 'The vision of the senses melts and dissolves', says H. W. Garrod, commenting on *The Prelude*, xiv. 188–205, 'but it melts into the revelation of permanent supersensual realities.'[2] A reader who confines himself to a selection of Wordsworth's poems might be puzzled between these two views, but any one who follows the development of his entire poetry will recognize that the passage from *The Prelude* and Garrod's paraphrase of it, are correct. The aptest, if not the only vehicle, for conveying 'supersensual realities' is the language consecrated by great religious writers and thinkers, which Wordsworth always used when he needed it, and never used without self-committing belief. Another world to tell of there is — not indeed one which he discovered, but one in which he believed. When in the closing stanzas of *The Power of Sound* he endeavours to give utterance to 'supersensual realities' they inevitably elude the precision of statement in which he conveyed sense-impressions. But the conclusion is one of the great passages of English mystical verse, perhaps the greatest Wordsworth himself ever wrote.

The ode opens with a panorama of the immense range and powers of sound and ascends at its close to a paean of praise to God uncircumscribed by His creation. The poet passes from the animal to the human world — from the lion's roar and the songs of birds to the sailor's prayer, the huntsman's horn, the peasant's

---

[1] *The Egotistical Sublime*, p. 124.   [2] *Wordsworth*, p. 130.

whistle, the pilgrims' chorus, the war-chant of Liberty, and so to
music and its power to soothe, fortify, subdue. At the seventh
stanza, he rises towards the sublimation which is his goal. Music,

> flowing from the heart
> Of divine Love, where Wisdom, Beauty, Truth
> With Order dwell, in endless youth,

proves its Orphean power over beings in whom reason is deranged
or non-existent: it is in fact inspired sanity. And in the myths of
Amphion and Pan we are reminded of the divine energy of early
poetic imagination. Thus, in the tenth stanza, we reach the third
stage:

> To life, to *life*, give back thine ear,

and the poem ascends to a higher strain:

> For terror, joy, or pity,
> Vast is the compass and the swell of notes.

These sounds are all controlled 'by one pervading spirit', which
involves the inaudible music of the spheres. Harmony is com-
pounded of 'discords just' as well as 'smooth tones', and the
inarticulate notes have a burden of spiritual meaning. They are
the endless 'praise and gratulation' to God poured forth from 'all
worlds, all natures'. Wordsworth has here drawn on some of the
great sources of imaginative power — Platonic idealism, Hebrew
sublimity, Apocalyptic prophecy. Intimations of Immortality
were once founded by him on the 'shadowy recollections' of childhood which link man with his spiritual home,

> Uphold us, cherish, and have power to make
> Our noisy years seem moments in the being
> Of the eternal Silence.

But how can the praise of Silence be reconciled with belief in God
as the Lord and Giver of Life? The poet himself asks and answers
this question in the conclusion and culmination of the poem:

> O Silence! are Man's noisy years
> No more than moments of thy life?
> Is Harmony, blest queen of smiles and tears,
> With her smooth tones and discords just,

Tempered into rapturous strife,
Thy destined bond-slave? No! though earth be dust
And vanish, though the heavens dissolve, her stay
Is in the WORD, that shall not pass away.

The greatness of the poem lies chiefly in the last three stanzas for
which the preceding ones are a necessary preparation. We may
miss the natural music of Wordsworth's best-loved poetry, but
what the ode lacks in charm is made good by its power. To convey
the mystical vision impersonally was a harder task, and perhaps a
more important one, than to relate it to an individual mind,
whether of the Wanderer or of the poet himself. *The Power of Sound*
is Wordsworth's greatest attempt to communicate the ineffable.

His exploration of the sense-and-soul relation is exemplified in a
few other poems of a more modest kind in the 1835 volume. Their
merit has been more generally recognized, for they recover the
charm of the personal note. The group called *Evening Voluntaries*
consisted in 1835 of nine items of which the last two are hardly
worthy of their place. In 1850 one of these is omitted, and eight
fresh items are added, changing a harmonious collection into a
miscellany of evening poems in different styles. As the scope of the
present chapter ends with the year 1835, it seems legitimate to
confine our attention to the first seven of the original series,
identified by their position in the original order. Wordsworth here
returns, with many differences, to the theme of his first considerable poem, *An Evening Walk*. Both works lie outside the period
of his complete dedication to Nature. In the wayward course of the
early poem, his mind is open to many impressions with little
self-direction: in the later, the 'love of Nature' is subordinate to
religious faith:

By grace divine,
Not otherwise, O Nature! we are thine.[1]

Only the second *Voluntary* is explicitly religious, but it shares with
the rest a peculiar serenity of mood and tranquillity of rhythm
which Wordsworth never attained so consistently before. The
Voluntaries are a group of vesper meditations, mostly by lake- or
sea-side, in lingering twilights.

[1] 'Not in the lucid intervals of life.'

The fourth *Voluntary*[1] is based on visual impressions, but in the others, the active powers are sounds and silence. In the first *Voluntary*[2] the 'village church-clock's iron tone' is strangely distinct in the stillness, and the few remaining sounds of 'Man's toilsome day' make palpable the spirit of the late hour. The third *Voluntary* ('By the Side of Rydal Mere') opens with the effect of the deepening twilight on the songs of different birds. In the sixth,[3] 'the gentleness of heaven broods o'er the sea', and the poet's mind and affections are on timeless things. The seventh ('By the Sea-side') on the calm after a storm at sea suggests that the mood of the moment requires some articulate voice of 'thanks and praise', such as would be heard elsewhere in Europe: 'vesper lays' on Calabrian shores, or 'Lutherian harmonies' from the northern seas. These *Voluntaries* form an epilogue to *The Power of Sound*.

Another poem of this time, *Devotional Incitements* (1832) celebrates the 'divine monition' which Nature addresses to the spirit of Man, not only in the 'canticles' of birds and brooks and the 'constant worship' of the sun, but also in the 'incense' of violet and thyme, thus adding the fragrance of flowers to the 'mighty world' of eye and ear. By its refined beauty, it well deserves its place among the later 'Poems of the Imagination'. An equal or even higher distinction belongs to *The Primrose of the Rock* (1831), which in its fifty-four lines comprehends the essence of Wordsworth's faith in the 'emblematic'[4] course of Nature and in the revelation founding Man's knowledge of the God of Love. It is a spring poem in two parts. The first part describes briefly how the return of spring brings new life to a 'coy primrose' rooted in a rock. From the transient life of the flower the poet's mind passes to the more lasting but invisible root that sustains it, to the enduring rock to which the root clings, to the 'constant' earth which encloses the rock, and to God, the upholder of all:

> So blooms this lonely Plant, nor dreads
> Her annual funeral.

[1] 'Soft as a cloud.'   [2] 'Calm is the fragrant air.'
[3] 'The Sun, that seemed . . . .'
[4] See *Thoughts on the Seasons* (1829).

The spirit of the second part can only be conveyed in the poet's own words:

> Here closed the meditative strain;
>   But air breathed soft that day,
> The hoary mountain-heights were cheered,
>   The sunny vale looked gay;
> And to the Primrose of the Rock
>   I gave this after-lay.
>
> I sang — Let myriads of bright flowers,
>   Like Thee, in field and grove
> Revive unenvied; — mightier far,
>   Than tremblings that reprove
> Our vernal tendencies to hope,
>   Is God's redeeming love;
>
> That love which changed — for wan disease,
>   For sorrow that had bent
> O'er hopeless dust, for withered age —
>   Their moral element,
> And turned the thistles of a curse
>   To types beneficent.
>
> Sin-blighted though we are, we too,
>   The reasoning Sons of Men,
> From one oblivious winter called
>   Shall rise, and breathe again;
> And in eternal summer lose
>   Our threescore years and ten.
>
> To humbleness of heart descends
>   This prescience from on high,
> The faith that elevates the just,
>   Before and when they die;
> And makes each soul a separate heaven,
>   A court for Deity.

In no other poem of Wordsworth are the natural and the religious elements of his inspiration fused together with such beauty and simplicity.

CHAPTER XVI

The Mind's Internal Heaven

THE Reform Bill was passed without a revolution and the British Constitution survived the change. Wordsworth could therefore write, in his last decade of composition, with a less encumbered mind. After the *Yarrow Revisited* volume of 1835, he ceased to plan poems on a large scale. He was content with 'effusions' or occasional pieces, or with the ideas suggested by his Italian tour of 1837. The character of his latest poetry results from its natural evolution. Long before, he had declared that there is a contemplative state of mind, in which words are but 'under-agents' to

> The thought, the image, and the silent joy,

and old age is the season of contemplation. But his interest in public events remained active; his mind was alert as ever and he laboured tirelessly on the revision of his past work. Some of his last poems might have been produced in his most vigorous years. In others, he discards most of the graces of poetry — he had never desired many — and is content to convey his thoughts and visions in verse at a low pitch of metrical energy. And he could still be 'surprised by joy' or by elegiac inspiration, as one or two rare poems bear witness. Near the end of 1835 he wrote his *Extempore Effusion upon the Death of James Hogg* — a magnificent personal elegy on five contemporary poets, with Charles Lamb added to their number. An 'effusion' for Wordsworth, is an unpremeditated composition, often unusual or unique in its verse form. This elegy belongs to the present chapter chiefly by its date, for in spirit it approximates to the 'Classical Sublime'. It has some analogy with Dunbar's *Lament for the Makaris*, and the refrain in that elegy, 'Timor mortis conturbat me', is paralleled by Wordsworth's question, 'Who next will drop and disappear?' But the late medieval lament contains no equivalent to the tragic note in the line:

> Our haughty life is crowned with darkness,

which carries on the thought of the central passage:

> How fast has brother followed brother,
> From sunshine to the sunless land!

'Sunless', however, is not a confession of hopeless grief, for it is only the *mortal* powers of Coleridge that are frozen at their source. But the spirit of the poem equally excludes a reference to the New Jerusalem, which has 'no need of the sun'. It seems most likely that 'sunless' is a reminiscence of the phrase 'sine sole' descriptive of the 'tristis domos' in *Aeneid* vi, and occurring shortly after the reference to Laodamia. The elegy has Wordsworth's natural sublimity of style with a literary sublimity engrafted upon it.

In strong stylistic contrast to the *Effusion* is the poem *Written after the Death of Charles Lamb*, which was originally an 'Epitaph' of thirty-eight lines. This short composition was in the style of the nine Epitaphs which Wordsworth translated from the Italian poet Gabriello Chiabrera whose work he described as subordinating 'what was peculiar to the individual to a sense of what he had in common with the species'. But generalization is inappropriate to so intensely personal a life as Lamb's: he therefore added about ninety lines intended 'to do some little justice to the sacred friendship which bound the brother and sister together'. In this supplementary passage — not stylized, like the preceding lines — he seems bent on removing the last veil of verse formality from the sympathetic insight with which Lamb's private life is outlined. The elegy invests it with a half dreamlike, half sacred character. This, too, is the manner of the lines on St. Francis.

A Cuckoo at Laverna has already been mentioned among the travel-poems suggested by the tour of 1837, but it has other aspects, reflecting Wordsworth's later thought. The lines are the raw material of what might have been made a very considerable poem. The phrase 'baptized imagination' has wide implications, so too has the comparison of the monks with the poet:

> Ah! not like me who walk in the world's ways, . . .

In his brief discussion of the poem, Hale White remarks that for Wordsworth 'the common distinction between sacred and profane is nothing', but he overlooks the later evolution of the poet's

thought. Once indeed there had been no such distinction, but
here it emerges, even while no breach is felt with the inspired
poetry of his earlier years. Wordsworth can now recognize the
spiritual illumination which allowed St. Francis, 'rapt though he
were above the power of sense', to bestow 'divine affections'

> On sun, moon, stars, and nether elements,
> And every shape of creature they sustain,

without condemning his own dependence upon the senses for the
inspiration of his early manhood. Saint and poet are not the same,
though their once separate paths were now converging. As if to
emphasize his meaning Wordsworth has placed, immediately after
the St. Francis poem, a sonnet *At the Convent of Camaldoli*, on a
Monk who, since entering the cloister, has painted a picture of his
'lady-love'. The poet imagines him as exhorting the Brethren to
destroy the work, or to remove it:

> That bloom — those eyes — can they assist to bind
> Thoughts that would stray from Heaven? The dream
>   must cease
> To be; by Faith, not sight, his soul must live; . . .[1]

The distinction between sacred and profane was not questioned
by Wordsworth at this time, nor was the distinction between
earthly and heavenly love.[2]

Wordsworth's most concerted work during this decade was his
series of fourteen *Sonnets upon the Punishment of Death* (1839–40).
A few years before, when the death penalty was removed from
about two hundred offences, some members of Parliament
objected on principle to the infliction of death for any crime
whatever, and it was in opposition to this view, in the existing
state of society, that the sonnets were written. Wordsworth found
his task 'a painful road' and the subject repels many readers,
though the sonnets are themselves poetically impressive. They are
little praised by critics, who often regret the side taken by the
poet on a highly controversial question. Professor Harper has a
special objection of his own: 'What does it matter, [Wordsworth]

---

[1] The Monk is speaking in the third person.

[2] In the next sonnet (XVI), the Monk prays for their final reconciliation.

seems to say, whether life be long or short, happily or painfully ended, if the soul is fit for eternity?' This, though a grotesque simplification of the poet's thought, rightly recognizes the change in his outlook since the time when the world was for him

> the place where, in the end,
> We find our happiness, or not at all.

But it does not follow, as Professor Harper implies, that he disregarded 'happiness and equal justice in this world', seeing that 'the only important life is yet to come'.[1] The best summary of Wordsworth's attitude to the death penalty is at the end of the sonnet, *Conclusion*:

> Strike not from Law's firm hand that awful rod,
> But leave it thence to drop for lack of use:
> Oh, speed the blessed hour, Almighty God!

Anyone who may still be inclined to judge these Sonnets harshly should remember that the volume of poems in which they appeared (1842) also contains the first publication of *Guilt and Sorrow* with its revised and merciful ending: 'his fate was pitied'. That the sentence of death on the Sailor in that poem should have been carried out is dismissed as an 'intolerable thought'.[2]

One of the conspicuous features of these latest poems is the satisfying finality with which they close certain lines of thought which run through the earlier work. For instance, there were limits to Wordsworth's enjoyment of a fine sunset, however spectacular: he could not forget that it was one of Nature's 'transient shows' and that 'the immortal Mind craves objects that endure'.[3] He takes leave of this thought in the last line of a sonnet ('The most alluring clouds that mount the sky') published in his volume of 1842:

> The house that cannot pass away be ours.[4]

Again, the poems addressed over many years to Mary Wordsworth end in the recognition that her spiritual strength is drawn from sources not subject to time:

> Thanks to thy virtues, to the eternal youth

[1] Harper, op. cit. ii, p. 424.   [2] See p. 20.
[3] *Miscellaneous Sonnets*, Part II. xi, xii.   [4] Ibid. III. xxviii.

> Of all thy goodness, never melancholy;
> To thy large heart, and humble mind, that cast
> Into one vision, future, present, past.[1]

It is well known how strongly Wordsworth deplored any threat to the beauty, seclusion, or ancient customs of Lakeland, but his power to meet changes — whether inevitable or not — with the faith of a spiritual seer ought to be more widely recognized. A poem called *The Wishing-Gate* is deservedly included in Arnold's anthology, but it represents familiar aspects of Wordsworth's poetry: its sequel, *The Wishing-Gate Destroyed*,[2] with its courageous conclusion illustrates a feature of his later mind which is equally important for a complete picture:

> Not Fortune's slave is Man: our state
> Enjoins, while firm resolves await
> On wishes just and wise,
> That strenuous action follow both,
> And life be one perpetual growth
> Of heaven-ward enterprise.
>
> So taught, so trained, we boldly face
> All accidents of time and place;
> Whatever props may fail,
> Trust in that sovereign law can spread
> New glory o'er the mountain's head,
> Fresh beauty through the vale.

Wordsworth's indignation at the obtuseness with which 'a false utilitarian' outlook regards 'the pillage of man's ancient heart' needs no apology in our days. He had often resisted the encroachment of railways on the peace of Lakeland, but he had resilience enough to view the whole question, from time to time, in a different light. The last of all his *Miscellaneous Sonnets*, written in 1845, distinguishes between two types of men: those who plan at a distance, without heed of 'local sanctities', and those who, with their instincts rooted in rural life, are happy in retaining the power to feel them. Hardly a great poem, this sonnet is memorable as the last word of a fighter in an unending struggle:

[1] Ibid.
[2] The gate was in fact not destroyed, but Wordsworth's error does not affect the poem.

At Furness Abbey
(Composed 21 June 1845)

Well have yon Railway Labourers to THIS ground
Withdrawn for noontide rest. They sit, they walk
Among the Ruins, but no idle talk
Is heard; to grave demeanour all are bound;
And from one voice a Hymn with tuneful sound
Hallows once more the long-deserted Quire
And thrills the old sepulchral earth, around.
Others look up, and with fixed eyes admire
That wide-spanned arch, wondering how it was raised,
To keep, so high in air, its strength and grace:
All seem to feel the spirit of the place,
And by the general reverence God is praised:
Profane Despoilers, stand ye not reproved,
While thus these simple-hearted men are moved?

As a final illustration both of the unity of Wordsworth's poetry
and of its self-transcendence, the lines he wrote in 1844 'So fair,
so sweet, withal so sensitive' have an interest for our present
study beyond their positive value as poetry. Many persons,
however, have loved the stanza on the daisy's 'star-shaped
shadow' and wondered at the vitality of eye and fancy in a poet of
Wordsworth's advanced age. He had long before written three
poems 'to a daisy' — the single flower — and years later he was
strongly moved, on one of his travels in the Clyde, by the unexpected words 'That's the very field where Burns ploughed up
the Daisy' — the immortal 'One', among the myriads forgotten.
The continuity of the same poetic impulse in widely sundered
periods is remarkable enough. But this last poem goes beyond its
predecessors: its conclusion subordinates the power of vital
observation to the spirit of adoration:

Fond fancies! wheresoe'er shall turn thine eye
On earth, air, ocean, or the starry sky,
Converse with Nature in pure sympathy;
All vain desires, all lawless wishes quelled,
Be Thou to love and praise alike impelled,
Whatever boon is granted or withheld.

Outward stimulus is transcended by inspiration from 'the Mind's internal heaven'. Love of Nature has become an aspiration towards a purely spiritual relation with the Deity.

It only remains, after this attempted survey of Wordsworth's poetry, to recapitulate our chief conclusions on his later work, together with some comments on its modifying effect on our view of his 'great period'. The closing years of the Napoleonic Wars found Wordsworth at the end of his large poetic schemes and also without his chief motive for sonnet-writing. *The Excursion* was finished and the 'paramount duty' of hope in the cause of national liberty had ended at Waterloo. In *Laodamia* (1814) he had found a subject which, though of literary origin, had the force of natural inspiration and enabled him to appeal to feelings which were 'sane, pure, and permanent'. It was the earliest of his poems in the style of the 'classical sublime'. In the most personal of these poems, the *Ode to Lycoris* (1817), he expresses his need as 'a bard of ebbing time' to cultivate the *art* of hope, one result of which resolution was the ode *To Enterprise* (1821). But poetry of the classical type could not be in the fullest sense 'sublime': it was not one of 'the grand store-houses of enthusiastic and meditative Imagination'. These he found to be 'the prophetic and lyrical parts of the holy Scriptures, and the works of Milton'.[1] 'However imbued the surface (of Milton's mind) might be with classical literature', he writes, 'he was a Hebrew in soul; and all things tended in him towards the sublime.' Nothing less could permanently satisfy Wordsworth himself, who had described the aspirations of man many years before in the great lines:

> Our destiny, our being's heart and home,
> Is with infinitude, and only there;
> With hope it is, hope that can never die,
> Effort, and expectation, and desire,
> And something evermore about to be.[2]

The writing of the *Ecclesiastical Sonnets* revealed to Words-worth the value to his poetry of the framework and language of

[1] 'To which I cannot forbear to add those of Spenser.' *Preface* to the Edition of 1815.

[2] *The Prelude*, VI. 604–7.

historic Christianity. The original attraction of the subject lay in his power to treat the strength and weakness of monastic life, in his impartial admiration for the martyrs on both sides in the Reformation, and above all, in his devout religious reverence. To quote Hale White once more: 'Wordsworth worshipped the true God alone, from the days of the "Lyrical Ballads" to his death, and set up no shrine to Baal.' In the heart of the subject lay a deeper attraction than he had at first perceived. More than any other power on earth, the Church was committed to fostering the sanctity of family life, and sonnets added later, such as 'Baptism' (1827), 'Confirmation' (1827), and 'The Marriage Ceremony' (1845) bear witness to this conviction. The concluding poems of the series strike a new note. Hitherto Wordsworth's poetry had associated the hope of heaven with other minds than his own, usually with persons in humble life. Now he himself recognizes, in the great cathedrals and churches, a testimony to the power of this belief:

> They dreamt not of a perishable home
> Who thus could build.

The short poem *To a Skylark*,[1] which was written a few years later (1825), though well known, has a significance which may easily escape notice. It is like an afterthought to the *Ecclesiastical Sketches*. The last line describes the bird, which links its low-lying nest with some imagined goal in the sky, as

> True to the kindred points of Heaven and Home.

The simple phrase, especially as coming at this stage in the development of the poet's thought, is extraordinarily pregnant. The antithesis and the union of 'Heaven and Home' lie at the very centre of Wordsworth's poetry, though with varying implications. The phrase is an epitome which simplifies the complexity of his work and casts a retrospective light on some of his greatest poems. Wordsworth's genius, at once domestic and unworldly, expressed itself with differing emphasis as it shifted its focus from nature to man and from man to God. While hope prevailed as a 'genial

---

[1] 'Ethereal Minstrel!'

power' there was no need to postulate 'another' heaven, but
what about the years when 'life requires an art'? Yet Wordsworth
believed in heaven, even when he did not emphasize its distinction
from earth. The relation between home and heaven lies at the
heart of the little poem *Stepping Westward*. The antithesis underlies *Resolution and Independence* where the homeless Leech-
gatherer, secure in 'God's good help', shames the well-housed poet,
insecure in his earthly hopes. In *The White Doe of Rylstone*,
Emily, deprived utterly of home and its affections discovers, while
still on earth, 'a more divine and loftier way'. In the *Evening of
Extraordinary Splendour*, the poet beholds 'an intermingling of
Heaven's pomp' with the 'ground which British shepherds tread'.
In *The Primrose of the Rock* the antithesis is both expressed and
resolved in the two parts of the poem. These are but a few from a
multitude of possible illustrations. Wordsworth taught that
human happiness and virtue depend upon the affections of home
and family and on the hope of a Heaven of which nature presents
an image and emblem. To present these truths with power and to
vitalize them with invention was one main purpose of his poetry.
But to disengage the thought of Heaven was not enough: it
must be invested with sublimity. This is the task attempted in
The Power of Sound. Starting with the most spiritual of the senses
the poet leads us finally beyond Heaven itself to the apocalyptic
vision of the Creator as the Eternal Word. Wordsworth's later
poetry culminates in this glorious ode.

   This forward-looking vision on a grand scale is matched on a
lower plane in some of the latest sonnets. The poet's tour in 1833
to parts of Scotland and of Northern England stimulated some
final hopes for the new age which he saw emerging in the industrial
areas on his route. While regretting that 'the strength of
backward-looking thoughts is scorned'[1] he was determined to
face the other side of the truth. He knew well enough that the
useful encourages itself, but he also perceived that the useful
need not necessarily be unlovely — could indeed, by imagination,
be made sublime. This discovery he expresses in the sonnet
already quoted — *Steamboats, Viaducts, and Railways*. But he
had no belief that Science could solve all the problems of

[1] *Itinerary Poems of 1833*, xliv.

knowledge or satisfy the entire needs of the human spirit. 'Conquering Reason, if self-glorified' would always meet some impassable 'gulf of mystery' in a universe which was 'infinitely wide'.[1]

> Science advances with gigantic strides;
> But are we aught enriched in love and meekness ?[2]

If 'old poetic feeling' is to be sacrificed to the 'harsh features' of new 'Motions and Means', the loss must be salved by a 'prophetic sense' of what communications rightly mean to the future of the race; progress must be an ascent. The Italian tour of 1837 quickened and refreshed the inner springs of his thought. In the monastic ideal he saw a possible approximation of Home and Heaven — a vision with which he sympathized profoundly, while keeping his own independent way as a poet.

Wordsworth's imaginative sympathy with the Tractarians, which we have noticed in several places, was deeply rooted in his upbringing, memories, and the natural constitution of his mind. Different as the two men were in many respects, he had certain close affinities with J. H. Newman. The moral crisis which Wordsworth faced in early manhood had its counterpart in the life of Newman, who thus sums up the tendencies in his thought about 1827: 'The truth is, I was beginning to prefer intellectual excellence to moral. I was drifting in the direction of liberalism.'[3] Had Wordsworth, in his last twenty years, looked back on his subjection to the influence of Godwin and his escape from it, he might have described his early position in terms similar to these. It is not surprising, therefore, that in Wordsworth, Newman should have recognized one of the literary precursors of the Tractarian Movement. In his article 'The State of Religious Parties' (1839), after mentioning Coleridge as one who 'instilled a higher philosophy into inquiring minds, than they had hitherto been accustomed to accept', thus interesting the genius of his age 'in the cause of Catholic truth', he then couples Wordsworth with Southey, as having 'addressed themselves to the same high

---

[1] *Itinerary Poems of 1833*, xiv.
[2] *Miscellaneous Sonnets*, III. xli ('To the Planet Venus').
[3] *Apologia pro Vita Sua* (1864), Part III.

principles and feelings, and carried forward their readers in the same direction'.[1] As a poet, Wordsworth anticipated the Tractarian movement through his characteristic belief in Imagination as 'the mightiest lever' in the moral world. Hence, in reviewing the course of the Reformation in his *Ecclesiastical Sonnets*, he deplores the iconoclasm which destroyed images and abolished rites, still powerful as 'devotional incitements'. This is the theme of his sonnet 'Regrets' (III. xxxiii):

> Would that our scrupulous Sires had dared to leave
> Less scanty measure of those graceful rites
> And usages, whose due return invites
> A stir of mind too natural to deceive.

We may recall how far Wordsworth is carried by Catholic sympathies in his remarkable sonnet 'The Virgin' and the later poem on St. Bega. His sense of *religio loci* was another link with the Tractarians: few of the modern pilgrims to Italy have been more deeply steeped in a feeling for 'local sanctities' than Wordsworth was in 1837. Newman's conversion to Rome in 1845 did not alter the poet's attitude to the first Tractarians. He replied in answer to an enquiry in 1849[2] that 'late events' had left his opinion unchanged. 'I foresaw', he said, 'that the movement was for good, and such I conceive it has been beyond all question.'

Some of Wordsworth's later poems are neither 'inevitable', like the best of his early work, nor new like the *Ode to Lycoris*, or *The Egyptian Maid*, or *The Power of Sound*. For a few years after 1820 his occasional verse sometimes suggested a loss of poetic vision. But the lapse was temporary, and in its final phase his poetry often shows the illumined sanity befitting advanced years. The master-force of Wordsworth's life was an unworldly enthusiasm which, had his native place and date been different, might have led him to devote his whole strength to the promotion of a religious revival. But his presence at the birth of modern democracy turned his mind irresistibly towards the laws which govern the well-being of human society. He was saved from the attractions of abstract theory by the awakening of his imagination through

---

[1] Ibid., Part v.

[2] Reported by Ellis Yarnall. See Batho, *The Later Wordsworth*, p. 301.

the medium of his early passion for Nature. The task of his life
was to combine three forces — ethical idealism, hope for Man
as a social being, and the imaginative love of Nature — in
original poetic forms. Few writers of any age have more effectively
turned the minds of their readers to an exalted love of beauty,
natural and spiritual. It was inevitable that in the course of a long
life in a revolutionary era the aspects of truth he held up for love
and admiration should undergo some changes. Many of his critics
have strangely ignored this principle of vitality. Why, for instance,
is it usual to recognize the mind of a true poet in the lines on Fox
but to see only the 'growing conservative' in the passage on Burke
added to *The Prelude*? Imagination and intellectual love, Wordsworth tells us, are 'each in each, and cannot stand dividually'.[1]
The record of his poetic life after 1814 — his renewed delight in
the classics, his extended interest in Nature, in history, and the
future of nations, as proved on his travels; above all, his devotion
to the historic Christian Church — witnesses to an ever-expanding
'intellectual love'. Only at the end of his career can we rightly
appreciate the fulfilment of the promise with which Coleridge is
coupled at the close of *The Prelude*:

> what we have loved,
> Others will love, and we will teach them how.

The doctrinal element in Wordsworth's later poetry may be more
effectively enforced by teachers of religion, but no poet is a more
powerful advocate of the religious attitude. In the fields of culture,
higher education, literary taste and criticism, his poetry and its
influence are indispensable today.

[1] *The Prelude*, xiv. 206–9.

G.U.W.

Select Bibliography

ARNOLD, MATTHEW. 'Wordsworth' (Preface to *Selections*, 1879; reprinted in *Essays in Criticism*, Second Series).

BATHO, EDITH C. *The Later Wordsworth* (1933).

BEATTY, ARTHUR. *William Wordsworth: his Doctrine and Art in their Historical Relations* (1922).

CLAYDON, W. A. 'The Numinous in the Poetry of Wordsworth', *The Hibbert Journal*, vol. xxviii, no. 4 (July 1930).

COLERIDGE, S. T. *Biographia Literaria*, ed. Shawcross (1907).

COMPARETTI, ALICE PATTEE. Critical edition of *The White Doe of Rylstone* (1940).

DARBISHIRE, HELEN. *The Poet Wordsworth* (1950).

DE QUINCEY, THOMAS. *Reminiscences of the English Lakes and the Lake Poets* (1834, etc.).

DE SELINCOURT, E. *Dorothy Wordsworth* (1933).

DE SELINCOURT, E.: *see* WORDSWORTH, WILLIAM.

DICEY, A. V. *The Statesmanship of Wordsworth* (1917).

GARROD, H. W. *Wordsworth: Lectures and Essays* (1923).

GROSART, ALEXANDER B.: *see* WORDSWORTH, WILLIAM.

HARPER, GEORGE MCLEAN. *William Wordsworth* (2nd ed., 1923).

HUTCHINSON, T.: *see* WORDSWORTH, WILLIAM.

JONES, JOHN. *The Egotistical Sublime. A History of Wordsworth's Imagination* (1954).

JORDAN, JOHN E. 'Wordsworth's Humor', *P.M.L.A.* (March 1958).

KER, W. P. *Form and Style in Poetry*, ed. R. W. Chambers (1st ed., 1928; 2nd ed., 1966).

KNIGHT, WILLIAM: *see* WORDSWORTH, WILLIAM.

LACEY, NORMAN. *Wordsworth's View of Nature and its Ethical Consequences* (1948).

LEGOUIS, ÉMILE. *The Early Life of William Wordsworth*, trans. J. W. Matthews (2nd ed., 1921).

LYON, JUDSON STANLEY. *The Excursion. A Study* (1950).

MOORMAN, MARY: *William Wordsworth. A Biography. The Early Years 1770–1803* (Oxford, 1957).

NEWMAN, CARDINAL JOHN HENRY. *Apologia pro Vita Sua* (1864).

POTTS, A. F.: *see* WORDSWORTH, WILLIAM.

READ, HERBERT. *Wordsworth*, appendix (1965).

ROBINSON, H. CRABB. *Correspondence of H.C.R. with the Wordsworth Circle*, ed. Edith J. Morley, 2 vols. (1927).

TODD, F. M. *Politics and the Poet* (1957).

WHITE, WILLIAM HALE. *An Examination of the Charge of Apostasy against Wordsworth* (1898).

WORDSWORTH, BISHOP CHRISTOPHER. *Memoirs of William Wordsworth* (1851).

WORDSWORTH, DOROTHY. *Journals*, ed. Knight (1897).

WORDSWORTH, WILLIAM. *Ecclesiastical Sonnets*, ed. A. F. Potts (1922).

— *Poetical Works*, ed. T. Hutchinson (Oxford, 1910).

— *The Poetical Works*, ed. E. de Selincourt and Helen Darbishire, 5 vols. (Oxford, 1940–9).

— *The Prelude*, ed. E. de Selincourt (Oxford, 1926).

— *Prose Works*, ed. Alexander B. Grosart (1876).

— *Prose Works*, ed. William Knight (Eversley edition, 1896).

— *The Letters of William and Dorothy Wordsworth*, ed. E. de Selincourt, 6 vols. (Oxford, 1935–9).

Note: Wordsworth's prefatory essay to *The Borderers* is printed in *P.W.* i, pp. 345–9.

Index

PRINTED IN GREAT BRITAIN
BY ROBERT MACLEHOSE AND CO. LTD
THE UNIVERSITY PRESS, GLASGOW